MW00440522

POETRY NATION

poetry nation

The North American Anthology of Fusion Poetry

EDITED BY

Regie Cabico

&

Todd Swift

Véhicule Press

Véhicule Press gratefully acknowledges the support of The Canada Council for the Arts for its publishing program.

Cover artwork, design, and calligraphy by J.W. Stewart
Cover imaging by André Jacob
Typesetting by Simon Garamond
Printing by AGMV-Marquis Inc.

Copyright © Regie Cabico, Todd Swift, and the authors 1998
First printing November 1998

00 99 98   4 3 2 1

CANADIAN CATALOGUING IN PUBLICAITION DATA

Main entry under title:

Poetry nation : the North American anthology
of fusion poetry

ISBN: 1-55065-112-9

1. Canadian poetry (English)—20th century.
2. American poetry—20th century.
I. Swift, Todd, 1966-   II. Cabico, Regie

PR1227.P73 1998   C811'.5408   C98-900195-4

Published by Véhicule Press in its 25th anniversary year.
P.O.B. 125, Place du Parc Station
Montréal, Québec, Canada H2W 2M9

http://www.cam.org/~vpress

Distributed in Canada by General Distribution Services
1-800-387-0141 (Ont./Qc) 1-800-387-0172

Distributed in the United States by LPC Group
1-800-626-4330

Printed in Canada on alkaline paper

For Allen Ginsberg

&

Ian Stephens

Contents

ACKNOWLEDGEMENTS 22

FOREWORD
Bob Holman 23

INTRODUCTION 25

SECTION ONE

FUSION BOMB

Allen Ginsberg 29
DEATH & FAME

Andrea Thompson 31
FIRE BELLY

bill bissett 36
loving without being vulnrabul

Bob Holman 37
THE DEATH OF POETRY

Bob Redmond 39
THE POET

Clifton Joseph 40
SHOTS ON EGLINTON

Denise Duhamel 41
THE DIFFERENCE BETWEEN PEPSI AND THE POPE
HAPPY ENDING

7

Ellyn Maybe 44
I Have Never Fallen In Love With Anyone
Who Felt Comfortable In America

Fortner Anderson 46
The Bovine Spongiform Encephalopathy Blues
My Friend

Hal Sirowitz 51
No More Birthdays
Does God Exist?
Damaged Body
Different Versions
Two Burials For The Same Person
How To Wash Clothes

Ian Stephens 54
Home, Grand Metis, Quebec 1995

Jill Battson 55
Hitching

Kimiko Hahn 56
The Unbearable Heart

Lee Gotham 57
I'd Love To But…

Marc Smith 58
My Father's Coat

W. Mark Sutherland 59
Fuck
Art Blakey

Melody Jordan 61
Strange Apartment In Brooklyn

8

Nothing Happened
Everything is Ice Cream
(and the world is a very hot place)

Micki Siegel 64
Skintones
Penmanship

Miguel Algarin 65
Nuyorican Angel of Wordsmithing
(Note for a Poet)
Nuyorican Angel Papo
(The Bi-Sexual Super Macho)
Nuyorican Angel Of Despair
(December 31, at the End of the Millennium)

Nicole Blackman 68
Girls
Liberation Barbie

Patricia Smith 71
Biting Back

Paul Dutton 73
T' Her

Penelope 74
Stein Tribute

Ras Baraka 75
For the Brothers Who Ain't Here

Regie Cabico 77
Antonio Banderas In His Underwear
In A Legendary Light
Check One

Sandra Cisneros 81
You Bring Out The Mexican In Me

Sheri-D Wilson 83
Bukowski on the Block

Tony Medina 86
How to Become a U.S. Citizen
Bloodsong

Todd Swift 88
Trick
U R Scully 2 Me
Curing
D.O.A.

SECTION TWO

<u>POUND UNPLUGGED</u>

Adeena Karasick 91
Albeit Erstwhile

Audrey De la Rosa 93
I am not white, señores

Barbara Tran 94
Love and Rice

Beth Lisick 95
Monkey Girl

Carmelita McGrath 96
The Half-life of Taffeta

Cheryl Savageau 98
Looking For Indians

TOO'KAY
AFTER LISTENING TO A READING OF ROMANTIC
POEMS ABOUT COLUMBUS:
ONE MORE THOUGHT

Chris Bell 101
From THE LEGEND OF CHEEBAH-HA
THE QUEST FOR IMMORTALITY

Cindy Goff 104
THE POLE IN HIS BACK WAS AS STRONG
AS MY FAMILY TREE
APPALACHIAN FLOOD
THE FIRST SOBER MORNING
ADDICTION

Daniel O'Leary 106
From TARSUS

David McGimpsey 108
IN MEMORIUM: A.H. JR.

Donald McGrath 114
THE STABLE

Eileen Tabios 115
RAPUNZEL, ENRAPT

Eric Sigler 116
DEAD WITH THE DEAD

Evelyn Lau 117
VANCOUVER PUBLIC LIBRARY OPENING GALA,
MAY 24, 1995

Gerry Gomez Pearlberg 118
THE DEATH OF SUPERMAN

Jason Camlot 119
KIT DISCOVERS SOUND
PHONO KIT
CRYPTO KIT...

Jeffrey McDaniel 129
POETRY NATION

John B. Lee 130
THE SERGEANT PEPPER SONNETS

Lois-Ann Yamanaka 132
YARN WIG

Louise Bak 134
DOUBLE-TAKE
M.
HETEROFLEXIDOME

Lynn Crosbie 137
LOVE LETTER FROM GARY COLEMAN

Marcella Durand 139
CITY OF PORTS 2

Mark Cochrane 140
MAPPLETHORPE

Maureen Seaton with Denise Duhamel 141
EXQUISITE MAJORITY
LET ME EXPLAIN
XENA: WARRIOR PRINCESS

Michael Holmes 144
(BRAMALEA LIMITED)
"IN HIGH SCHOOL EVERYONE YOU HALF KNOW
DIES ON FRIDAY"

Nick Carbo 146
Ang Tunay Na Lalaki (THE REAL MAN)
IS BAFFLED BY CRYPTIC MESSAGES
MAL DE OJO
FOR MY FRIEND WHO COMPLAINS HE CAN'T DANCE
AND HAS A SEVERE CASE OF WRITER'S BLOCK

Paul Beatty 149
STALL ME OUT

Raymond Filip 150
MOTORMOUTH

Robert Allen 151
From VOYAGE TO THE ENCATADAS
II GALAPAGOS TED: HIS PERILS

Richard Harrison 153
LOVE AND THE HOCKEY POOL

Richard Tayson 155
REMEMBERING THE MAN WHO MOLESTED ME
SACRED ANUS

Stan Rogal 157
VOWELS

Steven Heighton 158
ELEGY AS A MESSAGE LEFT ON AN ANSWERING MACHINE

Steven Ross Smith 159
BREN GUN GIRL. 1941
From THE BOOK OF EMMET
FLUTTERING 4.
FLUTTERING 8.
FLUTTERING 9.

Timothy Liu 161
THE SIZE OF IT

Wayne Keon 162
HIGH TRAVELLIN
TO TEOTIHAUCAN

SECTION THREE

MEDIA BYRONS

Anne Elliott 166
WHEN I RETURNED FROM MY MOTHER'S FUNERAL,
HE SAID I WAS TOO REBELLIOUS
RECIPES
SHE THOUGHT STARVATION WAS SOMEHOW HOLY

Beau Sia 169
A LITTLE KNOWN TRUTH ABOUT
FINANCIAL SUCCESS

Ben Porter Lewis 171
WAYFARER DUMMIES

Buffy Bonanza 172
AUTONEUROTICA

Carl Hanni 173
NOT MAKING IT IN MEXICO

Carl Hancock Rux 175
RED VELVET PANTS LULLABY 00

Catherine Kidd 177
From I-SOCKET

C.D. Jones 180
COMING OF AGE

Cheryl Boyce Taylor 182
Wind
Plenty Time Pass Fast,
Fas Dey So

Daniel Roop 186
Handing Out Poetry

DJ Renegade 188
Subterranean Night-Colored Magus
(3 Moods in the Mode of Miles)
Father, Son And The Wholly Ghost
Mama After Midnight

Evert Eden 193
Mandela
Big Breasts

Edwin Torres 197
15 Minutes
Catching the Rise in the Palm of My Hand
With Heart Sky Drowning

horehound stillpoint 200
All Right I'm Okay, You're Okay, Everybody is Okay
and Nothing Human is Alien and All That, Fine, But
There are Still a Few People I Would Like to See Take
a Long Hike Off a Short Pier
Reincarnation Woes

Ian Ferrier 204
You Want Me
Exploding Head Man

Joe Blades 206
Continuation (of Services Rendered by the Falmouth
Lifeboats of the Royal National
Lifeboat Institution)

Justin Chin 207
EX-BOYFRIENDS NAMED MICHAEL

Kélina Gotman 209
GLOBULAR MUD

Kevin Sampsell 210
ULYSSES
ANSWERING MACHINE LOVE
JACK NANCE
RIKKI LAKE
DAVID DUKE

M. Doughty 213
IN THE MIND OF THE MIND
I'LL BE YOUR BABY DOLL, I'LL BE YOUR SEVEN DAY FOOL
ROOTLESS
FOR CHARLOTTE, UNLISTED

Mary Elizabeth Grace 216
SHE
SEPTEMBER NEVER COMING

Mercedes Baines 217
CLIT SING ALONG
THE LAST TIME I SAW YOU

Minister Faust 219
REGGAE IS

Nancy Dembowski 222
LIFE ON VENUS

Noel Franklin 223
BLOOD QUANTUM
(UPON PURCHASING THE LATEST BOOKS OF SHERMAN ALEXIE
AND MARGARET ATWOOD ON THE SAME DAY)
LONG DISTANCE EX

Phlip Arima 227
Jane—waiting for the light to change—
Be Quiet

Rittah Parrish 228
The Rules

Robert Priest 231
Elvis/Bacchus iterations
Parallel Universes
The Death Of Elvis 1
Vote Shit
When You Call Someone Dickhead

rob mclennan 234
Dukes of Hazard Monologue

Sean Thomas Dougherty 235
I'm Looking for Lorca in Your Letters

Sky Gilbert 236
Romantic Possibilities of the Telephone

Taylor Mali 238
Labeling Keys
Switching Sides

Tish Benson 241
No Parts Spared

Wayde Compton 243
Come To
Band

SECTION FOUR

IN/FUSION

Alex Boutros 248
From BABY BOY BLUES

Alexis O'Hara 249
NIPPLE'S HINDSIGHT REVENGE

Anne Stone 250
SALINE

Carol Rosenfeld 253
DIKE-OTOMY

Cheryl B. 255
YOU ARE NOT THE HETERO DIVA

Christian Langworthy 257
HOW COULD I INTERPRET THE EVENTS OF MY YOUTH,
EVENTS I DO NOT REMEMBER EXCEPT IN DREAMS

Crystal Williams 259
IN SEARCH OF AUNT JEMIMA

David Jager 261
WORDS
CADILLAC BOMB

Death Waits 263
SCREENPLAY IDEA

Donal Power 264
PORNO
EXCAVATIONS

Elena Georgiou 266
A WEEK IN THE LIFE OF THE ETHNICALLY INDETERMINATE
LESSONS IN HONESTY

Emily S. Downing 273
WAR MOVIES: MEN IN ARMOR IN ARMS

Golda Fried 274
THE DINER
STICKY AISLES
THE POETESS IN LATE AFTERNOON UNDERWEAR

Guillermo Castro 277
BALLOONS FROM HELL
FASCIST MANIFESTO
SHIP OF FOOLS

Heather O'Neill 279
INSOMNIA
WEDDING DRESS

Jeffery Conway 284
PRE-APPROVED OFFER TO A POET IN DEBT
STARSTRUCK II
THE ALBUM THAT CHANGED MY LIFE

Jonathan Goldstein 294
5000 EJACULATIONS

Julie Crysler 296
THE FURY
SNAKE CHARMING

Mark Bibbins 301
YOUR SHIRT
BLIND
ORACLE
THE PARTS OF THIS WE REMEMBER

Ron Drummond 304
ATTENTION TO GRAY
THE CROSSING

Shafiq 305
TACKY TACK

Thoth Harris 307
THE IRWIN ALLEN EXPERIENCE

Tina Chang 308
FACE
ODE TO SOY SAUCE
OR MARTHA STEWART COOKS CHINESE

ALPHABETIC LISTING BY AUTHOR 313

CONTRIBUTORS' NOTES—CANADIAN 315

CONTRIBUTORS' NOTES—U.S. 323

CREDITS—CANADIAN 331

CREDITS-U.S. 335

Acknowledgements

[Regie Cabico]

I wish to thank Michael Lassell, Micki Siegel, Nicole Blackman, Douglas A. Martin, Justin Chin, horehound stillpoint, Goldalee Semel, Laverne Williams, Francine Witte, Dani Nikas, Diane Mendez, Eva Baer-Schenkein, Nancy E. Young, Golda Soloman, Jaclyn Piudik, Clare Ultimo, Stephen Cardella. Jin Auh, Daniel Luna, Dan Bacalzo, Tim Driscoll, and Tristin Taormino.

The Writers Voice: Glenda Pleasants and Kathleen Warnock; In Our Own Write: Carol Rosenfeld, Barabra Raab; The Asian American Writers Workshop: Derrick Nguyen, Peter Ong; The Nuyorican Poets Café—1998 Slam Team, Kieth Roach; Dixon Place: Catherine Porter & Ellie Covan; A Different Light Bookstore—Richard Labonte, Walter Vatter; Realness & Rhythms: Emanuel "Manny" Xavier; Big Fat Press: Anne Elliott; Poets House: Catherine Coy Leslie Sullivan; Poets & Writers: Fay Chiang, Roger Bonair-Argard; August Aichorn: Marcy Kraver; Phatitude Literary Magazine—Gabrielle David, Karen Chow; and Guillermo Castro.

Acknowledgements

[Todd Swift]

First I wish to thank my parents for their continual support. Other relations who made my work possible by showing that poets need not become lawyers (though they themselves did) are Bev Swift and John Swift. And Melita Hume, my grandmother, whose homemade anthologies and catalogues astound me still. Not quite part of the family drama, I also must thank Dr. Judith Vogel of the Montreal Jewish General.

Then there are the friends of poetry, who allowed me to travel light and fast over the world of words in their safe company: William Furey, who first worked with me on a reading series; Dan C. Mitchell and Jasmine Chatelaine who helped build my poetry dream home, *Vox Hunt*. Jake Brown, for being the best competition in town. Tom (Bone) Walsh, who first put me on the multimedia stage. Michael Brown in Boston, who pushed me into my first Slam. Jason Camlot for helping me wade through the enormous amount of fresh poetry in Canada. And the late pioneer of CBC radio broadcasting, John Bishopric, whose long poem is still unpublished, a loss to us all.

During my stay in Budapest, Hungary as a lecturer at ELTE University, much legwork was needed to be done back in the "real world," and Ian Ferrier and Fortner Anderson, Montreal's fathers of wordplay, were able virtual facilitators. Alex Espinosa, who generously allowed me to use one of Ian Stephen's unpublished poems also deserves credit for his kindness. This book could not have been assembled from its too-many working parts without the diligence and expertise of Simon Dardick, who luckily believed in the madcap scheme from the first stanza. Finally, let me thank my wonderful Sara Egan, who has graced me with the only support any of us needs, (com)passionate love.

Foreword

The great Canada-U.S. border is an invisible and exact 3,987 miles, making it the longest border in the world. It scoots round the Great Lakes, sweeps elegantly across the Great Plains, zigzags Rockies, laces around the knob of Maine, and won't rest till it explodes on both ends of the Pacific/Atlantic construct, waters which won't meet again till they gush below the Pole, rush into the locks of the Panama Canal, surge past the cape of Good Hope. It's real, too, this border. You get nervous when you cross it. You can get turned back; you better be on your best behavior. And please memorize the dollar versus dubloony ratio while you're at it.

Breaking down borders is what poetry is all about. It's what this book is all about. It's why the lines of a poem refuse to lock-step the plank to the page end. This anthology is a grenade to borders between generations, gender, sexual orientation, race, class, formal training, academic degrees, aesthetics—these divisions dissolve herein. Serve up brand-new non-brand recipe marking new era for old art, an aspic where each poem glistens and it's poetry itself that jells. In doing so, this book crosses the world's longest border sans identity papers. That it zaps nationalism is a signal, naming a new, all-inclusive Nation of Poetry in the process.

It's the breaking down of borders that calls the sweet fertility of poetry imagination into being. In the lineage that isn't, in the rush to the pen of democratizing design, first shouts in this book to the elders included herein whose work has always been open to all poetries—to inspire, not categorize. Ginsberg and Stephens, Dutton, Algarin, Cisneros—poets who created the ground in which these poems now flourish.

In the same breath let it be said that it is the *Saying* of these poems which allows them to be heard. A dynamic pulling of the poem from the page into the honest air has been the root of the Millennium II

PoetryRenaissance. The poem resting in, but not confined to, this or any book, now twirls Rumi-esque as spoken or sung, on television or the Internet, direct or mediaized, feminine, marvelous, tough. Poetry traditions now include rock music and abstract expressionism, contact improv and deconstructivism and cultural activism; herein you'll find the fruits of hiphop and rap, of poetry slams, of dub and pidgin and the delightful lurch of French into English into French and then the whole thing swishing down the tubes into dot dot dot Pure Sound.

To Cabico and Swift, let's be clear—a crowning chorus of thanks. Two young poets whose jobs—as always in the realm of Po, self-defined— include not only to write/perform but also to create events framing the poem and now a venture into the world of tradition, this anthology of a hundred or so, and in so doing seeing a Poetry Nation unbounded by old frames—prose poems mix it up with rap, identity kits blossom into love lyrics, Language lambs lie next to Slammer lions. Our deft editors portaged all boundaries. Et bien sûr, they get their poems in here, too. Bravo!

And who else is here? Who else has something to say? These words of sweet rasp and battle, flooding borders and barriers with singular views, visions, consciousnesses. Here's the ex in "taxonomy"! An axe to "digitalization of culture"! Hopping in ecstasy, that roar that rock'n'roll left behind on your battered eardrums now slowly heals into meaning. Mssrs. Reg and Todd have picked up fragments, redone mirror.

So crack open your favorite aircube, lash on the vid'n'virtual wires, and prep for an all-nighter. The poetry bus has landed, jammed with more species than Noah even. Here's your poetic license, here's your passport to the world of poetry, here's your poetry nation. Where the word ends and the dream begins, where the dream ends and the word begins, where ears are fists and tongues are whips, where the poem bathes naked in a mind, a book is calling.

Whether you answer or not, the poem is calling.

Bob Holman

Introduction

Over 120 contemporary poets from both Canada and the United States are included in this collection. It is one of the first anthologies to equally represent American and Canadian poets on such a scale. All of them, and none of them, is a Fusion Poet, for the simple reason that there is no school of Fusion Poetry per se, but a virtual, possible school—a way of appreciating the myriad of poets at the end of the millennium and their numerous positions and personae—their multi-messaged, multimedia approaches to poetry.

Poetry Nation is divided into four sections, which celebrate poetry activists, academics experimenting with the spoken word, Slam and multimedia performers, and new voices. What keeps *Poetry Nation* from simply being just another Who's Who of Poets is its thesis that there is a "third way" in the creation and reception of poetry in the 1990s. We have sought to rejoice in eclecticism and enthusiasm, verve and energy, but also, and always, excellence.

Poetry with a capital P is alive again (after repeatedly being pronounced dead in the public imagination ever since Plato), at least as much, if not more so, than when it flourished on campus and in coffee-houses in the 50s and 60s. College kids flock to Yawp!, a spoken word and music series in Montreal, or Julie Crysler's events at Buddies in Bad Times in Toronto. They snap their fingers at the Green Mill in Chicago or listen to Nicole Blackman create a poetry performance installation at Beyond Baroque in Venice Beach. Or stay till three in the morning to hear a tourist from Japan read Ginsberg's "Howl" in Japanese at the Nuyorican Poets Café's Open Room after the Friday night poetry slam.

Poets now zoom across the Net, are screened on videos, lasered onto CDs, and thrust onto stages from Lollapalooza to the Apollo Theater. A renaissance of chapbooks, zines and small presses are inscribing fresh new voices onto the page, and impressing them onto the stage, in record numbers. It is a great time to be an emerging poet.

We believe it is far too easy and reductive to classify poetry as either written or spoken, for the college or the bar, as slick or slam. In reality, many serious poets—the kind who get published in books like *Best American Poetry* and who teach as professors at universities and win or are nominated for major awards like the Pulitzer or the Governor General's—read or perform their work for audiences, and get their message across, wonderfully. Also real is the border-breaking excellence of many spoken word artists whose capacity for literate language play on the page is often breathtaking and eye-catching, whose success also depends on the aura of the performer/ poet propelled into action.

Ultimately, whatever the delivery system employed, good writing is, we believe, good writing. As poets ourselves, we looked for innovation and creativity. Works that inspired and moved us and shaped the landscape of this Fusion movement.

We decided that we would attempt to make a kind of sampling of this decade and include those poets and performers most actively attempting to make this new kind of wordspeech work. To provide historical context we included a few guides—forerunners and pioneers like the inescapably necessary Allen Ginsberg—those who made this open, direct and human language, in all its brazen candour and indelicacy, the new songbook of North America.

We believe the best poetry being written and performed today is by an emerging generation of poets who "fuse"—in Luis Rodriguez's striking image, the worlds of the oral and the written traditions. These are poets comfortable in print or squinting under the stage lights. These are the Fusion Poets. Whether they be first and foremost elegant writers of text or hardcore rappers, they work with a full awareness of the variety, the eclecticism, the wild multiplicities of media and meaning available to any creative imagination in the infobahn age. They contain multitudes, opposites. Are one and many.

Fusing poetry energizes the written word and the performed word by juxtaposing alternatives in a never-ending series of passionate strategies

for renewal. These Fusion Poets are writers who want to be seen, heard
and read, and be excellent at every stage of the way. In the process, they
are opening up the discourse for new subjects, attitudes and experiences
for all of us, in whatever nation we find ourselves.

Regie Cabico,
New York City

Todd Swift,
Montréal/Budapest

Section One

FUSION BOMB

Allen Ginsberg

DEATH & FAME

When I die
I don't care what happens to my body
throw ashes in the air, scatter 'em in the East River
bury an urn in Elizabeth New Jersey, B'nai Israel Cemetery
But I want a big funeral
St. Patrick's Cathedral, St. Mark's Church, the largest synagogue in Manhattan
First, there's family, brother, nephews, spry aged Edith stepmother 96, Aunt
    Honey from old Newark,
Doctor Joel, cousin Mindy, brother Gene one eyed one ear'd, sisterinlaw
blonde Connie, five nephews, stepbrothers & sisters their grandchildren,
companion Peter Orlovsky, caretakers Rosenthal & Hale, Bill Morgan—
Next, teacher Trungpa Vajracharya's ghost mind, Gelek Rinpoche, there
    Sakyong
Mipham, Dalai Lama alert, chance visiting America, Satchitananda Swami
Shivananda, Dehorahava Baba, Karmapa XVI, Dudjom Rinpoche, Katagiri &
    Suzuki Roshi's phantoms
Baker, Whalen, Daido Loorie, Qwong, Frail Whitehaired Kapleau Roshis,
    Lama Tarchen—
Then, most important, lovers over halfcentury
Dozens, a hundred, more, older fellows bald & rich
young boys met naked recently in bed, crowds surprised to see each other,
innumerable, intimate, exchanging memories
"He taught me to meditate, now I'm an old veteran of the thousand day
    retreat—"
"I played music on subway platforms, I'm straight but loved him he loved me"
"I felt more love from him at 19 than ever from anyone"
"We'd lie under covers gossip, read my poetry, hug & kiss belly to belly arms

round each other"
"I'd always get into his bed with underwear on & by morning my skivvies
    would be on the floor"
"Japanese, always wanted take it up my bum with a master"
"We'd talk all night about Kerouac & Cassady sit Buddhalike then sleep in his
    captain's bed."
"He seemed to need so much affection, a shame not to make him happy"
"I was lonely never in bed nude with anyone before, he was so gentle my
    stomach
shuddered when he traced his finger along my abdomen nipple to hips—"
"All I did was lay back eyes closed, he'd bring me to come with mouth &
    fingers along my waist"
"He gave great head"
So there be gossip from loves of 1948, ghost of Neal Cassady commingling
    with flesh and
youthful blood of 1997
and surprise—"You too? But I thought you were straight!"
"I am but Ginsberg an exception, for some reason he pleased me."
"I forgot whether I was straight gay queer or funny, was myself, tender and
    affectionate to be kissed on the top of my head,
my forehead throat heart & solar plexus, midbelly. on my prick, tickled with
    his tongue my behind"
"I loved the way he'd recite 'But at my back allways hear/ time's winged
    chariot hurrying near,' heads together, eye to eye, on a pillow"
Among lovers one handsome youth straggling the rear
"I studied his poetry class, 17 year-old kid, ran some errands to his walkup
    flat,
seduced me didn't want to, made me come, went home, never saw him again
    never wanted to…"
"He couldn't get it up but loved me," "A clean old man." "He made sure I came
    first"
This the crowd most surprised proud at ceremonial place of honor—
Then poets & musicians—college boys' grunge bands—age-old rock star
    Beatles,
faithful guitar accompanists, gay classical conductors, unknown high Jazz
music composers, funky trumpeters, bowed bass & french horn black
geniuses, folksinger fiddlers with dobro tamborine harmonica mandolin
autoharp pennywhistles & kazoos
Next, artist Italian romantic realists schooled in mystic 60's India, Late fauve
Tuscan painter-poets, Classicdraftsman Massachusets surreal jackanapes
with continental wives, poverty sketchbook gesso oil watercolor masters from
    American provinces

Then highschool teachers, lonely Irish librarians, delicate bibliophiles, sex
    liberation troops nay
armies, ladies of either sex
"I met him dozens of times he never remembered my name I loved him
    anyway, true artist"
"Nervous breakdown after menopause, his poetry humor saved me from
    suicide hospitals"
"Charmant, genius with modest manners, washed sink, dishes my studio guest
    a week in Budapest"
Thousands of readers, "Howl changed my life in Libertyville Illinois"
"I saw him read Montclair State Teachers College decided be a poet—"
"He turned me on, I started with garage rock sang my songs in Kansas City"
"Kaddish made me weep for myself & father alive in Nevada City"
"Father Death comforted me when my sister died Boston 1982"
"I read what he said in a newsmagazine, blew my mind, realized others like me
    out there"
Deaf & Dumb bards with hand signing quick brilliant gestures
Then Journalists, editors's secretaries, agents, portraitists & photography
aficionados, rock critics, cultured laborers, cultural historians come to
witness the historic funeral
Superfans, poetasters, aging Beatnicks & Deadheads, autographhunters,
    distinguished paparazzi, intelligent gawkers
Everyone knew they were part of "History" except the deceased
who never knew exactly what was happening even when I was alive.

Andrea Thompson

FIRE BELLY

I was once
a nappy headed
barbie wielding
cartwheel turning
little girl

deliriously playful
and obliviously brown

adolescence brought
scalp burned

straightened hair
    initiation
skin grown fairer
with hormone change, and
less playing with the sun

brought passing
accidentally
getting dates, being in
on nigger jokes told
by a soon to be embarrassed
kid at the party
who doesn't know my history

Jeff Garland waited for me
behind the same snowy hedge
three years in a row, him
a big gangly teenager
and me still just a kid
but I never did
take the long way home, no

just stood my ground
and fought tooth and nail
reclaiming my right
to walk down the street
with my head held high

and the colored girls go
do, do, do, do, do, do, do, do…
hmm

and the boys who do
date me
eventually
are heroes
for not listening
to the teasing
are brave in heart
and soft in skin

also
often
later

    disappointing
  as they mistakenly
  stake flag on me
    brave explorer
      first to see
    this exotic
     and erotic
      foreign
      colony

      now
      the dic
      tionary
      states

that something that is
exotic is such that is
from elsewhere, overthere
overseas, once upon
a time in a kingdom
far, far away. Not
native, not from here
here my dear
beats the heart of pre
judice, assume first
think later

Mr. man on the street
this girl will not
give you the answer
you may so want to hear
when you ask where
I am from

I will not
banter in Swahili
or the long drawl of Patwa
will not enthrall you
with captivating tales
of the ivory coast

of lazy days spent
wit muddah and sistah
singing folk tunes
while weaving
from the loom
under the broad shade
of the coconut palm

no
not this girl
this girl will tell you
that she is from a land where
the people all share
a fire belly ferocity
about their belonging

a land
of strip malls, snow tires
backyard barbecues, Safeway
parent's day, carport, camping
and toboggans

and if any further questions
do not insinuate exile, I will
expand upon the blood
which is new to this soil
and tell ya'll
it's from the land of Buckingham
marmalade, BBC, Royal Brigade
and a little
nosh with tea

and that the blood that is
from the rest of me
tells a tale
of North Star
railroad, underground
of near escapes and
bondages broken
of hundreds of years
working the land
and buried in the soil

and that I am slave
and I am slave master

but
I am not
a hot chocolate
sweet ginger
coco, oreo
honey dipped
brown sugar
butterscotch
coffee, caramel
cinnamon girl

I am not dinner
at the afro-congo
down-to-the-bone
brown-girl-cafe

where am I from?
no, really from?
no, my parents?
parent's parents?
before that? No?
original
origin - al
origin - al
origin - al al al ly?

let me tell you

I come from a land
of snow job
and fire belly
where the neighbors
are Garlands
and the natives
are brown.

bill bissett

loving without being vulnrabul

manee timez
i *was* considring th wayze uv sunnee
n murkee possibiliteez yet ther was is ar
onlee th wayze that can happn he sd as i was
am accepting ths evreething opend up 2 b
sew much eazier yes as iul nevr b as i was
onlee th inkredibul non logikul un translatabul
wayze uv being as i am wun n multipul n
present within WHAT GOWD th WATR N
SEE KREESHURS wer FLOODING thru
evn th closd windos thees opnings involv
not being pressurd he went on by annee othrs
my selvs or schedules accepting YES th
kontra dicksyuns embray sing th process sure
unknowing th goal like whats th point ok xcept
we b 2gether ar flying undr th giant looming sew
neer sew far sew manee manee ITS A NU GAL
AXEE star flamingoes constellaysyun bneeth
th selestshul shaydee evr reeching branches
comets shooting hi liting go on suddn path wayze
luxuriating in th sensitiv breezes yes th ocean
ripping thru us in all direksyuns each wave n
us disapeering now they see it is not how it is
if yr not vulnrabul how ar yu in love he askd
its a nu kind uv loving i sd n its reelee possibul
may b n is reelee mor wundrful whn it can happn
uv kours not always me ium ths close 2 happee
ness i sd yet th scene changes melting in anothr supr hot
spell whats th point uv lerning lessons if we cant
remembr them
our specees skreemd in 2 th deep turquoise whale
nite teeth sew rippuling shine swet dripping off
them tusks prodding gnashing our legs off blood
spurting **sharks interrupting our picknick
ing** *or* us trappd in anothr ice age brrrrrr big
time *or caut in a suddn tidal wave* its th big wun
fine ride it out arint we sew small
squishd undr all ths watr is it still calld

th atlanteek *or* burreed undr an un
announsd erth quake ar they evr ANNOUNSD
WHAT AR YU SAYING

dont give yr heart   unless
  dont give yr heart   s h a r e   its a
dont give yr heart   transplant

Bob Holman

THE DEATH OF POETRY

You were invited there
You overslept again
What's your excuse this time
You missed the boat/vote/rote/moat/bloat/goat..., You missed the goat

The book was printed up
The words all ran together
The pages blank with ink
So the faux po's use invisible stink

It was a fluke that you were inside of the coffin as they swung it up on their
    shoulders
On the way to the graveside
Wasn't it a real nice graveride?
You're finally inside-in
Real nice riptide

Woho! The Death of Poetry
Mercifully fast
Only lasted a millennium or two
The art of the past

No mo po
Get down to bidness
Po's no show's
Ho ho ho—Good riddance

The view was dark/hark/lark/bark/park/stark...The view was stark
The time was passing slo/emotion
The day was crambe repetita, fool and a balmy,
April is the cruelest ... coolest! ...

The creeps were creeping out
Launching eulogy missiles at the street
The word's worth opposite beat!
The drummer's melodizing feet

Typewriters on parade
Walt'n'Emily rolling grave
Nothing left save to save
The Death of Poetry

It was a computer thing—
A neuter thing
Belligerent knucklehead
Brat art teeth shred
Flesh word battery nozzle
Blue skinny grenade carousal
Itchy mean grouse rasp kiss
Whatta life death is
The Death of Poetry

Whatta life death is
The Death of Poetry

The Death of Poetry
Mercifully fast
Only lasted a millennium or two
The art of the past

Whatta life death is
The Death of Poetry

Bob Redmond

THE POET

for laura moran and the baby-sitters

after the famous poets read, they and the locals schmooze
but i and my backstage pass leave from the back gate
leave them, their kiss-ass and fuck me
and even their well-meaning banter
their after-work rant and rave
"i loved your stuff!"
"are you a writer?"
"we should, we should really, we should get together"
i leave the hard business of selling and buying
and meeting and being on and up
leave that networking and overtime word-ing
leave hammersmith echoes to bandy about each other
like a traffic jam honking in red and blue

i go home, for the three year old whose poet-mother is working late
at her other job, pulling guinness for finnegan and frat boys
deserves a break and i assist and take
the quiet child with me

yes, i have landed the labor of love tonight in my arms
i carry carward a half-mile and longer the tired girl
talking to her threads of the day's festival chaos
and pinwheel splendor
coo-cooing the cor-cor, darling corey, sleepy corey
little girl getting heavy, heavier with every corner and crossing

i trade steps with the other poet-pulled-nightwatch,
mother's friend melody who shares conversation and by turns
the child's sleepy bones
little girl, tired girl
whose nodding head is full not with tv or purple toys
but poetry, her mother tongue, her future tense
full with the cadence of tracie morris, bob holman,
everton sylvestor, naomi shihab nye, bye-bye poets
you won't sign my book, shake my hand

you won't even see your own until later
for now they are but memory or longing
while i, i go home with the poem itself
i am carrying the precious breathing poem
to watch and ponder
this long-haired child of eyes
of ears, of honest weight
this child who sleeps
this child

who is only just beginning to sing

Clifton Joseph

SHOTS ON EGLINTON

I was caught in a cross/fire
on Eglinton Avenue just/the/other/day.
this was no night/time shooting in the wild/west
it was about three in the afternoon i would say
you didnt have much time for thinking
you had to rush your ass out/the/way
hoping none of the children
would be ricocheted DEAD
on the sidewalks where they were at/play.

shots rang/out on my block on Eglinton Avenue just the other day
two young/bloods-with-guns bicycled from the alley/way
pumped hot lead into another
and rode down Oakwood Avenue
on their getaway. Shots rang/out on my block
just the other day.
mouths hung open wide
but nobody knew what to say. But
I want/to/know: "What the 'france' is going on?" when
this-is-the-way-that-the-brothers-play!

shots rang out
on my block
on Eglinton Avenue. Just the other/day.

while "my/man" was eating some curried goat.
And everybody dropped/grabbed the floor like a sweet/heart
knowing it was no joke. But
some serious/settling-of-scores
over cash/money, badness or some dope
yeahhhhHHHHHHHHHHHHHHHHHHHHH
the death/smoke................. of-crack/coke.

Shots rang out
on my/crowded block the other/day
those cats wasnt into no-Africa
wasnt into no-"Ites/Green/Gold"-and/that
was just some cold/blood-ed/gangster-ism
and did I say that it was black/on/black
BLACK-ON-BLACK/ON-MY-BLOCK
as if the system and the killer/cops
was/not heavy on our backs, HEAVY/HEAVY
on-our-backs, these "mo/fo"-hooligans
doing crime that is black/on/black. Tell me:
"Why are we so messes/up?
why some of us so whack
that black/blood stains my block
from crimes that are black/on/black
from crimes that are black/on/black
from crimes that are black/on/black.
and the thing that hurts
and hurts so bad
is that the shhhht aint over yet.
the shhht
aint over
yet!

Denise Duhamel

THE DIFFERENCE BETWEEN PEPSI AND POPE

I have this blind spot, a dark line, thin as air, that obliterates
a stroke of scenery on the right side of my field of vision
so that often I get whole words at the end of sentences wrong

like when I first saw the title of David Lehman's poem
"The Difference Between Pepsi and Coke" and I misread
"Coke" for "Pope." This blind spot makes me a terrible driver,
a bad judge of distances, a Ping-Pong player that inspires giggles
from the opposite team.
        I knew a poet who dressed up as a cookie
and passed out a new brand in a crowded supermarket.
The next day he gave Pepsi Challenge to passersby
in a mall.
    I felt old-fashioned admitting to this poet that I prefer Coke,
that wavy hyphen that separates its full name Coca-Cola.
Like the bar let down in the limbo dance, the Spanish tilde comes
        down until
not even a lowercase letter can squeeze under it.
I searched for that character recently, writing to David Lehman,
telling him about an electronic magazine, the address of which
had this ~ in it. I couldn't find it, although I stared
at my computer keyboard for more than a few minutes.
I only noticed it today in the upper left hand corner, above the tab,
the alternate of ', if you hit the shift key. I wonder if I also have a
        blind spot
in my left eye. I wonder if the poet who dressed as a cookie
is happy in his new marriage. I wonder if you can still get a bottle
        of Tab
anywhere, that awful soda my forever-dieting aunt used to drink,
with his pink logo, its "a" all swirls, looking like @.
            Yesterday,
when my husband was waiting at an intersection, he said, *Is*
        anyone coming?
I looked from the passenger seat and said confidently, *We can*
        make it.
Then we were almost run off the road. I said
I'm sorry I'm sorry through the exchange of honks and fists
and couldn't believe when my husband forgave me so quickly.
            Not only that,
but *I'm a bad proofreader,* I thought to myself as I made a mental list
of ways that I felt inadequate. One friend also recently noted that
        maybe I
talk too much about myself, so I told her the Bette Midler joke,
Enough about me, what do YOU think of me? which doesn't *really*
bring me back to David Lehman and his poem, but does make me
        realize

how far away I strayed from my original point
which was that I thought his poem would be funny because of the
        title,
not the real title, but my mistaken one. I started to guess his poem
in my head: Pepsi is bubbly and brown while the Pope
is flat and white. Pepsi doesn't have a big white hat. The Pope
can't get rid of fender rust. Pepsi is all for premarital sex.
The Pope won't stain your teeth.
                            But "The Difference
Between Pepsi and Coke" is a tender poem about a father
who the speaker reveres and I wonder if David Lehman's own
        father
is alive or dead which is something I often do—wonder
how much is true—when I read a poem by someone I like
which I know is not the right way to read a poem even though
Molly Peacock said at her reading that she is the "I"
in all of hers and doesn't use the word "speaker" anymore.
                                        Still,
I feel like a Peeping Tom, although this is really about what I can't
        see,
my blind spots, and how easy it is for me to doubt my decisions,
how I relate to the father in Lehman's poem who "won't admit his
        dread
of boredom" and panics and forgives. How easy it is to live for
        stretches at a time
in that skinny dark line, how easy it is to get so many things all
        wrong.

HAPPY ENDING

I lost my virginity in a hotel
although on the police report I said it was stolen.
My virginity contained my only picture ID
and concert stubs that proved I'd seen Kiss and Queen.
I wanted it back. I wanted to slip my virginity
into my pocket where I'd last seen it,
the smooth red leather and jingling coin pouch,
the tight metal snap. I looked at each stranger
in the elevator—*Dis you take it? Do you recognize me
as the one you had for lunch?* I sniffed the cubicle of air

for the scent of my sex on someone else. I sniffed
the lit buttons after each man had pushed one
hoping I'd left my smell on his hand. I finally went home
and wept, the blood on my panties three cherries
that won me nothing in the slot machine.
I watched a black and white TV, doodled on a hotel napkin
as my mother cried she didn't know me anymore.
I was grounded until the mail came several days later.
A kind stranger had sent me back my virginity
in a padded envelope so I could keep it
or lose it again, this time sober, with a boy my own age.
I checked the crotch of my panties I'd hidden under my bed.
The blood dots slid off like new pennies or cinnamon hearts,
then disappeared. My mother put down her iron and smiled,
braided my clean shiny hair as the whole world sang
a song about what a good girl I was.

Ellyn Maybe

I HAVE NEVER FALLEN IN LOVE WITH ANYONE WHO FELT COMFORTABLE IN AMERICA

I have never fallen in love
        with anyone who felt
        comfortable in America

people who wear the 60's
        on their eyebrows like a birthmark

who wear turn-of-the-century Russia
        like a boat with a hull made of flame

people who wear Montreal
        like an almanac
        that is a forbidden book
        floating on their adam's apple

people who wear a TV
        under their arms

like a deodorant
trying to decide
where the antenna belongs

people who can recite 80 poems
    but can't remember their
    driver's license
    have my respect

people who can
    sing 100 bottles
    of sandpaintings on the wall
    backwards
    in the time it takes
    to pour the shotglass
    that pulls its trigger slowly

people who talk to dogs
    and trees
    and are afraid
    to ask the time
    and yet somehow know
    are beloved

people who wear anthems they make
    with paisley and parsley
    and mesh together a bell
    that rings through the soundproof sky
    the government is trying to sanction

people whose fingers tell stories
    of peace and love and thunderclouds
    overcome by a dish of lightning
    with a side of stars

people who don't listen
    at the most popular
    time of day
    to the most popular
    radio station
    because they'd rather be wishing

people who have cars
    so full of bumperstickers
    the engine is only incidental

the people
    who miss card catalogs

the people who miss
    cream rising to the top

the people who yearn for deja-vu
the people who love Leonard Cohen's voice

Leonard Cohen

these are the ones I sing to
    in my overbitten sleep.

Fortner Anderson

THE BOVINE SPONGIFORM
ENCEPHALOPATHY BLUES

Oh you'll shiver and shake
you'll grunt and scream
as he cracks open the world
and eats your dreams.

Tonight

Under the brittle stare of the blue-eyed moon

I engage a sacred travail

lift my tool out of the shadows and into the glare

long and cool and sharp.

Out of spittle and jism I'll spin the threads

with the blood of pedigree rat and pentium chips

I'll weave a sticky sieve to catch the fleshy bits.

I'll scoop the bloody mess into crystalline vials, and

we'll be up all night on a genetic hack

growing two eyes two hands a nose and a sweet-smelling crack.

> mais sans histoire
> sans mémoire
> il est nulle
> il est faux

So, I'll spin a yarn to cover his squalid little tale.

Oh I yam what I yam what I yam.

Under the stars of the well-oiled heavens
who shimmer in silence from zenith to horizon

Who shall be witness, a witness to the world
as I build me a man.
Golem, Golem, Golem..... Golem

It's nano-robotics and yesterday's dead
mechanical conception in a plexiglass tray
stainless steel needles and a glass syringe
sirloin tips and critical mass
the corpse of a cat and a color TV.

My man
Oh, he'll walk the walk and talk the talk.
He'll strut, strut, strut.

Who shall bear witness, witness on the world

> Cut the meat and chew the gristle
> Tear the flesh and crush the muscle
> Crack them bones
> Crack them bones

His eyes shall bathe in the dark liquid of the heaven's cream
and his ears shall sail on the warm breathe of the aether's song
                    Beautiful people

                        pour road kill and pets
                        into a great big kettle
                        Grind 'em up and feed 'em to cattle

Oh I got the bovine spongiform encephalopathy blues

                                                again.

Oh my man, he'll make things right

            because, you know, we'll all be in a terrible fix
            with that di-oxy-ribo-nucleic re-mix

My man, My man, My man,

shall know of the creatures that walk upon the earth
and know of the creatures that fly in the heavens
and know of the creatures that swim in the sea
and he shall know of the plants of the forests and plains

                        Oh, that crazy rhinoceros
                        is so simply preposterous.
                        It's so sad, soon so dead
                        just like the rest of

My man

Shall take them one by one and two by two

the serpent and the ape and the sheep and the honeybee.

With flesh-covered hands

he will take the seed of the ewe and the seed of the honeybee

and in his own hot core he will mix the seed
to birth mutton the taste of honey and mead as thick and black as
ram's blood.

He shall take the seed of the serpent and ape

and in his hollow bosom he will plant the seed

and birth a slouching tower of meat and bone and scale.

Man made new.

Tonight let him rise

out of the stinking pool of wasted life and broken souls

and speak

his tongue lolls about that grinning hole.

I am, he shall say

I am

your man.

MY FRIEND

My friend, you are falling forward
stumblebum, clown or star.
Toward an end
the fire or a hole.

As you lean into night toward another morning
we'll raise our arms and cup our hands
soon it will rain down all the tender morsels of your passing.

The TV will bray
the radio will weep
till this bed's awash in the bloody tears
        and traces of bilious love
of those you'll leave behind.
Tonight my friend, will you teach me how to die?
Lean close and whisper me all those hard-fought secrets

teach me the cough, the grimace, and the rattle
  at the end.

It will be glorious
to die under the hot lights to thunderous applause
filled with all the pomp and chatter
I need.

On these boards
we'll vomit up what's left of our lives
cough blood and shit bile into the stinking sheets
    and laugh as the blood boils under our brittle skulls.

Now grab ahold, and ride this gurney
we'll plummet through the septic corridors
johnny shirts flapping through the rushing airs.
We'll reach out bent hands
    shriek to the startled managers and barristers
we'll cry out secret verses to those stolid faces
lost to our hyped loves, ecstatic failures, and fabulous demise.

And when
the words whistle past
and stop
we'll fall back here
I'll wipe the slaver from your chin
you'll comb my hair.

Maybe we'll roll the bones for your dreams
you knew it would come to this
they're all packed up so nice and ready to go.

All the souvenirs, taken from the shelves
Mom & Pop
and the days, and nights, and the day
all caught now in my tongue and eye.

You must help me, my friend
extract them all
one by one.

Tear out the broken arrows
uncover the sores

open each bloody stone
and unravel the words and time.

We shall remember them each
and lay them aside.

Tonight, my friend, you must help me
die
as these words whistle past.

Hal Sirowitz

NO MORE BIRTHDAYS

Don't swing the umbrella in the store,
Mother said. There are all these glass jars
of spaghetti sauce above your head
that can fall on you, & you can die.
Then you won't be able to go to tonight's party,
or go to the bowling alley tomorrow.
And instead of celebrating your birthday
with soda & cake, we'll have
anniversaries of your death with tea
& crackers. And your father & I won't
be able to eat spaghetti sauce anymore, because
the marinara sauce will remind us of you.

DOES GOD EXIST?

There's no proof that god is up there,
Mother said. But no one can prove
that he isn't. Only the dead know.
But they're too busy being dead
to tell us. So if I were you
I would go to temple, & play it safe.
If He's dead all you lose is the time
you spent praying. But if He exists
& you didn't go, you'll be in big trouble.

You won't like Hell.
You never liked hot weather.
And then how can I visit you?
Angels aren't allowed inside.

DAMAGED BODY

Don't swim in the ocean while it's raining,
Mother said. Lightning can hit the water,
& you'll be paralyzed. You don't like
to eat vegetables. Imagine having
to spend the rest of your life being one.
Someone will have to wash you,
take you to the bathroom, & feed you.
Children will tease you. But
you may be lucky, & get struck
by only a small voltage. Then you'll be
a smart vegetable, like an asparagus.
You'll be able to make your bed by yourself,
like wouldn't it be nice to eat a chocolate
        ice cream cone,
the thought will flicker, & then go out.

DIFFERENT VERSIONS

The difference between the Christians
& the Jews, Mother said, is that they have
Jesus, who spoke in parables, & we have
Moses, who spoke in commandments. None
of them spoke in English, because
they lived in the desert, & Lawrence of Arabia,
who gave English lessons when he wasn't
fighting wasn't born yet. We started
our religion first, & then they copied us. They
claimed that they improved on the Bible by adding
the New Testament. But you & I know that when
you try to improve on something by making it
bigger, like putting more bread crumbs in the
        meat loaf,
it's never as good as if you just left it alone.

TWO BURIALS FOR THE SAME PERSON

According to Jewish law, mother said,
if your arm gets chopped off,
you can't just throw it away, but
you have to bury it in a cemetery, because
it's considered a part of you. And
you can't have a tombstone for your arm
in New York, & then another one for your body
in New Jersey. All the parts of you
are supposed to be buried in the same place.
So, if you lost your arm when you lived
in New York, & then you happened to die
in California, your surviving relatives
couldn't bury you there, but would have to fly
you all the way back to New York,
so you'd be reunited with your arm.
And just because you're dead doesn't mean
the airline will let you fly for free.

HOW TO WASH CLOTHES

Just before your mother died, Father said,
she took me into the laundry room,
& showed me how to do a wash. She
had me put the five quarters in,
then showed me the button to push.
She wouldn't let me go upstairs,
but made me wait until the machine
was finished. It was like being stuck
in a car behind an eternal red light.
Then she showed me how to operate
the dryer. She wanted me to become
more independent. It worked. I don't
have to get married again.

Ian Stephens

HOME,
GRAND METIS, QUEBEC, SEPTEMBER 1995

1.

Northern lights smeared across the sky
Pastel, greens and yellows
The changing gusts blowing
      through the trees
Broken leaves along the black street

Sweetheart, where is the knife?
In the black river
Where urchins grovel
And crab claws wrestle
Where shrimp hearts listen
To the plunging gray whales
Elegantly pushing through the gulf

Where are your lips of dreams?
Your milk, your fortune?

2.

Time is the killer, each
Dawn merciless sunset
Tireless and cruel

Home is timeless, tranquil, still
As laughter
As an embrace
As warm as a fire
As clear as a moonlit winter meadow

A smile and around the world
The cancer stops
The missiles erect

Time is the killer—I would stay
Here forever.

3.
And the killers gallop in gangs
And we must respect them
They take the evil and the child

Sweetheart, where is the gun?
The hearts we held as one?

Jill Battson

HITCHING

This is a story that involves running from a dominant father
California, Key West
touches of unwelcome male hands on your jock 18 year old body
the man with the B&D suitcase
you handcuffed to the bed that night in Pennsylvania
when it was minus 2 out and all you had on was a Blue Jays wind-
breaker
and the wind whistled through that like
no tomorrow
rolling the man for his wallet and car keys
driving to New Orleans for Mardi Gras
the big breasted woman naked to her waist dancing to the southern blues
on the balcony below you
disgusting your virginal sensibilities with their size and volatility
Key West the red spotted bandanna close to your eyelids
volleyball on the beach, smoking hash and drinking long island iced tea
into the night with the cuban hustler
who had 3 ounces of gold hoop in his earlobe
and that afternoon you met Tennessee Williams
a sad softened man with a penchant for morning martinis
never writing a thing after 1978
the girl who left her station behind the bar
walked up to you and dragged her warm pussy along the
blond hairs of your sun-tanned, hitchhiking hard leg
before kissing you full on the mouth
just to feel your surprise
and the vacant eyed man with ten dollars to his name

who fixed you up with a 79 malibu and drove with you
to the west coast
where the summer of love was still in full swing
yes, this a story about a dominant father smacking his wife in the
mouth
and you running and running
getting out of the house into the indigo softness and tarmac toughness
of your real world.

Kimiko Hahn

THE UNBEARABLE HEART

In the train hour along the Sound, distant from the details of grief
I look up from the news toward the salt marshes
clamped beneath a snow we thought we would not see this year;
now fallen twice this past week mother died, instantly, 10:30 p.m.,
broadsided by an Arab kid fleeing a car of white kids with baseball bats;
a snow only matched by my father's head as I reach to touch him
as I have never touched him. He wishes
he could see her once more, to say goodbye,
as Ted and I said goodbye to the body that was mother's.
Grief comes in spasms: the smell of banana bread, I think of the rotting fruit
my sister and I tossed before father came home from Yonkers general.
A flashlight she bought my youngest daughter
who always rummaged under grandpa's side of the mattress.
The orange day lilies the florist sent to our apartment:
the lilies from the woods she brought to my wedding.
And after I told my six-year-old, grandma died in the accident,
after tears and questions she suggested, maybe now is a good time
to explain what the man has to do with babies.
So I chose one perfect lily from that vase
and with the tip of a paring knife slit open the pistil
to trace the passage pollen makes to the egg cell—
the eggs I then slipped out and dotted on her fingertip, their greenish-white
translucent as the air in this blizzard that cannot cool the unbearable heart.
As I write this, I still demand your attention, mother.

And now that she's gone how do we find her—
especially my small daughters who will eventually recall their grandmother
not as a snapshot in the faults of the mind
but as the incense in their hair long after the reading of the Lotus Sutra.

Lee Gotham

I'D LOVE TO BUT...

It's been weeks since i unplugged my printer, my telephone, my fax machine and modem. I'd like to see an analyst, but I'm afraid that'd be a cop-out. My best friend is the bottomless cup and I think he may be killing me. I can explain: You see, there's warm reassurance in the speed of the traffic, the height of the bridges, and their low antique guard-rails... it was all so long ago. Explanations are always reassuring; but I find this disconcerting. An artist's life should transcend explanations! Life should transcend artists' explanations! Explanations should... Explanations, expectations, expurgation... Too clean to see too plainly... Ex-communication. Shouldn't the should-word be annexed from the language?

Perhaps I'm only having a caesura, a minuscule crimp in my normally ebullient (if limping) course through life. Chased at gunpoint, one leg already inevitably bullet-riddled, you're entitled to collapse in the bushes, a fevered intoxicant sleep come upon you. Aren't the bad-guys obliged, on principle, momentarily to lose your trail? Isn't that the formula? How else is the beleaguered rhyme-writer meant to regroup and confront his or her nemeses? Surely we've all taken that fugitive pause in the stairwell? That raincheck on the career-deciding dinner date, business lunch, trendy gallery schmoozing session? Even the seasoned brown-noser needs a minute to catch his breath.

Marc Smith

MY FATHER'S COAT

I'm wearing my father's coat.
He has died. I didn't like him,
But I wear the coat.

I'm wearing the coat of my father,
Who is dead. I didn't like him,
But I wear the coat just the same.

A younger man, stopping me on the street,
Has asked,
"Where did you get a coat like that?"

I answer that it was my father's,
Who is gone now,
Passed away.

The younger man shuts up.

It's not that I'm trying now
To be proud of my father.
I didn't like him.
He was a narrow man.
There was more of what he should have done,
More of what he should have tried to understand.

The coat fit him well.
It fits me now.
I didn't love him,
But I wear the coat.

Most of us show off to one another
Fashions of who we are.
Sometimes button to the neck.
Sometimes over-priced.
Sometimes surprising even ourselves
In garments we would have never dreamed of wearing.

I wear my father's coat.
And it seems to me
That this is the way, most of us
Make each others' acquaintance—
In coats we have taken
To be our own.

W. Mark Sutherland

FUCK

handle
hyphen
hyperbole
verb
noun
adjective
conjunction
food
fatigue
metaphysics
insult
base
best
or
beautiful
voice
of
emptiness

ART BLAKEY

pum pum pum
ppp pum

tishshshshsh
tehtehtehteh

tah
tehtehtehteh
tah
tehtehtehteh
tah

pishshshshsh
tishshshshsh
pishshshshsh
tishshshshsh

tototototototo
tototototototo

pishshshshsh

tehtehtehteh
tah
tehtehtehteh
tah
tehtehtehteh
tah
tehtehtehteh
tah

tish
tehtehtehteh

tish
tehtehtehteh

tish
tehtehtehteh

tototototototo
tototototototo

pum pum

Melody Jordan

STRANGE APARTMENT IN BROOKLYN

It's all punishment from here on out. You will awake from your fun night
with a hangover, too late. There will be nothing to eat. You will spend
money you don't have on food you don't want. You will be hassled on the
street. You will return to a strange apartment in Brooklyn to eat that
large box of mac n cheese. The smell of gas won't go away. You will become
upset while eating mac n cheese. Because it is orange. Because you can't
cook. Because of the one scene in Clan of the Cave Bear where Ayla leaves
to find her people. Because you understand why you have been alone and
unable to make friends your whole life. You will wish there was a radio.
You will want to watch TV like never before, because you know it is
broken. You will be bored. You will write a poem, it will suck ass and make
sense to not even you. You will call people they will not be home. You will
call people they will not want to talk to you. You will write a poem, it
will be good, really good, you will realize you have written this before.
You will realize it is by someone else. You will mutter why does she keep
writing everything before me. You will be bored. You smoke. You smoke too
much. You sit. You smoke. You smoke too much. You will be homesick. You
will realize you have no poem. You will realize you have no home. You will
be homesick for nowhere. You will want coffee. There will be none. You will
want to take your mind off nothing. Nothing looms. You will brush your
teeth for the sixth time today and think of all the mirrors you have looked
in and the face that always looks back. You will try to remember what it
felt like to be touched, on your hand, softly on your face but it just
turns to scratching. The construction work outside grows louder. You will
want to drink. There is no alcohol. There is no god. So you leave. You will
be hassled on the street. You go and you drink at a bar in Manhattan. You
leave the bar in Manhattan. You return. You leave, you stumble. You have
images of never remembering where you have stayed, a fantasy of yelling
into the night without a specific point. You have always wanted to go to
CBGB's. So you find it. The band is disappointing, but the bathroom is an
excellent place to puke. And you do. You stumble towards the subway.

NOTHING HAPPENED

2 A.M. I'm tired
2:15 I can stay the night
2:20 I shouldn't stay the night
2:25 I'm making the bed
2:30 God, what a pig
2:35 He needs me to stay over
2:40 I decide I should stay the night
2:45 I'm leaving
2:50 Nice hug
2:55 Can I use your toothbrush?
3:00 He changes his clothes in the kitchen
3:05 One pillow
3:06 I can use it
3:10 I'm a mature adult
3:15 I'm going straight to sleep
3:20 I'm a giddy teenager!
3:25 I'm tired
3:30 I wonder what his heartbeat sounds like?
3:35 fast
3:40 I am your higher power
3:45 He tells me he sleeps sideways
3:50 He turns over
3:55 Starting to sleep
4:00 Should I sleep sideways?
4:05 Is it O.K. that I'm here?
4:06 Is anything really O.K.?
4:07 Eagles, Liz Phair, Unwound song ramblings
4:08 I lay next to him sideways
4:10 I'm tired
4:13 Does he really like Ginger better than Mary Ann?
4:14 He lost his virginity to Ginger
4:15 I move away
4:16 I lost my Ginger to Mary Ann
4:20 Pretend to sleep (—wish I had some weed)
4:25 cuddle
4:30 Am I a cuddle junkie?

4:35 kiss
4:36 KISS!
4:37 kiss?
4:38 What's wrong with being a cuddle junkie?
4:39 What's wrong with being a hedonist?
4:39 and a half: He pulls away
4:40 What's wrong with this person?
4:41 Why do I care?
4:45 Sometimes when things are made unclear they come up again later
4:46 I don't know what you're talking about.
4:47 That's exactly what I'm talking about.
4:48 giggle
5:00 sleep
5:01 He's kissing the back of my neck
5:02 wiggle
5:03 little wiggle
5:04 Full frontal wiggle!
5:06 Back touching!
5:07 Too much
5:09 Tired
5:10 Is there ever a right time to do the wrong thing?
5:11 Too little
5:15 Too late.
5:20 In every way

In every way

EVERYTHING IS ICE CREAM
(and the world is a very hot place)

Everyone is given one ice cream cone.
Every other hour—
Everyone is given one flavor of ice cream.
Throughout his/her existence
Some people are given two scoops of ice cream
We do not know why
But we laugh at them when it melts on their hands.

You scream
I scream
Everything is ice cream.
(and the world is a very hot place)
So hot, in fact,
That if we do not eat the ice cream immediately it will melt.
There are a lot of ice cream headaches because of this....

(I am thinking of this now...)

Micki Siegel

SKIN TONES

Your skin is warm gold
mine pale pink
what do we look like
lying together
on the blue sheets
still and quiet after love
arms and legs entwined
like a statue
so finely sculpted
it is impossible
to find the seam
between the two figures

PENMANSHIP

You make love to my words
my words are dreamings
through a hole in the sky

Miguel Algarin

NUYORICAN ANGEL OF WORDSMITHING

(Note for a Poet)

I. Nuyorican Aesthetics:
 It is a moral imperative to give poetry to the people. It is a
media twenty-first-century picturetel event when a young poet
can read on *Unplugged*, transferring via MTV the heat of passion.
Electronic verse has changed the craft of writing poetry. We can
interact *live* with Tokyo, London and Rome simultaneously; once
the poet reaches millions, he/she learns how a verse can heal
human pain.

II. Illness, Inspiration and Metaphor:
 a. Use the first person instead of the third person if it isn't pathos.
 b. Imaging Pain and Pleasure
  i) without becoming maudlin or melodramatic;
  ii) without eliciting pity from the reader; and
  iii) provoke a feeling of interaction between the person who is
   ill or enraptured (the metaphor-maker) and the reader's
   imagination.

III. Cultural Worker: A Humble Servant

IV. Poet's Burial:
 a. Instructions for ceremony should be written as a poem.
 b. The community walks in a processional honoring the bard.

V. Meditation:
 a. Concentration: Empty the mind totally.
 b. Analytical Concentration: Put one objective in mind.
           Keep all other concerns out.

NUYORICAN ANGEL PAPO

(The Bi-Sexual Super Macho)

I.
The Fourth of July fireworks
went unseen by me.
If you could not see them
then I would not see
the New York skyline
ablaze in colored fire.
The red, white and blue
would climb to the moon
without my fourth of July
Coney Island, Bushwick, Brooklyn
churchgoing,
newfound friend,
we parted in the name of fear,
the not falling in the black hole
of speedy passions
and underdeveloped love.
I drove you home,
shook your hand as we opened the trunk
to get your pack,
but you know, really,
I almost pushed you back
into the car, the hearth,
the fireplace of warmth,
the wheels that would have,
could have crossed the Williamsburg Bridge,
into Loisaida,
driven us into a nest of dreams
and corruption,

and purity and cleanliness
entwined in next to perfect lust,
yes, no, instead,
I didn't see the fireworks.
Instead, i sat thinking about
how nice it was to have left you
without our rushed desires fueling
the blazing Fourth of July skyline of New York.

II.
I tried
to separate
where we should start to touch.
I tried postponing, first with "Straight out of Brooklyn,"
then food,
but you were on an impulse
to burn fire,
to scorch passion,
I should have left you in Bushwick,
without numbers exchanged,
I could have lied about my name,
yet could'ves and would'ves
live in conditional tenements,
where on the third floor
we committed unconditional love,
knee to knee
nude from the waist down,
lust-fueled hands full
of belly buttons, buttocks and meat.

NUYORICAN ANGEL OF DESPAIR

(December 31, at the End of the Millennium)

so free that liberty weighs 'round my neck,
so without restraint that ropes tie my mind to Somalia,
so world-wide-bright-eyed gone wild
that Africa is the brilliant white-and-black
of an opaque 1934 Tarzan flick,
a dream that rides me to the burial grounds
so I couldn't leave my house until Ted Koppel
showed me how valiantly the US Somalian
relief operation yields the best
Channel 7 Eyewitness Nightline News
foreign occupation television special.
I couldn't leave my house, so I didn't get to find out
if my date was a he or a she
cross-dressed either way.
You see, I've already seen *The Crying Game*
and I'm not taking bets on who's a she or he,

but forget that,
do you know what surprised the Marines,
it wasn't Somalians,
it was a sea of extra-terrestrial lights
and television pre-occupation news teams,
"It's an eerie sight, " said a two-star general
as he arranged his would be-presidential hair
for a 2000 run for the White House T.V. shot.
It isn't that the Somalians need food and relief
you see, we also need great T.V. viewing
and Allah knows that we have to have it,
and Allah delivers,
the warlords perform in the theater of operations,
yes, Allah is great,
so during the morning talk shows we're dismayed
by how our kids are traumatized
by skeletal two-, three-, ten-year -old Somalian children—
what counseling should we do for them?
Well maybe the good Samaritan thing to do
is turn the T.V. off and let your children eat,
then turn it on again
when you want to see the great moral
imperative of our armed nation
dump marines on a lit beach
with a civilian army of world correspondents
eagerly waiting with microphones in hands
while our Marines crawl on their bellies
up to the microphones to say,
"Hey, these Africans don't have bullets,
they're just hungry."

Nicole Blackman

GIRLS

When he leaves,
he leaves a space,
a big or little airless place
that begs to be filled.

68

A part of the weekend that says
"What are you going to do now?"

And you think if you fill it up
you'll survive.
So work and clean and call
and cook and write and drink
and read and sleep and shop
and say this is fine this is fine.
You can do this.

Laugh and go out drinking
with your friends when it's over.
Call everyone you know and say
"Whatever," shrug, clear your throat.

It's kind of like losing a dog.
You'll miss him
but maybe it's better this way.

His friends are still your friends
sometimes
and they watch you
because they send him messages
about how you're doing.
Sometimes they figure now is their chance
and they tell you they've always had it bad
for you.
Be careful with his friends.

So cut your hair
and learn to play guitar.
Walk fast and yell back
at bike messengers who tell you
what they'd do to you
if you were theirs.

Stop wearing his coat and sell his CDs.
White out his name in your address book.
Buy new perfume and learn to masturbate
with the showerhead.
Turn the pain into something you can use.

And when it feels like you're imploding,
like you're the only one
who wants to lie down in the street,
know that there will always be girls
who stream through this city
with their mouths slightly open
trying to breathe
and waiting to be kissed.

LIBERATION BARBIE

I'm visiting Barbie again today
but I get so upset seeing her like this
with all her bodies frozen forever
in clear cellophane coffins
like Eva Peron on display to the masses.

Barbie's dream houses are cardboard
and her surfboards, horses and Corvettes have a
shiny shiny hot pink shine.
God, she must be sick of pink.

When I was a kid, all she could do was
hang out at the beauty salon
eat at the ice-cream parlor
or stand awkwardly on a fashion runway.
These days she's a rap singer, a doctor,
or a Naval petty officer.
But she smiles like a porno star
no matter what she's wearing.
Ken's molded hair and painted
bright white smile look painful.
At least he has a molded lump for a crotch,
Barbie only gets a weird dent between her legs.

Behind real glass, wearing real silk, are the real dolls
with really big price tags
($295 for a Collector's Edition of the Bob Mackie Barbie)
One young mother,
fending off an adrenalized munchkin says

That's stupid. You're just paying $290 for the dress y'know
and I know she's never paid $295 for anything ever
no not ever.

Across from the pink wall are the Other Dolls,
not nearly as desirable, but they try.
90210 dolls, Shani dolls, Asian dolls, Happy To Be Me dolls
with small breasts, thick waists and short legs.
After closing time, Brenda Walsh and Barbie hang out and
trade clothes, discussing late night sexual encounters
with Dylan and Ken.

Barbie's hair just gets bigger.
No doubt, millions of little girls in Mattel focus groups say
My favorite part is her hair.
Yes, I like playing with her hair the best...
So the hair keeps getting bigger
and curlier and blonder.
Pretty soon, you'll just buy boxes of Barbie hair
with no Barbie at all.

Patricia Smith

BITING BACK

Children do not grow up
as much as they grow away.
My son's eyes are stones, flat, brown, fireless,
with no visible openings in or out.
His voice, when he cares to try it on,
hovers one-note in that killing place
where even the blues fidget.
Tight syllables, half spoken, half spat,
greet me with the warmth
of glint-tipped arrows. The air around him
hurts my chest, grows too cold to nourish,
and he stares past me to the open door of his room,
anxious for my patented stumbled retreat.
My fingers used to brush bits of the world

from his kinked hair,
but he moved beyond that mother shine
to whispered "fucks" on the telephone,
to the sweet mysteries of scalloped buttons
dotting the maps of young girls,
to the warped, frustrating truths of algebra,
to anything but me. Ancient, annoying apparatus,
I have unfortunately retained the ability to warm meat,
to open cans, to clean clothing
that has yellowed and stiffened.
I spit money when squeezed,
don't try to dance in front of his friends,
and know that rap music cannot be stopped.
For these brief flashes of cool, I am tolerated in spurts.

At night I lay in my husband's arms
and he tells me that these are things that happen,
that the world will tilt right again
and our son will return, unannounced, as he was—
goofy and clinging, clever with words, stupefied by rockets.
And I dream on that.
One summer after camp, twelve inches taller than the
summer before,
my child grinned and said,
"Maybe a tree bit me."
We laughed,
not knowing that was to be his last uttered innocence.
Only months later, eyes would narrow and doors would slam.
Now he is scowl, facial hair, knots of muscle. He is
pimp, homey, pistol. He is man smell, grimy fingers,
red eyes, rolling dice. He is street, smoke, cocked cannon.

And I sit on his bare mattress after he's left for school,
wonder at the simple jumble of this motherless world,
look for clues that some gumpopping teenage girl
now wears my face. Full of breast milk and finger songs,
I stumble the street staring at other children,
gulping my dose of their giggles,
and cursing the trees for their teeth.

Paul Dutton

T' HER

for Monk In' Mabern

'roun' midnight
'n' you
'bout 12 'clock
'n' 'round, I guess, oh,
you
'bout midnight I w'z
12 'r so 'n' I w'z lookin' 'round 'n'
'bout midnight I s'z
'tsbout 12 I s'z
you 'n'
so I took 'n' s'z
'round here somewhere I think
'roun' midnight
I s'z I gotta
'cuz you gotta be 'roun'
'bout 12 it's gotta be 'bout
mus' be 'roun' midnight
anyway 'n' you gotta be
at least somewhere I s'z 'n'
so 'roun' midnight
I took a li'l look 'n' saw
'tsabout 11:59 I s'z you
'n' someone s'z oh yeah
'cuz I know you
'n' I know
'roun' midnight you might
y'know be somewhere
'n' someone s'z you, y'know
'n' so I took a li'l 'n' s'z
well 'tsaroun' midnight
so I gotta look where
'n' someone s'z take a li'l
so I took some 12 'r midnight
'r mebbe 1 'r 2 'n' s'z
you mus'
'n' lookin' for you 'roun' midnight

'cuz y'know
you mus' be somewhere 'round here
'roun' midnight
'r 1
'r 2
'r 3
I gotta
y'know
gotta
'roun' midnight
'n' anyway
mus' be at least 12
'n' I gotta get
gotta fin', y'know, someone
gotta fin' you
'roun' somewhere
'round, I guess,
midnight

Penelope

STEIN TRIBUTE

Turn the TV on off
Off on the TV on
         and off.

Get a glass of red wine
Red wine
         no ice
No ice in my red wine.

Turn the sound on
      The sound of TV on.

Get your rocks off

　　rocks off

Watching shows
　　by
Xerox, Xerox, Xerox.

Ras Baraka

FOR THE BROTHERS WHO AIN'T HERE

This is for the brothers—who aint here
For the strong brothers who are missing in action
For cool daddy pimp Long Legs who had seven children
three of them on crack
for my main man Big Willie Graham
who was shot by two white cops
before taking three of them with him one of them was black
For Wausi Changa found strangled in his apartment
after coming home from a Black Nia F.O.R.C.E. meeting
For Larry Witherspoon—who went all the way through college
tried to marry some caucasian woman
too bad she was the boss' daughter
This poem is for the makers, the breakers, the no-stuff takers
the mixters, the tricksters, yeah and the cabbage lickers
This is for the brothers who aint here
Echoes of laughter
cloudy puffs of smoke
white washing wizards in the midst of darkness
You aint good for nothing black man
Death to you
Death to you black man
Dead black man
Black man dead
smells of death, movements of death, thinking of death,
dead thoughts living death,
death, death, death, death
This is for the brothers who aint here

You still the same you were
When you first got here
Serving somebody else's cause
but only now you think you serving your own
And will kill anybody—who tells you otherwise—
if he's black that is.

For the brothers you don't see
Before I go to bed at night
Burning tears like fire roll down my cheeks
As I think about all the brothers that could have made a difference.
But was too tough, too wild, too sane—to do s.
What happened to you black man?
where are you?
Where are those pyramid builders, those creators of sciences
and languages,
those starters of civilization, are you?
Where are you?
Where are you?
Where are you, black man?
This is for the brothers who aint here
I could scream until my voice disappears,
Think until my head bursts
Write until my fingers fall off
You evil sons of bitches
I want to squeeze you—until your very essence disappears
from thought
But, that will make me sane
And I'm insane—that's right
Crazy as hell, off my rocker, out of my mind

For the brother who aint here
The community protectors, devil rejecters,
for the doers, and takers, the revolutionary makers—yeah.

For the brothers who aint around no more
I'm so sorry black man—so sorry
Sorry that we had to be oppressed
Sorry we didn't just wipe these devils out
Sorry for all the women we beat up—out of our hatred
Sorry for all the other brothers we killed out of ignorance
Sorry for being weak in times of courage
Sorry for being dead and taking you with me

Sorry for letting them destroy everything we had
Sorry for being everything opposite of what we were created to be
Sorry for all the dead drug dealers in fancy cars
Sorry for the lack of unity and run down communities
Sorry for not raising our children up to be warriors
Sorry for getting killed before I even became a teenager
Sorry for being born into slavery
Sorry for these sorry schools
Sorry, I'm so sorry black man, so sorry
Black man I'm so so so sorry
I'm sorry black man
Sorry
Black man
Kill.

Regie Cabico

ANTONIO BANDERAS IN HIS UNDERWEAR
"...I don't want to be overexposed."—*Vanity Fair*

His back and clavicles are draped
        in a gossamer robe, reserved for
    an Iberian Zeus.
Only his hands protrude,
        curved over an invisible
    steel backing. Sitting among

a flock of palm trees, he doesn't
        mind the sun
    against his chiseled brow,
nor bother with the photographer's
        lens thrust skyward.
....His head tilted, a typical

model pose. Chest and loins
        exposed, he parts
    his legs accepting the glare
of the heated bulbs. The camera

pulses and clicks
as an unexpected sea breeze

surreptitiously licks his calves.
　　Wrapped around his ankles,
　white slippers kiss his
feet. Engrossed in deep
　　contemplation, his right hand
　twirls a red silk tassel

between his index and middle
　　fingers, brushing the bronze
　of his inner right thigh.
Perhaps he knows his fans:
　　mortal men, nymphs, Madonna,
　talking horses and pigs alike,

will ooh and ahh
　　at the elastic riding high
　up the hip, each voluptuous
swoop and arch of his
　　super star-studded quality,
　spilling full-frontal

and oh....so generously!
　　He sits content. The wealth
　of flesh, unseen to use,
coyly tugging the black-lycra
　　band of his briefs
　　—branded HOLLYWOOD.

IN A LEGENDARY LIGHT
for Marilyn Monroe

I walk with simple people
who wish me to believe

that I am not an instant...
I lock the door and hear a knock.

An Angel
        peeks from the corner
                of a mirage

        and says my mother is the gardenia
a nurse kept
                in her breast pocket.

My father's a secret gauze, crinkling,
        the day I breathed...

I don't thank Fate, nor count my muses
but give praise to mathematics,

the number 7's
breathless proportions.

When I was a model, I spoke as a model.

When I was an actress, I spoke as a girl
enamored by sunless rooms
and yellow bars of spotlights.

(If the camera won't love you, who will?)

My nose was crooked like a long bridal veil
plink, plink, plink, I got married.

I knelt at the tabernacle of chaos.

plink, plink, plink, I got married
and mistook vodka for water.
One gallon of sleeping pills and I dream of Neptune.

Playboy parts scattered like bones on glassy paper.
A centerfold, the portable trap of my vulgar self.

I pretended to be a baby chick
locked to what its eye first seizes.
A quiet blonde-shell without a libretto
whose skirt flutters in rough pentameter—
a GI's obscene flag.

I consider myself a missionary to the suburbs,
like McDonald's or a really long rope.
A dimestore magic trick in legendary light.

"May Day May Day" cries the tabloids
like the lack-luster pages of my weekly planner.

Housewives want to be me
but I'm only a glass bottle
poised in a publicity still.

I'm just a woman. Bewildering June.
Norma Jean. Lightheaded and I have strange dreams.

CHECK ONE

The government asks me to "check one".
I say "How can you ask me to be one race?"

I stand proudly before you a fierce Filipino
who knows how to belt hard gospel songs
played to African drums at a Catholic mass—
and loving the music and suffering beats
and lashes from men's eyes on the Capitol streets—

South-East DC with its sleepy crime
my mother nursed patients from seven to nine
patients gray from the railroad
riding past civil rights.

I walked their tracks when I entertained
them at the chapel and made their canes pillars
of percussion to my heavy gospel—
my comedy out-loud, laughing about,
our shared stolen experiences of the South.

Would it surprise you if I told you my blood
was delivered from North off Portuguese vessels
who gave me spiritual stones and the turn in my eyes—
my father's name when they conquered the Pacific Isles.
My hair is black and thick as "negrito," growing abundant
as "sampaguita"—flowers defying civilization

like Philipino pygmies that dance in the mountain.

I could give you an epic about my ways of life or my look
and you want me to fill it in "one square box."
From what integer or shape do you count existing identities,
grant loans for the mind or crayola white census sheets—
There's no "one kind" to fill for anyone.

You tell me who I am, what gets the most money
and I'll sing that song like a one man caravan.
I know arias from Naples, Tunis and Accra—
lullabies from welfare, food-stamps and nature

and you want me to sing one song?
I have danced jigs with Jim Crow and shuffled my hips
to the sonic guitar of Clapton and Hendrix,
waltzed with dead lovers, skipped to bamboo sticks,
balleted kabuki and mimed cathcali
arrivederccied-a-rhumba and tapped Tin Pan Alley
and you want me to dance the Bhagvadad Gita
on a box too small for a thumbelina-thin diva?

I'll check "other."

Sandra Cisneros

YOU BRING OUT THE MEXICAN IN ME

You bring out the Mexican in me.
The hunkered thick dark spiral.
The core of a heart howl.
The bitter bile.
The tequila *lágrimas* on Saturday all
through next weekend Sunday.
You are the one I'd let go the other loves for,
surrender my one-woman house.
Allow you red wine in bed,
even with my vintage lace linens.
Maybe. Maybe.

For you.

You bring out the Dolores del Rio in me.
The Mexican spitfire in me.
The raw *navajas*, glint and passion in me.
The raise Cain and dance with the rooster-footed devil in me.
The spangled sequin in me.
The eagle and serpent in me.
The *mariachi* trumpets of the blood in me.
The Aztec love of war in me.
The fierce obsidian of the tongue in me.
The *berrinchuda, bien-cabrona* in me.
The Pandora's curiosity in me.
The pre-Columbian death and destruction in me.
The rainforest disaster, nuclear threat in me.
The fear of fascists in me.
Yes, you do. Yes, you do.

You bring out the colonizer in me.
The holocaust of desire in me.
The Mexico City '85 earthquake in me.
The Popocatepetl/Ixtaccíhuatl in me.
The tidal wave of recession in me.
The Agustín Lara hopeless romantic in me.
The *barbacoa taquitos* on Sunday in me.
The cover the mirrors with cloth in me.
Sweet twin. My wicked other,
I am the memory that circles your bed nights,
that tugs you taut as moon tugs ocean.
I claim you all mine,
arrogant as Manifest Destiny.
I want to rattle and rent you in two.
I want to defile you and raise hell.
I want to pull out the kitchen knives,
dull and sharp, and whisk the air with crosses.
Me sacas lo mexicana en mí,
like it or not, honey.
You bring out the Uled-Nayl in me.
The stand-back-white-bitch in me.
The switchblade in the boot in me.
The Acapulco cliff diver in me.
The *Flecha Roja* mountain disaster in me.

The *dengue* fever in me.
The *¡Alarma!* murderess in me.
I could kill in the name of you and think
it worth it. Brandish a fork and terrorize rivals,
female and male, who loiter and look at you,
languid in your light. Oh,

I am evil. I am the filth goddess Tlazoltéotl.
I am the swallower of sins.
The lust goddess without guilt.
The delicious debauchery. You bring out
the primordial exquisiteness in me.
The nasty obsession in me.
The corporal and venial sin in me.
The original transgression in me.

Red ocher. Yellow ocher. Indigo. Cochineal.
Piñón. Copal. Sweetgrass. Myrrh.
All you saints, blessed and terrible,
Virgen de Guadalupe, diosa Coatlicue,
I invoke you.

Quiero ser tuya. Only yours. Only you.
Quiero amarte. Atarte. Amarrarte.
Love the way a Mexican woman loves. Let
me show you. Love the only way I know how.

Sheri-D Wilson

BUKOWSKI ON THE BLOCK AH-HA

> "peace and quiet are in your future"
> —Fortune Cookie

Look, Bukowski's underwear
on display in plexiglass cubes
you've got Bukowski on the rocks, okay
you've got the handkerchief he used to blew his nose
a ripped unwashed undershirt
petrified

in a mock plexi-glassed closet
you've got his socks
his empty shoes
just to set the mood of streets well-tread
not a word that he said
not a word that he said
"there is hardly anything as sad as a run-over cat"

You've got his pastel plaid arrow
shirt and baby blue jacket
he wore to the races
his driver's licence, his un-
spent money, bottle opener, unsmoked cigar
you've even got his unused band-aid on display
like he planned his scars in advance

Come on!
where are the rejection letters that said he stepped over the line
the toilet where he puked
his big yellow cat
the hopeless nights
with classical music on the radio
and another bottle of plunk?

Bukowski's licking cunt he's gonna share chicken and coleslaw with later!
Blam Wham!
that's when my rant
hit the Flitcroft cobblestones
hard
slide it in
slide it out
that's when I got tossed from the "American Realist" show
now you see it
now you don't
please, adjust clothing
before leaving
Bukowski's life reduced to T-shirt sales
and what would he say?

ching ching
outside my hotel window
one whore screams at another

you fucked my fuck you fuckin' fuck!
ha

ching ching
in a doorway a fifteen year old
with a needle between her teeth hisses
kiss and a fix
kiss and a fix
for a fiver
ha

ching ching
and O, Imperial does mean something
'cause in wine
size does matter

I say
wako scumsucker looking for a scab

In the gallery down on Flitcroft Street
you watch your wallet
close as a second skin
and what can I say?
at St. Paul's it costs four quid to pray
and there's no end to my
generosity

Bukowski thought balling was "making it"
and a low rent brand of romance
now he's on the block ah-ha
is irony the language of slaves?

London, 1996

Tony Medina

HOW TO BECOME A UNITED STATES CITIZEN

- Place a TV on your altar
- Wallpaper the cross on your rosary with dollars
- Sing "The Star Spangled Banner" while rinsing with Scope or Listerine
- Paint each and every individual one of your pubic hairs red white and blue
      (in that order)
- Bang your head against an ATM door for the stars
- Shoplift a loaf of day-old bread for stripes
- Watch *The Brady Bunch* for the rest of your life, chanting: "Uh, my nose!"
      "Uh, my nose!" "Uh, my nose!" or *"Marcia-Marcia-Marcia!"*
- Eat at McDonald's three times a week
- Name your first born John Wayne or Elvis, even if it's a boy
- Have respect for sailors
- Memorize the names: the Niña, the Pinta and the Santa Maria
- Snort decaf in shopping malls
- Soak your feet in cappuccino
- Give your corns and bunions electric shock treatment
- Show up at "Whites Only" surprise parties in Tennessee thrown by the FBI
- Impersonate J. Edgar Hoover impersonating Barbara Bush
- Place your right hand on the bible and repeat these immortal words of
      Justice Clarence Thomas: "Hey, who put pubic hairs on my Coke?"
- Lip synch the entire sound track to *Shaft*
- Perform all the stunt scenes of the house negroes in D.W. Griffith's *Birth of a
      Nation*
- Send a bottle of E & J or O.E. to every Indian reservation still standing
- Hang a picture of Hitler in your living room next to the one of Jesus, the
      Pope, and the most recent President
- Purchase a copy of Newt Gingrich's book *To Re-Write America*, and read it as
      if it were the new Gideon's bible
- Repeat the only line from that old capitalist spiritual: *Oonga boonga/ Oonga
      boonga* until you get sick, swallow your tongue, or die of lethargy
- Sell your daughter to U.S. troops for a VCR and Polka lessons
- Believe everything they tell you in school and everything you see on TV

BLOODSONG

Didn't I tell you
that the heart
is a mouth
on paper
that the paper
is a flame
split into lips
pursed like an arrow
and that arrow
bleeds into the drum
of one's tongue
trapped in memory's ear
Didn't I tell you
it is hard
for the wound
to forget
the migrating blood
forced out
by exile
or eviction
that one man's journey
is another man's
fast removal
from the face
of the earth
that some travel
in the hulls
of slave ships
while others
hug the bottom
of rafts
swallowing
oceans
of mud

Todd Swift

TRICK

Karla is 8.

Her whole body is folded like a napkin used in a trick.

It will take a long time to smooth her skin back, removing the creases.

Folded and folded over again.

A red napkin.

Folded and folded, then swallowed.

Out it comes, from someone's ear.

Slowly, knotted.

Nobody says: it isn't the same one.

For her next trick Karla will stay under water, silent.

Until she wants to.

U R SCULLY 2 ME

A man, age 30, in Spokane, Washington
sees a woman, age 24, and falls
in love with her. He has no knowledge
of her name. He barely has an idea
of where she comes from. Her profession,
if she has brothers, sisters, the possibility
of scar tissue on her thighs, this is all unknown
territory. Still, he knows. Somehow
he knows about something deep, buried
like the truth, inside of her body. More
than a name or a mark, a fact of light,
an emanation from her skin, from what is beneath,
concealed within. He feels he knows her soul.
Whatever that is. The truth surrounds her like a glow,
a crash site on fire behind the firs. She smiles
and goes onto the bus and is gone. He will not
ever see in her the flesh again as long as he lives.

The Haunted Man travels for miles
with two compasses and a piece of white chalk.
He measures his relation to the North Star.
He marks each telephone pole. His exact distance
from the Moon is charted. He begins to scatter
chicken feathers outside of houses of worship.
He chants a single word which contains the idea of her.
He is speaking in a lost tongue. He marks an X
on the door of a house and knocks. It opens.
A woman opens the door. She is dark
where the other was fair. They are entirely
not the same person. She is the sister
of the other one, and falls in love
with the Haunted Man at once. They marry.
The first woman dies in a plane flying to the wedding.
He attends the funeral. It is a closed casket ceremony.
He marks the priest's gown with chalk.
He and his wife never talk. They never have sex.
They lie beside each other, barely breathing.
Their eyes never make contact. One is alien.
The other is alien, also. They never touch,
like the lovers on the Grecian Urn. Nothing
is more strange than how we come to yearn.

CURING

I have discovered a cure for blindness. It involves glass. You must crush it like you were churning butter. Spread the grains upon a kerchief, stolen from a peasant girl in the fields. Strip naked. This must be done three weeks before harvest (the moon removed) when the sky is the colour of veins under an old woman's skirt. Begin to dance as if dogs were after you. Smear the shards across your genitals like jam. Whimper like the wind worrying for the damned. Be careful to bleed against a wall where recently two lovers have been; gently. Move away from the spot, appearing ashamed. Bind your wounds with splinters. Apply broken eggshells lightly to the open, wandering eyes. In the morning, all is changed: they will not stray again. When you return the kerchief, she will thank you, smiling. Look indirectly at her now. You are in the sun.

D.O.A.

dedicated to Vincent Lang, d. Memorial Day, 1996

I would like to report a love affair
that is very over. My own.
Her luminous poison is all through my system,
I've been running through busy streets like doom,
my silk tie flying over my shoulder,
knocking the fedoras off completely strange men,
not noticing the runs up the legs of secretaries,
skewed hems, refusing to pay anyone
for rides on the trolley cars, going up and down.
My heart has the limited life span
of a May fly. It's due to explode any time now,
and when it does I will immediately die.
The Grim Reaper's got me on a very short leash,
so short it feels I've been unleashed by him.
I have twenty-four hours, maybe a week
to find the guy who did this to me
and settle my accounts. I want information.
Give it to me straight, Doc. Every second counts.
Talk! Could anything toxic in my bloodstream
have come from something as nice and red
as my gal's lipstick? There's gotta be
a better explanation. Her kiss is her alibi.
Sure, that's it. Fate's had it in for me, ever since
I got here, already lonely and walking dead.

POUND UNPLUGGED

Adeena Karasick

ALBEIT ERSTWHILE

In incumbent umbrage, abyss splurge
shattered absence abandoned in
a shacked-up schemata act
echolalic rhetoric, a
conjugated silence of
mucosa aroma

> when my body brims with tolerance
> when it no longer holds me
> when I'm burning between

secretum retreats or
incriminate imminence

as cerea slits silence
viscose slick risks
distance when what's

> sacred, *secare, escarre*
> *eskhara éscarts,*
> succours

in the carnage of

> *mourning when mourning is*
> *of mourning and dwells in*

desiccated articulacy
as a reticent negligent
agenda atrophies in

a symbolic bloc rocks
in proxy locs.

    or a provocative glottis wrought

as an impossible *gloss. glas. gliss.* listens when
linguae langue linguis lingers

                in *onoma*
                   eponyma

And opens in immensity

in remnants, residuals, articulated in
exhortative sorts, exitin'in
fermata grafts damaged as
a resident hesitant

when desire slides in the absence of
studded space, echoes,
screams

in the horror of

         high mourning, if mourning is
            half mourning

to close in on
its silence accumulates,

as wretched homonymies,
anonymies, eponymies

in the residue of
recreant shrieks and bleakly ambiguous in

the scars of
tolerant hollers.

        if full mourning is of mourning
        remainders what follows for the
        mourning of mourning in the

metonymy of intimacy
crawling with contingency

mourning to mourn
the already-mourned

all that is irreplaceable, *plaisible,* possible
as the private, arrives,
survives

and the destinerrancy
of desire.

Audrey De la Rosa

I AM NOT WHITE, SEÑORES

    I am not white, yet my skin is white as magnolia. my grandmother, Rosario Ibañez—mooorish mulatta wed an Argentine banker named Ramon. He heaped stones on her body and forced her to carry coal on her back, the coal pressing her vertebrae. She bore ten of his children, all with black eyes and tight curly hair. I am not white señores. My maternal grandmother was Basque, and her husband a gaucho with skin the color of mate. He lived in the wilds of Patagonia, the wide plains.

    I come from earth, from horses and the wide plains...

    My great-great grandmother, a Tehuelche Indian from the North, killed her own daughter with a machete. Her skin was the color of smoke and ashes.
    I am not white señores, although seeming to be, my pallor only outward. Inwardly, I am smoke, mate, ashes. I have danced the Chacarrera by the Niger to the beat of a puma skin drum. I have felt the coldness of your blue stares; your paleness has grown maroon at my outrage, the outrage of living among you, breathing the same poisons. I belong among horses, tero birds even papagayos singing in the radiant light of the Patagonian plain. And you do not understand my language nor my native tongue.

I come from a race that cannot be conquered. I am wild as puma,
angry as urraca birds screaming.

For too long I have worn the pearl strands of a lie, but I tell you now,
I am smoke, mate, ashes spilling into the radiance of Patagonia's sky.

Barabara Tran

LOVE AND RICE

He jumped off the water buffalo and I knew we'd be married.
He turned it easily, pushing its head to the side.
The orange diep trees were like blazes of sun
just hanging in the air below the clouds.
Untainted masses spread across the sky.

I told Mother that night he was my lover.
He knew nothing of it.
I thought of nothing else as I wrung the sheets.
That he was my cousin didn't matter,
there was no room for shame.
Grandmother would notice the sun setting
and know her clock needed winding,
know she had missed her bananas and rice.

That first time I touched him, I thought of nothing but fruit.
There was no electricity then; night came early.
I took a long bath pouring water
gently over my body, watching it drip
between the wooden slats.
Soon, I'd be carrying
a weight inside me.

Beth Lisick

MONKEY GIRL

Oh, Monkey Girl. Oh yeah, Monkey Girl. Gung Hay Fat Choy! I was born in the year of the monkey.

I was walking around the Chinese New Year parade. There I am drinking a warm beer, I had my paycheck in my sock, and this old lady I'm standing next to asks me what year I was born.

"1968," I tell her. "The year of the monkey." That much I'm sure of.

"Oh. Monkey is naughty!" she tells me and clucks her tongue. "Monkey is sneaky. You are naughty monkey, I know."

Well, oh yeah, Monkey Girl. Gung Hay Fat Choy, Monkey Girl!

"I know all about you."

Then one of those guys, the kind working for the environmentally progressive energy corporations in between getting his master's and his bachelor's, approaches me, his gigantic hand extended. "Hi! I'm Steve! I'm a rat."

"Rat is clever," the old lady says. "Rat work hard. Rat make good mate."

"So, why don't we blow this teriyaki stand and get a drink," he says.

I tell him teriyaki is Japanese. Mr. Stanford Rat Boy is not so smart after all. "Yeah. I'll let you buy me a drink."

So I go along with this for a couple of …months. And I can't even think of my own excuses why at this point. I just keep thinking, monkey is naughty. But he's a rat, and I have to keep reminding myself of that.

I have two recurring nightmares: one about my dad's '77 Pinto and another about rats. I'm naked in my bed and there are big lumps moving underneath my skin. They're rats that have burrowed there except there are no entry or exit wounds. They're just crawling between muscle and skin up my thighs, up my stomach and then busting out where my collarbone breaks. Their hideous yellow-tooth faces look a lot like mine.

The last rat I saw before this guy was in an East Village garbage can snorfling through a bag of used pampers. The rat before that crawled up my pajama leg as I slept in a smelly, drafty studio in Santa Cruz. And then there was Pippin, the only pet that was ever all mine. She choked to death in my fourth grade bedroom on a tennis ped I gave her to sleep in while I was away at my family reunion in Ozarks.

Gung hey you, you fat choy! You were born in the year of the rat?

Now sometimes I read my horoscope and if I don't like it I can just pretend I'm the self-involved Cancer, the brooding Scorpio, instead of the happy-go-lucky Sagittarius. However, for some reason, I deeply believe in this rat thing. This Chinese lunar calendar business. It must be all that advertising about the mystique of the Orient. Ancient Chinese secret, uh?

Just give me a horse. 1954. 1966. I'll gladly swat the flies from his butt. Or a snake. 1965. I have no problem sucking poison.

Rooster. '69. I've been known to enjoy a cock.

Dragons. Tigers. Oxen. Cool!

Dogs. Pigs. Rabbits. Sheep. Cute. Kind of '80s country kitchen wallpaper material, but cute enough.

This monkey girl just wants to go to the monkey bars, hanging upside down while all the blood pools inside my head and I think I'm somewhere else. Somewhere far away from Pintos and tennis peds, family reunions, the Ozarks and this dirty, clever, hardworking rat with the six figure income who only wants me because I'm naughty.

Carmelita McGrath

THE HALF-LIFE OF TAFFETA

You were adamant that I should have kept that dress,
danced in on New Year's Eve at the waterfront,
complemented by some gentleman's formal jacket,
swirling above legs wet from knee-deep snow.

I told you it was a size five,
would only fit half of me now,
gone green the way black does with age
like an old man's suit;
the boning that held the top up, did I tell you?
popped up and out one night while I was dancing,
my partner chortled: "She's wired, this one."

You pictured the dress
surviving in my daughter's dress-up trunk,
a costume, a put-on of her mother before she was one.

Kind of sad, I'll admit,
stuffing it in the green garbage bag
(it resisted crushing, kept puffing out as if alive):

it had gate-crashed, trespassed, high-stepped,
been worn with all the shoes danced to dust
across boundaries of countries, continents,
carried on ships, in cargo bays on planes
and once, just once,
squashed in a briefcase to a clandestine adventure
that, even now, only two people know about;

in its salad days, the dress crackled electrically
one night under a snowmobile suit
beneath snapping northern lights
on its way to the one formal dance of the year.

But surely taffeta survives somewhere,
must have a half-life like plutonium, invisible
but somewhere, making you and I
remember who we were, sending us on a wardrobe chase
to our former selves, who we were
on evenings when we wore gloves or smoked
long cigarettes, and believed like fanatics
in the power of champagne to show up at the right time.

Is there any of that left now?

The way the nights burned and glinted,
faceted as Murano glass, as bright
as moonbeams in old songs. And we fell silent;
on either side of the table, we were back,
hardly daring to tell stories hard to fathom now.

Who invented those girls? Surely,
not their parents, or a climate
complete with June snow and January fog.

Did you go home
and peer into some old album,
sing in your sleep
a snatch of a song from a hot night in Jamaica?

Me, I had a wild cavorting dream
that started on a train on top of a mountain
and ended in a town in northern Italy.

I woke imagining
taffeta somewhere
rustling under the moon
in the Robin Hood Bay dump,
festal in a merry company of rats,
crackling perhaps with a song once danced to,
empty of a wearer.

Cheryl Savageau

LOOKING FOR INDIANS

My head filled with tv images
of cowboys, war bonnets and renegades,
I ask my father
what kind of Indian are we, anyway.
I want to hear Cheyenne, Apache, Sioux,
words I know from television
but he says instead
Abenaki. I think he says Abernathy
like the man in the comic strip
and I know that's not Indian.

I follow behind him
in the garden
trying to step in his exact footprints,
stretching my stride to his.
His back is brown in the sun
and sweaty. My skin is brown
too, today, deep in midsummer,
but never as brown as his.

I follow behind him like this
from May to September
dropping seeds in the ground,
watering the tender shoots
tasting the first tomatoes,
plunging my arm as he does,
deep into the mounded earth

beneath the purple-flowered plants
to feel for potatoes
big enough to eat.

I sit inside the bean tepee
and pick the smallest ones
to munch on. He tests
the corn for ripeness
with a fingernail, its dried silk
to color my mother's hair.
We watch the winter squash grow hips.
This is what we do together
in summer, besides the fishing
that fills our plates unfailingly
when money is short.

One night
my father brings in a book,
and shows me the map
here and here
he says, all this
is Abenaki country.
I remember asking him
what did they do
these grandparents
and my disappointment
when he said no buffalo
roamed the thick new england forest
they hunted deer in winter
sometimes moose, but mostly
they were farmers
and fishermen.

I didn't want to talk about it.
Each night my father
came home from the factory
to plant and gather,
to cast the line out
over the dark evening pond,
with me, walking behind him,
looking for Indians.

TOO'KAY

This is the pie
that defines our Frenchness
in the winter season

the Christmas Eve pie
of twice ground pork
cooked slowly
seasoned lightly with salt and pepper

we make dozens to give away
but Uncle Raymond won't eat our pie
missing the spices his tongue demands

he calls it *tourtière*
says there's no such thing as *too'kay*

but there it is
written in Memere's book
the Indian k replacing the *r*
as foreign to Algonkin tongues

as the spices
memere leaves out

AFTER LISTENING TO A READING OF ROMANTIC POEMS ABOUT COLUMBUS: ONE MORE THOUGHT

His name
was my grandmother's
favorite curse word

Chris Bell

From TALES OF THE LAST CHEEBAH-HA
THE QUEST FOR IMMORTALITY

Chapter One
1. Arap Sang, being no one in particular's fool, quickly devised a plan to trick God out of death.
2. But Arap Sang did not want to take any risks himself.
3. So Arap Sang sought out one man, Waischu, who was alone.
4. This Waischu was such a lazy man that he did not even have the energy to be bored.
5. Arap Sang thought it would be easy to take this man Waischu and approach God without attracting attention from the other people.

Chapter Two
1. Arap Sang found Waischu sitting under the shade of a tree.
2. Arap Sang strolled up to Waischu as if he had just found him by accident.
3. 'Waischu!' Arap Sang cried.
4. 'May I join you?'
5. Waischu did not say 'yes' and he did not say 'no'.
6. Waischu did not say anything.
7. 'I have been walking a long time, trying to think of a way out of death,' said Arap Sang.
8. 'Why bother?' Waischu replied.
9. 'There's nothing we can do about it anyway.'
10. 'Let things work out the way they will, then take the credit.'
11. 'But this will only work out one way,' retorted Arap Sang.
12. 'Then what are you worried about?' Waischu asked.

Chapter Three
1. Arap Sang began to think he had made the wrong choice.
2. This Waischu was either too stupid or too smart to go along with his plan.
3. So Arap Sang had another idea.
4. 'Well, I suppose you are right, Waischu,' Arap Sang said.
5. 'I should not worry about it.'
6. Waischu did not reply, so Arap Sang said good-bye and walked off.

Chapter Four

1. Arap Sang strolled off over the horizon, out of sight of Waischu.
2. He circled around, snuck up behind Waischu and climbed up the back of the tree.
3. Arap Sang hid amongst the leaves, picked a green fruit and let it drop in Waischu's lap.
4. Waischu lazily took the fruit up and ate it.
5. Arap Sang picked another green fruit and let it drop.
6. Waischu ate this one too.
7. This went on for some time.

Chapter Five

1. Waischu had never eaten green fruit before, and when he grew sick from it he did not know where this sickness was coming from.
2. Waischu decided he was dying.
3. Arap Sang yelled down in a loud voice:
4. 'Waischu! You greedy pig! Now look what you have done!'
5. Waischu was frightened and thought this was God talking to him.
6. Waischu struggled up and made his way to God's mountain.
7. Arap Sang followed Waischu all the way to God's mountain and into it without being seen.

Chapter Six

1. Waischu climbed to the top of God's mountain, crossed over the rim and down inside, and called for God.
2. 'God!' cried Waischu, 'I think I'm dying.'
3. 'So what do you want,' God replied, 'immortal life?'
4. 'Well, no,' said Waischu.
5. 'So you want to die, then,' said God.
6. 'No!' cried Waischu.
7. 'Make up your mind,' God growled.
8. Waischu saw there was no way out of it, so he asked for immortal life.
9. 'Immortal life!' roared God.
10. 'Are you crazy?
11. 'Anyway, you can't have immortal life because you were born too late.
12. 'So, you must die.'
13. 'What, now?' shrieked Waischu.

Chapter Seven

1. 'You have the wrong man!' Waischu cried.

2.   'I only ate too much green fruit and felt sick!

3.   'It is Arap Sang who is looking for immortal life.'

4.   'Arap Sang!' God bellowed.

5.   And Arap Sang, who was hiding and thought he had been discovered, crept forward.

Chapter Eight

1.   'So, you want immortal life?' inquired God.

2.   'Yes,' said Arap Sang, who had overheard everything and had a new plan.

3.   'Well, you can't have it,' said God.

4.   'Ohhhh, I know what you are going to say!' cried Arap Sang, wringing his hands.

5.   'You are going to say that I cannot live with the people...'

6.   'Well, no,' God interjected.

7.   '...That I cannot live with you...' Arap Sang wailed.

8.   'Certainly not!' roared God.

9.   'You are going to say that I cannot live on the earth or in the sky, or the mountains or trees or stars!

10.   'In fact, you are going to say that I cannot live in any place that can be named!'

11.   'No!' cried God.

12.   'Are you sure?' said Arap Sang.

13.   'Of course I'm sure,' God bellowed.

14.   'Well, then,' said Arap Sang, 'if that's your final word, and you have said 'no', then I cannot live anywhere that can be named.

15.   'And if I cannot live anywhere that can be named, then I must live in between things.

16.   'I must live where the mountain meets the field, and the day the night, and life death, because there is always a little space in between things, though it be very small and often overlooked, and so is not named.'

Chapter Nine

1.   God fell completely silent and stayed that way for a long, long time.

2.   'You are giving me a headache,' God said at last.

3.   'Go away.'

4.   And from that day on, God never listened to any arguments.

5.   When a person is meant to die, they die.

Cindy Goff

THE POLE IN HIS BACK WAS AS STRONG
AS MY FAMILY TREE

Building the scarecrow was difficult. No one would give up
old- clothing. I put cooked spaghetti in its head
for brains and hard-boiled eggs in its face for eyes.
The neighbors couldn't understand
why I needed a scarecrow since I didn't have any corn.
They called the Audubon Society and complained
because it frightened away birds.

In the middle of the night I laid my head on his chest,
and listened for a trolley. In an attempt to make him talk,
I built bonfires all around him.
He jumped on me,
and put me in a harness to plow his ego.
I felt like a gymnasium
where prized ear corn were on display.
His penis was fifty crickets rubbing their legs together.
After he came, he wouldn't hold me;
he just went back to the way he was standing.

I got fired from my job because I wore dresses
sawdust flowed from between my legs
and I couldn't explain it.
I was so scarred by his hay thighs
I couldn't wear bathing suits.
Now I can't even cross my legs
because his ghost is between them.

APPALACHIAN FLOOD

Rats scramble vertically on bricks.
A limp fox turning over and over
floats by clothing
caught in young dogwoods.

Windows are still windows
but with unrestricted access.
A wedding gown and a water snake
curl around a chandelier.

Beneath the water, objects move
but don't float: dictionaries, brass beds,
trampolines, tractors.

Beneath the flood, the earth is full
like it never had a backbone.

THE FIRST SOBER MORNING

No one is awake in the campgrounds
of the dismantled carnival. The hermaphrodite sleeps
with the levers of her rollercoaster.
The nymphomaniac is curled up in a Ferris wheel seat.
The fat lady sleeps sitting up in front of a carrousel mirror.
And the young college student, who just wanted to earn money
for Europe, is middle-aged now. She snores on a straw bed
in the geek pit.
I'm so afraid of telling them
we will not be moving to a new town.

ADDICTION

I stroll backward through the garden's maze
made of high hedges and sundials
        and commune with gravestones.
I'm learning the language of engravers
whose chisels trick my stubborn spirit
into my hands full of habits
        and I am one of those habits.
I who do not control the teachings of algebra
or the preachings of physics
have unraveled the moon like a moth.
My mouth is full of meteors

that alter my weather daily
and whose dust belongs
behind museum glass
    instead of infecting words.
Soon I will speak through ravens
but first I must gather my bones
and construct an alphabet.
My eyes have nothing to do
but rest on stones benches
while the sundials point to a shadow
    that's trying to kill me.

Daniel O'Leary

From TARSUS

for Rainer Christ

Standing outside the gates of Alexandria
I think of the need for payment for all things,
And not with a wound in a bull's side,
As the Mithraists have it, at least not precisely,
But rather with a different wound that bleeds
Invisibly, over the histories of all races,
In the lined faces of lamed men.
And I am lame. I drag this blunt anchor
Through stones as if some business would flounder
If my attention wandered for one too many moments
To ripe April hill's shadings of green,
As if the shaved heads would have me head down
On a cross if I for one moment longer took breath
Of honeysuckle from a sea breeze.
So to Alexandria I come stinking of purpose,
Though truth be told it is a commodity
That does not burden me overmuch in my travel,
And I seem to myself at times an actor
In an allegory scraped together by boy priests,
Sons of eminent butchers, in an episode

In lost time, bad citizen screwing the clean.
But it has been too like this for many years.
I studied much as a green youth and squandered
The position my family might have guaranteed
Had I learned early a useless trade.
Instead I went to Athens, and from there to Rome
Itself, bartering innocence for a place at high
Tables. And I learned much that was to deny
Me sleep. I heard—how can I tell—magi, beautiful
Charlatans, speak against god-caesar chorused
By shining specters in candle-sputtering rooms.
I was men so eaten by love that their stone
Came alive under their God-tracing chisels.
And I saw too the locusts at work, the maggots
Fattening into swarms by warm water on the flesh
Of dumped slaves, each stink identical though born
Of Asia, Africa, and Gaul. And I learned only
A handful of alphabets. Stray voices saying always
The same sinking 'please,' voices horribly
Wrenched into lament for dead mothers, lost lovers,
Selves they had never been but only surmised
From the curling waters of a village river.
And to Alexandria I come seeking more of only this.
I have little left to expect. I have sent my spirit
Away, across the white tongue of Persia, north
To where the Gaels are said to peg their dead
To the ground, across Africa's strange dark core;
And it seems only here have I place to rest,
Though this species of rest will of necessity
Finish me. And when I am finished I ask of God
Or Gods or Fate only this, that I might know one
Certain thing. That I might for that brief passage
Before oblivion know the difference between
Evil and ignorance, between demons and angered deities.
Why must human beings batter one another to Hell
Even in their loving, even in their brief touching?
But the gates open. Now I must leave you on this hot
Dune. I pray for you, love you, and would that I could
Touch your hand.

David McGimpsey

IN MEMORIAM: A.H. JR.

A few weeks before he died
thin, thin from the cancer
Alan Hale was stopped by a teenager
who pumped gas at an L.A. station
& asked the gaunt skipper if he was alright,
if he was dieting or something
like Oprah, Lasorda or some other famous,
formerly overweighted.
"Yes that's right," the mighty sailing man said,
"we're doing the series again
& this time I'm going to play Gilligan."
& he drove out into the afternoon.
Now his body is out in the Pacific
mixing with coral reef & Catalina trash,
whole with the universe, taking time out,
resting forever from the question:
who was responsible for the fate of *The Minnow?*

Brave in diagnosis, brave in chemo,
brave in goodbye. From heaven send a message,
have a few hot dogs & smile.

Once, when you were in the greenworld
tempest in the uncharted areas of the sea,
you fell under the terrible curse of Kona.
Digging through the fine island sand,
making practical refrigeration
to store Mary Ann's guava jelly
you unearthed the idol head,
its mouth downturned,
its jagged teeth poised to cut through skin.

The curse of Kona, you said
(in-between frantic conjurings of fates
more terrible than being stranded
on an island full of idiots),
could only be cured by Watumbi's dance.

Only Watumbi's dance,
doctored to the rhythms of the tropical forest,
could deliver release into the world
of the relatively uncursed.
"Superstitions don't have to be ridiculed"
you said to Prof. Roy Hinckly Ph.D. (TCU),
who was irreverent in answering your call
for the dance but admitted
that he had seen many things
that defy the laws of reason in his years
as a castaway in the cancerous sun.
The Professor tried his best
but couldn't help start dictating all the triumphs
his Cartesian mind had brought them all:
saved them from the deadly Mantis Carni bite
with an antidote of ground clam shells & papaya roots,
saved them from marauding Marubi head-hunters
simultaneously translating their intent to kill
& finding a safe, inner-island cave
to huddle & coo about the lost USA;
saved the crew from long-term effects
of radioactive vegetables the size of trees.
The skipper set the Prof. straight, said, "son
it doesn't hurt to believe in the curse of Kona
or believe Jesus Christ is waiting for me, drunk,
on the other side; it doesn't matter tonight if I
send in a subscription for *Scientific American*,
anyway you have it we are stranded here on this island,
the two foot hole in the *Minnow* untouched
by doctoral insight—we won't be rescued tonight."

Stupid or no, you ran around the island
through nests of damselflies, crunching
the bambooish undergrowth at your feet,
burning; sweat tracking the folds of your neck,
burning salty-dog neck & chin.
Jonas Grumby,
you ran straight into a palm tree & conked-out.
A severe case of *bumpinus on the nogginus*
but when you came to, you still believed.

You had survived the wreck
of the infamous *USS Indianapolis;*

bobbed helplessly in warm water
American canapés for swarming tiger sharks,
banjo sharks, what you will.
From Guadalacanal with your purple heart
the scars zigzagging around your shoulders
like a complex tattoo of a jungle fire.
Through the years the colours started to dull,
even in the land of Gauguin
is there ever enough tropical variety?
I don't think I can just sit back & hear anymore
not if we must touch bottom of the dolphinless sea.
Dive underneath all the water
five miles deep in the Izu trench off Japan
& tell me what's there if you can.
Weren't you the leader?
There has to be a better government.

I can see the x-ray shadows.
I can see them come back after the triumph
of telling everybody you had it licked.
A shadow on the x-ray screen, a *mass,*
doctors / oncologists yapping before their knives
their cobalt, their interferon,
their understanding
there's a certain point of no return.
How did that storm come in & in 3 hours
sweep you out to sea?
Sweeping you out forever
& making you what you are?
Salut mes joyeaux naufragés.
I can see the x-ray shadows.

Monkeys throw plastic explosives overhead.
The rich couple, their money useless
still manage to have a certain
I-paid-my-way-through-Harvard kind of fun.
The Professor will work for them one day
& Mary Ann will take to the street
to sell her preserves.
You danced with Ginger Grant,
the most beautiful woman in the world.
Her ballgown bared of its sequins,

her red hair drawn back with a beret
of sticky orchids. She rehearsed
lines from a prison movie in your ear.
You danced in the courtyard
in front of the bamboo huts
that lasted for 12 lonely years;
through typhoons, dictators & rock stars.

Japanese lanterns, crepe paper & torches
giving the cleared part of the jungle
a sense of festival & backyard safety.
The coconut-Vitrola playing Paris accordion—
the air of the left lagoon bank
soft & warm, protected for the Tiki,
ready for the lost
& ever & always
260 nautical miles SW of Honolulu.

Hours spent, beautiful, swinging imperceptibly
in a navy issue hammock,
the silhouette of your belly on the wall,
candles flickering gently on the green palm fronds,
the captain's hat over your eyes.
Skinny Mulligan, what's-his-face,
above you, ready to fall out & rake hell.
Dreams of Malaysian food, of Australian wine
of sailor stuff from Seattle to Hong Kong.
Dreams of maybe getting married,
of strolling with prams through the San Diego zoo
sort of just like I-don't-know-who.
Hours spent reading the naval manual,
(not one for staring at Manuel's navel)
tying bamboo sticks together,
sharpening bits, things for survival he says
survival enough to kill the time.
No phones, no lights, no microwave.
Hours thinking about the fate of *The Minnow*.
One wrong weather report & that was it.
It happens to everybody in some way.
Did y'all fasten your anchor
when you threw your life overboard?
"When I get back" you prayed

"I'll do my best to clear my name, extend my commission
& still surprise the world by doing something nice
for that stupid kid."
Broadway impressarios could visit the island
as much as they wanted, proposing
a musical Hamlet or a musical Lear—
it didn't help one bit.
You said "I can't remember everything, it gets lost
deep into the bright afternoons.
It's amazing, I stayed fat through it all,
through everything. Isn't that funny?"

The Skipper & Gilligan will be friends forever,
despite their tragic mistakes.
The worst things will still happen,
they always do, despite our bonds.
Things settle in the damp roots of our lungs
in the red fibers of the fibers of our muscles & rot.
It was a wild time:
sand in everything, amazing inventions.
The sputum of the atoll-gods rippling lagoon water
like spacecraft tumbling back to America.
Don't let go of my hand because I'm dying
of cancer or drowning in the Irish sea.
Brave it out & bury nothing, let it drift
with everything still wet & alive.
Let it drift aimless,
just another tour gone astray.
Christmases, rainy seasons, mosquitoes,
all forgotten, just like last February
in the suburbs.

Ces après-midis disparaissent
et Gilligan et le Capitaine goûteraient
leurs tartes aux crème d'ananas
avec nous-autres. Goodbye little buddy.

Victrola dancing Ginger accordion lighted
ricewine crepe-paper Ginger perfume
jungle Paris red-haired moonlit Ginger.
You survive, not to cry
like Pagliacci,

but because life holds to you so well.
You wore your captain's hat proudly
receiving visitors to your family restaurant:
"The Skipper's Lobster Barrel"
on La Cienga Blvd. in Los Angeles, California.

Dozing through a little busride
through the birch forests of Upper Canada
the tinge of diesel seeping in the luxury coach.
The view out into the stretch of winter,
faded trees scratching the horizon,
squaring out the meager farmland.
Nothing there that wasn't frozen.
In the dark February plain
the voice of the seven stranded castaways
deep in the Boreal forest
"Skipper! Professor!"
I thought I heard somebody cry.
"I think the Howells have scurvy!"
Saying it was only a TV show
is like saying it was only a friend,
only my brother, only my father.

Put the antennae high, pay your cable bills.
To volcanoes fresh & lagoons anew.
He was like to ponder expeditious rescue.
He'd say "when I get back to civilization
I'll tell you what I'm going to do:
I'm going to have a tall glass of cold beer
& I won't spill a drop.
I'm going to order a steak, New York cut,
medium rare & two inches thick."
How thick? "Two inches thick!"
In the plate will rest the slightest residue:
blood, spice & fat
agents of flavour after the meat is gone.

Donald McGrath

THE STABLE

As the door creaks in, the sun
glides off its edge like water off a paddle.
The stable is one great cathedral
of gloom pierced by a blond plank of light,
a Milky Way of whirling motes.
Poking from the ropy, frayed walls
of a slime-green toolbox under a freckled window,
a glossy hammer handle with the initials JM,
rust-caked pipe ends
and the watery, jaundiced eye of a spirit level
are drenched in a lunar glow.
A curtain of hay is crosshatched in gold.
At its base lie the wrestling magazines.

Postage stamps scanned by the beam,
up close they reveal
scraggy, blood-matted hair, black leather
hoods and harnesses rivalling the arsenal
of tackling hanging in the horse's stall.
There's the liquid flip flip of pages, deep
reds and blues of summer clothes in shade.
Stripped down to underwear, rolled and tucked
beneath the belly and between the buttocks,
boys rub their bodies together, straddle
warm backs, lie in the hay practicing holds.
Rough straw arrows their skin, agile air
whips across it.
Someone keeps watch at the window.

Eileen Tabios

RAPUNZEL, ENRAPT

"stairs rising to platforms lower than themselves,
doors leading outside that bring you back inside"
—Clifford Geertz, on Michel Foucault

She locks the entrance to the turret containing a thousand diaries whose
papers are yellowed and leather covers cracked. Then she feeds the key to an
alligator. She is outside where ants clamber up the velvet folds masking her
thighs (she actually scents grass!). She understands gloves are old-fashioned
but has resigned herself to certain constraints: it takes time for the ink stains
on her hands to fade. But she has crossed the moat. And as she peers at the
stolid, gray tower which she once draped with her hair, that a man once
climbed, she shivers but smiles.

First, she must eliminate her guides. Her godfather—an emperor of two
continents and the eagles overhead—has sent a troop of retired generals. She
can feel their white beards swaying as they urge black stallions toward her. She
can hear the horses gasp as effort glazes a wet sheen over their hides. And
though the shimmer of air in the distance simply may be the temper of a
summer day, she lifts her skirts and breaks forth into a run.

Once, a man buried his face into her shaking hands. She treasured the alien
rush of warmth against her fingers as he spoke of sand, gritty but fine; of
waves, liquid yet hard; of ships, finite spaces but treasured for what they may
explore; of ocean breezes, invisible but salty on the tongue. "Like the potential
for grief?" she asked. He raised his eyes in surprise and she captured his gaze.
She pressed on, "I have read that grief is inevitable with joy." Still, she woke one
day to a harsh rope dangling from an opened window, and emptiness was
infinite by her side.

Now, she is taking the path opposite from the direction she saw the man
choose when he departed. As his hands left the rope, he looked up and saw her
lack of bitterness framed in the window. The forest respected her grief with a
matching silence. But she had learned from the Egyptians how to measure
intangible light, a lesson which revealed the earth to be round. Now, she runs
and as she begins to gasp, she can feel the sand between her toes, the breezes
tangle the long strands of her hair and the waves weight her skirts. And as she

feels his ship disrupting the horizon, a sheen breaks across her brow and she
feels her lips part. Enrapt, she knows she soon will take off her gloves. Enrapt,
she feels she is getting there.

Eric Sigler

DEAD WITH THE DEAD

Dead with the dead, I died.
Life no presence, death no decease.
Still as light singed into shade,
quicken this into release;
admit none dead, though I died.

Tears in the bucket I shed.
Sunk in the shaft, plunged in the pool,
bucket clapped on the stone side,
the waters return, they are cool—
admit no tears, though I cried.

Down to the deep, I went down
to the dark—dark without light.
Mandate passed down, down a rung—
vision down dark, dark my sight—
admit no rise, I went down.

Whorled in a rush, I rush on—
heart too troubled for breath.
Hard at the edge, I melt down.
Melt this life down into death.
Admit no death, though I died.

Evelyn Lau

VANCOUVER PUBLIC LIBRARY OPENING GALA,
MAY 24, 1995

I live in the house where I did not say
I love you. Every night I repeat it
as prayer, penance, incantation. I sit
in the black armchair to taste the memory of you.
The green couch. The burnt-orange floor. This wall
where the streetlight shines at 11 p.m....

Parties remind me of you. Tonight a man
said your name, and the room swam with grief.
The speaker smelled of Pierre Cardin. I leaned
into the staple of his elbow, to feel the flesh
and bone of the person who knew you, who once
shook your hand, shook your wife's hand.
Around us men and women tumbled
like chips at the bottom of a kaleidoscope.
Gowns like fish scales, tuxes like funerals.
Again, I whisper, *say it again. Love...*

but nothing more happens, though there are
performers on stilts, Shakespeare actors in velvet,
red volka, quail pierced by bone, though
we slide swizzle sticks into our purses for souvenirs,
laugh subversively. Though a man I once saw on his knees,
weeping, his back candy-cane striped,
his face a pomegranate of lust,
his penis a nub, a slug, a tuberous potato
is here tonight, splendid in his suit,
chin cocked, glass raised, wife stalwart by his side.
Say it again, I yell, *love*, but the diva
opens her throat, and no one hears.

Gerry Gomez Pearlberg

THE DEATH OF SUPERMAN

Remember that first tumble?
The one you took through space in a basket
like Moses through the dark wet channel of the midnight sky?
How those *My Favorite Martian* radio signals
clung to their oxygen tanks like
stars turning dime-store gold
on the undrinkable reservoirs of this daily planet?
Tonight, the American flag
over the Exxon station is so huge
that it frightens you as you pull off
the highway of angels.
You've reached the other side
of all your tumbling battles, Superman:
this town is Retrospect, a place to hang your hat.

And when the test comes back from the neon lab,
and when the waiting room waits for something good to happen,
and when the arms of Lois Lane
pan your sky like lighthouse beacons in the night,
and when she kisses you and calls you "Clark"—
how vividly you can imagine what it is to lose everything,
how graphic, how lustrous, how radiant the fear.

Loss is a one-night stand on an empty runway,
a white calla lily simmering in your hand.
Wave it in the air: surrendering flag.
Dangle it to the ground: trumpet for the lips of your heart.

Signatures of blood claim credit for catastrophe,
run rivulets down your face like an eyeliner masque.
As your body has completed the work of your mind,
your mind has exerted itself against your flesh.
The calla lily seems to mourn you,
its buried trumpet calcifying
in the underground cake of minerals and stethoscopes,
its tongue the color of dried ice,
a passenger pigeon pressed like a primrose
between the pages of a hardbound book.

You're that calla lily, Clark,
a series of dots torn from the page,
reconnecting in the night sky,
a blind constellation of heroic service
popped from your frame.
Take off your glasses,
your wristwatch, your tie.
You won't be needing them, man of steel.
Take off your shoes, those pants,
the red and blue spandex, the yellow belt,
the tattooed *S* on the tattoo of you.
Take back your body.
Touch it with your hands as if for the first time.
This is the first time.
Watch yourself in the mirror.
Turn off those X-ray eyes and what do you see?

You are naked
and your hair is
a blue-black crow
in a cypress
preening in the dark.

Remember its color.
Everything must die.

Jason Camlot

KIT DISCOVERS SOUND

Kit found work
in statistics
at the University of Peripheral Matter

counting words per
sentence for the great
canon he chose.

The results were startling.

In the first 5000 sentences
2455 even
2545 odd.

In the third 5000 sentences
2462 even
2538 odd.

In 40,000 sentences
20,001 even
19,999 odd.

Spenser used twice
as many Os
as De Quincey.

Swift averaged twice
as many complaints per
period as Schiller.

Chaucer used the least
number of simple
sounds anywhere.

The Chancellor
of UPM sent a memo
of congratulations.

On his lunch breaks
Kit composed nonsense
verse about insects.

The numbers clicked
like beetles in his desk
and taught him

love was meaningless
unless counted
over time.

He dreamed battalions
of smarmy bugs
on summer flesh.

Life is a prostitute
he wrote
to a freshman lover

but you
are pure
like rain.

All that counting.
He began to divide
his objects into sound.

He purchased
a hi
fi

and imagined
sound tattoos
by a diamond needle.

He baked
sound potatoes
wrapped in foil

and dipped
sound wieners
into mustard.

He purchased
a micro-
recorder

and began recording
everything
edible.

Dropped leeks
in China
town.

Freeze-dried
dragon
flies.

The sound
of still-born
onions.

Living the perpetual
bachelor's
life.

In the hiss of the world
in the hush of the phonograph-lady's throat
he heard cuts of living voice
and imagined sound tattoos
by the tip of a diamond needle.

He purchased
a micro-
recorder

and began recording
everything
audible.

The jumbled names of telephone conversations.
The squeak of his own greb steps.
The bell struck like an alarm of terror.
The wrapped crunch of shoulder cartilage.
The gurgle of his freshman lover's cheek.
The honk of a city moon.
The pivot and scrape, resistance to arrest.
The pop and crinkle of Twinkies ravaged.
The rubber thunk of dead pinball.

Evenings at home
labeling
little tapes.

The sound of lists piling.
The shuffling sound of general unemployment.

Snow falling general over populations.
Slap shots thwacking urban plywood.
The hiss of cappuccino machines like Madagascar cockroaches.
The pling of porcupine quills in a curious poodle's nose.
The clip clop of cleft-hooves.
The Os in Van Toorn's De Kooning.
The hoorah! of ardent fervor.
The man in apartment 12 scratching a nightmare
 onto his wall at 4 am, like clockwork.
Hospitals after midnight.

What's all this?
his freshman
lover asked.

Those are all
my
sounds.

The heraldry of Hockey Night in Canada.
Soft paper tearing.
Cigarette cellophane.
Wax candle thud.
Clink, a bullet in a tea cup.
He hits the goal post!
The sound of the old fur district, groaning.
The muted sound of a hand deep inside.
Whittling licorice sticks.
The quiet hum of autistic storms.
The waxy rub of crayon parents.
The empty tock tock of ignorance.
Beetles at work and ground moths in autumn.

What are all
your sounds
for?

They are
for
remembering.

For
remembering

what?

That
your pain
is elsewhere.

The shift of snow angels recently unbodied.
The crack of backgammon bones.
A tooth chipped on the lip of a urinal.
The indignant pause of national humiliation fabricated.
The clinks of a reticent dinner.
The whir of lost channels.
The frail little squeak of being observed by an enigmatic.
The press of violent assimilation.
The sad quiet of oblivion to their own doom.

But I
have
no pain.

Of course
you
do.

No
I
don't.

I will
be
your pain.

That
's
stupid.

The calming gurgle of life amnesia.
The muffled pops of a carnival in the hidden zone.
The sound inside an Egyptian kiln.
Rosaries scattered on linoleum.
Tap tap tap the fascist metronome.
Radio news storms.

Crinkling the pages of a thin nerve diary.

Kit
ended
the affair.

PHONO KIT

Thomas Edison™ crossed the Atlantic
to capture Tennyson's voice
on a wax cylinder.
This is to be read militantly
because the poem was
The Charge of the Light Brigade
which itself looks like a wax cylinder,
grooves containing sound in the nooks
of letters. Of the first ten words
in that poem he read—so much like
Ezra Pound's fascist broadcasts:
"Europe callin', Pound speakin', Ezry Pound speakin'…"—
three of the words are "half"
three of the words are "a"
three of the words are "league"
and one of the words "onward".
Turning in circles,
a scratched prison
spun for his ghost.
Many decades the cone was lodged
behind a steam radiator
"Eau et Gaz Sur Tous Les Etages"
in a decrepit third floor flat
where Kit played his Elfking '45
on a Realistic™ phonograph.
"I do what I can to keep
an even tone of voice;
now, when I drop my voice,
they turn on more current."
This is still to be read
militantly.

Discovered
by Kit in the spring of '68.
What the ... ?
like a defeated conch shell.
Kit softly returned its shape,
by his own device made it utter
the deep sounds of bulk
many leagues under
"All in the valley of Death"
were the first words
he could discern, but
"Awe Eee Uh Phahee 0 Hesh"

from the throats of ancient male fish,
Kit thought.
"All the world wondered"

Reminded of his youth,
his effigy parents and their substance,
all the voices possibly melted
into the coitus-dummies' thighs.
"Flashed all their sabres bare"
There was nothing he could do
but record the impurities as he heard them:

8 seconds of crackling
1 second of overload
8 seconds of crackling
3 seconds of mucous sound
2 seconds crackling
35 seconds horrible high frequency distortion
8 seconds mouth noises
19 seconds very dull tapping, as in a dream
4 seconds crackling
2 seconds nasal passage
4 seconds crackling
31 seconds of obscure whispers
"Some one had blundered"

There is no end
to this charge of history,
but the wax cylinder turning,
in Kit's decrepit flat,

the same martial voice,
the same sounds in between the words,
the repetition of the blunder,
the same six hundred slaughtered.
Like The Flight of Lindbergh,
all early recording is meant
for translucent pedagogy.

...CRYPTO KIT...

...crumpled and damaged is the tin plate kit of lucifer...
...breakfast on it once: a needle kit for the pin cushion esophagus...

...leave the fun kit alone for now, someone will later discover it...
...and lose their fingers, left in the fatal fun kit...

... the mercy kit was left unconscious for too many centuries...
... and now there is nothing but a comatose kit for torture...
... are you comatose for kit torture...

... the ring on his thumb was a kit tag, horrible...
... swollen up for the kit of inscription...
... the tattooed digit of kit #90989...

...review this literature kit, I'm sure there are deaths that amuse...
... even more than the fun kit murder pranks...
... even more than the fun kit epilepsy...
... even more than the fun kit...

... this touch for your own sake as well as for the kit's...
... because when you are happy the kit is happy...
... and the kit must always be happy...

... feel the kit ...
... be the kit ...

... if you touch a life kit as you pass away...
... and they can fold you up into a flat body kit...
... you may one day be admitted into the prestigious kit museum...
... and what a nice kit that is to be a part of...

... shag carpets where the virgin parents of kit child died...
...found grounded with Styrofoam and an electro kit inside her ...
and the physics kit more stunning than he would have suspected...
...their mouths frozen open like dew kits...

...you're a good kit...
...you're a good looking kit...
... vomiting before the tell me tell me kit...

... fortune or misfortune, there is no simpler choice kit...
... excluding perhaps the micro kit of deviant behavior...
... it used to be that a kit dismantled itself...
...but now a kit will corrode itself from within...

... leave the kit alone...
... his first attempt with the macho voice kit...
... now the cool cat kit lies in his own blood-puddle tonight...
...the flashy gun kit jammed perhaps...
... play the kit piano, he had said...
... or there will be no music kit tomorrow...

...the god kit falling like crab apples from babel...
...pieces from the kit burning with the wrath...
... the brimstone of a kit of sorrow...
... and a kit of fire socket tears...

... his body was a kit made by exploited hands...
...and the factory was a big kit made by exploited hands...
... and the big machines were exploitation kits...
... each with their own self-repair kits...

...and then there is the kit who swallowed the schubert megaphone...
... and now at his tomb he's called kit schubert...

Jeffrey McDaniel

POETRY NATION

In the capital square there is a statue of Jack Spicer
puking his guts out, the phrase *My vocabulary
did this to me* inscribed in the marble base.

In nightclubs, supermodels stomp their heels
and dream of their hearts being enlarged
with compassion implants
as the poet gets all the attention.

Guys in trendy rock bands mope like damp rats
whenever a poet walks into a room.

Everyone wants to be a poet, even the coroner
scribbling in his note pad at the crime scene
a drowned man is judged only by his piers.

*Car jackers pause in mid-heist...to consider the moon.
Hallmark is burned to a crisp.*

The back of Baudelaire's head
appears on every other thirteen dollar bill.

Homeless people stand in line for Pablo Neruda.
In hospitals they feed cancer patients Carolyn Forche.
In churches there are giant wooden replicas
of Emily Dickinson nailed to a cross.

Instead of NBC and CBS, there is WSMerwin,
the Walt Whitman channel, and Sappho at Nite.

The Constitution was written by Tristan Tzara.
All men are created equal under Dada.
The drug czar makes sure everyone gets enough.

Lucille Clifton for President!
Charlie Parker is the national bird.
Howl is recited before professional football games.
You can pay for groceries with words.

John B. Lee

THE SERGEANT PEPPER SONNETS

I
Remember how you wanted her
falling/backwards into your bed
her skirt flowing/into her body shapes
like warm butter/
while you listened to Sergeant Pepper
the/summer you were sixteen
and the music/moved in your skull
like the moods of smoke
when/twenty years seemed
such a long time and
John/Lennon's first son was a school boy
dreaming/diamonds.
Or the gravel road dust fuming/up
behind your uncle's truck
and you heard/"A Day in the Life"
in the blue cab
and/if anyone had changed the station
then/you'd have killed them
and struck out all
alone/because you believed in love
and music.

II
When Sixteen magazine ran the last fan/zene photographs
of the fab four in six/tyseven
mustachioed and gone to/grass
with the piccolo trumpet on Pen/ny Lane
and the swoozing organ rhythms/
of Strawberry Fields
two cool tree leaps a/way
from the bubble gum and braces set/
they left behind
the pre-pubescent or/ganisms
called "screaming girls" and took up/
the red roach and hookah water

bubbling/hot like dangerous chemistry
and/the Technicolor wash of a
psylocy/bin sunset the way the sea shares itself/
with the sky becoming cobalt blue:

you either drown or learn to swim;
you either fall or learn to fly.

III
I was just getting over my sister/singing
in the house like a shower
full/ of girl scouts when the radio
matured/ and the lamp cooled
like a child's forehead com/ing out of fever
and the rooms went glomm/y
with artificial shade
and the meat/smells of a shared harvest
long after we'd/lost
the wheat-gold hair of childhood
and gone/ to work in sweat-shops,
fast-food chicken joints/and the hot
fields of my father's bean rows/
where we followed the planter's graph like tough/
philosophical arguments easy/
to lose involving why those pulled weeds
sagged/ in our hands
like the failure of desire.

IV
my own Sergeant Pepper salad of snap/shots
would include Hitler and Curly How/ard
grandfather Lee and Tom the hired/ man
stuck there like two straw-infected dolls/
their pant cuffs leaking
the viscera of/ harvest barns,
the many masked Beatle boys,/ Dylan
Thomas and so many poets/
they would seem a heavy crop
of faces/ on a halloween shop wall
we'd never/ wear them out wearing
them out
and of course,/ Holden, the hopeless

catcher whom I read/
trapping the light in my own upstairs
hall/ coming in at the window like a
thief/ of words—the winter afternoon
the all-American assassin.

Lois-Ann Yamanaka

YARN WIG

My madda cut our hair so short.
Shit, us look like boys, I no joke you.
I mean more worse than cha-wan cut.
At least cha-wan cut get liddle bit hair
on the side of your face.
Us look almost bolohead
and everybody tease us, *Eh boy,*
what time? or *Eh boy,*
what color your panty?

I figga my madda sick and tired
of combing our long hair every morning.
She make us all line up
and us sit down one by one on her chair
by her makeup mirror. She pull
and yank our hair just for put um
in one ponytail, but I tell you
she pull um so tight,
our eyes come real slant
and our forehead skin real tight.
Ass why now we get boy hair.

One time we stay walking home from school
and Laverne Leialoha calling us *snipe*
cause us Japanee and we get rice eye
she say. Then her and her friend write
S-N-I-P on the road with white chalk
they wen' steal from school.

Us dunno if she teasing us
SNIPE for Japanee or
SNIP for our boy hair.

My madda she start to feel sorry.
She no can make our hair grow back
all long again. But she go down Ben Franklin
one day and come home with plenny black yarn,
the thick kine. She make us yarn wigs,
I no joke you, with short bangs
and long, long yarn hair in the back,
all the way to our okole.
Just like the high school cheerleaders or
like Cher on the *Sonny and Cher Show.*
My sistas and me make the yarn hair
come in front then we flip um back
like Cher do.

The other day my madda took us store
and all us wen' wear our yarn wigs in the car.
We stay letting the yarn blow out the window
'cause so long. But when we was ready for go out,
I wen' fast kine pull off my yarn wig.
Shame, eh? More better they tease me,
Eh, boy, than *Eh, yarn for hair.*

My sistas, they so stupid,
they wear their yarn wigs in the store.
The lady at the soda fountain
tell, *Oh-ma goodness! So cute!*
Harriet, try come, try come,
and the lady from the fabric side
come running over. *Oh-la cute yo daughtas!*
I kinda stay thinking maybe
I should have wore my yarn wig, too.
The fabric lady tell my madda,
You made um? Oh you so cle-va wit yo hands!
And they so adora-bull.

One sista start bringing her hair
in the front and acting like Cher.
My other sista pull all her hair on one side

and start acting like she looking
for split ends and her too go fling
her hair back.

Me, I order my vanilla Coke
and look at myself in the soda fountain mirror.
I see my sistas drag my madda
buy yellow and orange yarn
for make like Bewitch and Lucy.
I no look at myself no mo.
I pull my bangs real hard with both hands
and start feeling real bolohead.

Louise Bak

DOUBLE-TAKE

yellow earth scorched red

red sorghum rusted with blood

blood of thin white hare shot

shot by *sake*-gunners retching

retching over bleeding flesh

flesh of young slave girl's

    friend

friend who gnawed her pants

pants ravished with toothmarks

toothmarks like her own on

on soldier's bootless foot kicks

kicks her on to wooden board

board called plank of comfort

   woman

woman as cum-vessel for rice

rice extra-salted with tears

tears after those double "U"s

"U"sually "U"niformed maraud

maraud her mother and sister

sister watches the firefly's light

   eclipsed

eclipsed by a cloud of grenades

grenades air-popping a kernel

kernel of life they called *whore*

whore-before-*woman* beside hare

hare only knew 'til now that this

this was a **woman**-before-whore

whored by war.

M.

M. Chrysanthemum
M. Butterfly
M. Saigon
What next?

M. Bangkok?
M. Malay?
M. *Chin*-a (Pet)?

all silently chanting
Colonize Me
a mantra for the White-myth-maestro

dreaming of *wai tu yung* girls
dispensing rice cakes on open clam shells in a parade

pondering whether her waiting cunt
is slanted to match her eyes

imagining lotus blossoms teaching you
Hau tu Sekkusu

hoping her soul is as yielding as silk
not stone-washed like *Levis* denim

seeing *sum yung chic* on the Cantonese
cuisine menu, followed by *fuc me slo*

Occidentally constructing the myth of
Asian woman as exoticized cipher

en garde:

M. Commodifier
M. Pearl Fisher
M. Colonizer

your chrysalis is rupturing
and the butterfly is flying free
no longer your frenulum flutterer.

HETEROFLEXIDOME

I will miss you, Pun-jab-*me*-by-Nature
are only 22 with 2 more calendars
to charge through, or so that's what
the white-coat said at Toronto General

Hospital, where he stuck his finger
up your anus & you spat in his face.

I will miss you, whirling *Shiva Nataraja*.
You dance to the driving music of *Eros
& Thanatos*, in dark back-alleys & public
Lavatories, choosing to ravage darting
lovelies or egotesticle flutter-flies, who
turn you into a fire-hydrant hugger in
the *Trojan* dawns, as you romp to work.

I will miss you, *Krishna,* lover of *Radha* (II)
in multiple guises. You have the courage
to love, whom you choose, though you have
been beaten on the streets of Bombay only
to piss up the *CN* tower. You cry for the
first time on newly relaced docs because you
know you can't kick your way out of this one.

I will miss you, dream-catching Bhangranaut.
You taught me to respect myself at a picnic
on rose petals & 24-carat gold leaflets, on an
empty cemetery plot you mark off with curry
powder; working a *Ru-Paulian* sashay around
me thrice & once more for non-conformist
measure & I pray you will reach your eternal

heteroflexidome.

Lynn Crosbie

LOVE LETTER FROM GARY COLEMAN

my face is flaccid, and with time its ex-
terior went under. the bags and lines
are purple seamed, like fruit, on
a lady's hat. and shakes too, deep

black and blue midnight.
your elbow when it falls to the hip.
crooked and it crunches, splintered
wood, when it shattered. a nightmare
I had about cars and leather.
your hand, that bamboo tree, spread
ink flat thin from a languishing brush.
a soft movement, like sinew shrinking.
it blazes out, it holds the span of
my neck and fits, fingertip to shell
cartilage.

you can hear it crack. it's shaped
small, I am, a small man, and the
problem was my dressing in a boy's
clothing. the band of my hips, extends
to, the sand of my cheeks. in a shirt
with a hood, and eating always makes
you cry. your tears when I looked
over. I would have made a different
world.

to God: I grow in noise. my clothes
tear, I am visible, huge, pouring
over the chesterfield prop. I held
them in my wooden hands like grasping
pegs and soldiers.
now, like keys in the ignition or
the metal flash of my razor. these
icons of my adulthood, I will not
pout again or speak to the fish.
my heart is filled, and I feast no
longer. nor am I dwarfed by children.
they run from me and I am fragrant.

I have been hooked to the machine
for hours and I feel as if I am being
leaked out in pieces. and bits come
back, I didn't choose. to be ugly
and smirk to you about this, my first
ever ritual. you move me between your
knees and your spine is arched forward.

if it breaks into a clean half,
I'll cut you the rest. and I can move
with you. we. have marks on our bodies
like stigmata. the spots of scorpion bites,
and the welts from a chain, that stung
when we made an axle. crossing
one over one in inlaid relief.

it is night when I write you, and
strangers walk by my window.
their voices are sickening,
and the rage comes to me. I want to
bear you high above my shoulders,
and I spend tome, building an Egyptian
hammock. it's sewn around yielding
bars, and it sways under canvas. you
have the smudges of a fading
Nefertiti. like a knife in your eye.

my chest is a pair of bellows.
it blows and stirs.

the shingles of hair on your
sleeping cheekbone, a tendril

is sweet to my closed face,
all jowly and,
shaped for love.

Marcella Durand

CITY OF PORTS 2

Motionless billows of icy water vapor chill
in the upper atmosphere of greater dispersal;

tendrils cross the radiometric ether and spark
in blue tendons, the cartilage of air, over

the border of Canada seen in a slim line
of old growth forest and clouds of black flies.

We reached this far. An oval lake shiny
in the taillights on a car traveling

day and night over sea level bridges from
one key to the next, a string of towns and

a giant white cross blur to an imploding star
against a Connecticut navy sky and the stark forests

of an in-between state. In the process of euphoric metal
stress. Cosmopolitan. And with no warning, the highway

strikes with overbearing rivets, hooded, then
diamond-like bends to cross a field of water.

It is a tunnel closed at both ends. It runs
    halfway in granite, and half
        in liquid shifting sand.

Mark Cochrane

MAPPLETHORPE

Paint my lips. Airbrush my jawbone with talcum, my
jawbone is shaven raw-blue. Blush me, rouge me,
feather my scrolled wings of hair. I say to my wife.
I say, make me over like Mapplethorpe, lips open &
vulnerable. I say, a man like one idea of a woman.
Make me that. Later let me preen in leather, tough,
the same angle, but for now I pout into your f-stop.
Don't stop. Do me like that, yeah, like Mapplethorpe.
Closer now, cheeks lavender & brows blue, garish as
our ancestors, faces of baboons. Come to me with eyes
lined, lashes black, your broad gorgeous shoulders,

your freckled muscular neck. Let a man & a woman kiss
a woman & a man. Two palettes, & smudge, pigments
& oils: a diptych. There is gender all over our faces,
mixed up & blended over all of our faces & boy, boy
am I, am I ever, boy am I ever in love.

Maureen Seaton with Denise Duhamel

EXQUISITE MAJORITY

It's hard for me to get a good job.
I want a house, Nordic track, and a new PC.
Sometimes I wonder about the word *consequences*.
I mean, nothing runs in a straight line, right?
I put on a shirt that says *Made in Japan,*
not on the label, but on the front. *Model Minority,*
Ms. X, Mr. X, Baby American.
Non-nuclear and cut from nobody's mold.
If I were just a squiggle outline,
what color would I be? If I had sex with you,
would we smoke afterward? I worry about designer
clothes and my investment in American individuality.
(Tommy Hilfiger is the choice of certain gang—
members wearing two jackets at once to show off
their money. If I had to give my opinion,
I'd say—let the best designer win, man).
If you're the only one in first grade with crooked bangs
I guess that makes you a minority, sort of.
Or answer this: If all the animals in the world died,
what the hell would we eat?
Yesterday I saw Nell Carter on Prince Street.
I'm a New Yorker so I didn't stare.
I walked down the steps to the six train,
slid my token into the slot.
A silver bar twirled and let me in.

LET ME EXPLAIN

It was easy for Jim to take off his clothes,
his body firm as a futon, his penis
just the right size. The small towel fit around his waist
perfectly, covered everything. I, on the other hand,
had all this flesh to worry about, breast to pubis—
lumpy thighs, thick ankles, the largest ass
at "Plato's Retreat."

What feels good on flesh?
Fringe on a book mark. Tassels on a graduation cap.
Cold metal coins in summer.

My grandmother pushes out her false teeth to make us laugh.
She is so sad, her husband dead so many years,
her children nothing but disappointment.
When I sleep with her, I rub my feet all up her legs.
I am so little. Her legs are so strong. I dive down to touch her toes.

When I want a massage, Jim says yes.
I pretend to sleep—otherwise it ends up sex. Once,
a woman rubbed my back and I cried after she left.
My body was a shaved bear, cold and prickly.

What is bisexual? Would I still love Jim
if he were a woman? Would I embrace his vulva gladly,
his soft breasts with nipples as sweet as hard candy?
My best friend is Carole Jenkins.
She wears pants to first grade and carries me on her back
up the steep cobblestone hill when my asthma flares.
She gets bad grades, gets into scrapes. I love her
like my teenage cousins love James Dean. She's arrested

in a bar brawl years later, taken to emergency for stitches
    over her eye.
Carole has a girlfriend with false eyelashes and costume jewelry
who cries when Carole is thrown the book, cries
at all those black stitches, a lost game of tic-tac-toe.
I go to court to tell of the time my tongue stuck
to the icy fence at recess. How Carole ran to get warm water
to separate my tongue from the fence like a Band-Aid from flesh.

What stops the bisexual from taking over the world,
sleeping with the boss, the boss's husband, the boss's Doberman?
It's not safe, all this nondiscriminatory salivation.
It's unsanitary, not neat.

I was ok when she touched me—not too terrified
and Jim was kind to me, tender as a new father.
She had cool fingers, respectful. At first I thought it was Jim,
but he was in me, busy with stronger mechanics.
She was blonde and white marble,
older, so her skin had begun that velvet stage.
Her husband was a shadow behind her.

Susan is a woman who wants everyone—
all at once, on every side, as if she is a room with no corners.
There is no one she won't fuck. There is no one
she can't take in her mouth and level in five minutes.

Susan came on to me. I told her I liked Jim.
She laughed and then she slept with him.
Now I hate Susan, the way she twirls her long hair
    through dinner,
the way she sits too close to men and women,
that split down a couple, an ax through wood.
"I can fuck you, I can fuck your husband."
Someone who doesn't know diamonds from fakes.

God is hard on the bisexual woman—
a scornful subject for poetry.
God shakes his head at the woman
who loves whatever is there in front of her—
a chair, a cloud, a cheap wedding trinket.

There were small rooms big enough for a mattress
and four colliding bodies. My skin
was its own tight boundary, the air around me cheddar-sharp.
She was the light in our midst—plump lamb and halo.
I crossed over to her while my mind would let me,
while the angel of scent and glut perched on my tongue.
The men were busy with their eyes and hands
their paternal regard. We were busy leaving them.

XENA: WARRIOR PRINCESS

I run through the muck of New Zealand
side-kicking fiends. Sword-fighting demons
add to the quackery of my even-
tempered sidekick's medical practice.
I'm good with a sword and herbal poultices
to cure my own wounds. Don't mistake my bruises
for mistakes. Every one was destined to boost
TV ratings and jolt the audience
from microwave popcorn and frozen fishsticks.
You can be me for Halloween. In fact,
I come in all cultures now, scratch
my surface, I'm complete as Barbara Striesand.
She can keep her press-on nails, her dopey fans.
I have warrior work to do, silvery plans.

Michael Holmes

(BRAMALEA LIMITED)

"i like crazy people, especially those who don't see the risk"
                                        —John Lydon

the premier & his boys manufactured us muppets: a
bramalea ltd. reality where an alphabet of infernal sesame
streets spell whole subdivisions.

in nightmares it's their buddy paul, the more
mephistophelian of the moguls (the one that reminds me
of a megalomaniacal, paper-clip hoarding bert), whose
speculation relentlessly constructs the letter-of-the-day in
a viral pinwheel (your childhood, michael: brought to you
by the letters O & Y & the number 666). it was a
"planned community," the blueprint stolen from dante:
see, the residential inner circles feed the industrial
perimeter. . .

bramalea is the kind of cosmic joke you can play on
200,000 or so middle-class folks—one that only *mr.
snufflupagus* or *captain poetry* could fully appreciate.

i lived in the E section. on earnscliffe circle. just off
earl's court. one up from edinburgh. in bramalea,
geography is *very* important. at bss, my high school, there
were those from as far away as avondale & balmoral. an
interesting fact: you can fit the first five letters of the
alphabet into about four square miles. (now there's
something your primer won't teach you: it's not quite a
1:1 ratio.)

bramalea means that douglas coupland is never gonna *be*
the "voice of the X generation." we might produce a
few cool-looking books—lots of black, complementary
colours, great design—but nothing that'll ever catch,
nothing truly *popular*.

ever since watergate was broadcast to the sticks it's been
impossible to be urbane. there are stories, from the 50s &
60s, that older writers can still get away with, but for the
most part you've gotta accept that kids who grew up on
the children's television workshop & movies about nam
—a classic film genre & the only one created by a US
president—are gonna cringe at fond reminiscence. still,
i figure someone should write about bramalea (we called
it viet bram & brampucia), especially the libelous bits:
the best of it all being the damp corduroy headiness about
her—allison in jodhpurs—always game for a dry hump.
cause if there's nothing deliciously cosmopolitan going
for rubick's cube, duran duran, or roller disco you can still
make it by japan's "adolescent sex": how the you that you
are never looks as ridiculous as those people in group
shots nostalgia dresses up.

bramalea is like this. sometimes the radio gets into your
clothes: but it's noticeable only after you've gone cold
turkey.

bramalea is when you erase all the pre-sets & the best lies
come sweetly: how the car shimmied with the weight of
fast friends & classes ditched; when savings-time meant a

summer boon of 1/2 bag highs cheap & demented, the
kind that work up the glow of immortal teen-aged
night-sweats & the ABCs of cruising the streets with
grover & cookie.

bramalea is about how there are two kinds of people
in the world.

it's simple: you either *choose* to be an *ernie*, or you're
gonna be a *bert*.

"IN HIGH SCHOOL"

in high school everyone you half know dies on friday or saturday
night—they shoot themselves in the head with their father's hunting
rifle, or they take acid & lock themselves in their brother's van at 3
am with a skill saw & bleed to death—gracefully if pitifully—
drowned in the buzz of shimmying teeth. or maybe they augured a
lifelong struggle between workaday & the weekend & necktie
themselves to the visiting team's goal-posts. most often tho they buy
it in groups on the backroads—lose control on a stretch of
treacherous curves—coming home from the party, thru the glorious
fog, or over the mysterious black ice.

Nick Carbo

Ang Tunay Na Lalaki (THE REAL MAN)
IS BAFFLED BY CRYPTIC MESSAGES

he finds on cheap match covers.
                        PLEASE
            MAKE ME TASTE LIKE
                        A MAN
is the first one he reads after lighting up
an American Spirit cigarette on the corner
of Broadway and Houston. The painted Statue
of Liberty on the giant DKNY ad on the side
of the building winks her big blue eye

as if she understands what those words mean,
as if she could make him taste like a man.
The street sign changes to WALK
and the natural smoke of the natural cigarette
feels good in his lungs. He thinks
of the taste of fried garlic, of anise seeds,
of rambutan fruit, of broiled tuna—
none comes close to what a man
would taste like in his mind. He reaches
underneath his shirt and sweater to scratch
his left arm-pit. He smells his fingers
and thinks, *this is what a filipino man*
must taste like to American women.
To test his hypothesis, he sticks
his index finger in his mouth, pulls
it out with a slurpy sound and points upwards
as if he were testing the wind,
as if he were carrying a flaming torch.

MAL DE OJO

In the market in Garrucha there are stalls
that sell herbal remedies for love-sickness,
constipation, depression because of bad
grades in school, depression because your husband
is seeing another woman, depression because of illness
in the immediate family, gout, and bad breath.
A mixture of *matalahúva, canela,* and *perejil*
to ward-off the evil eye. From behind
small baskets filled with sticks of sandalwood,
the woman with large earrings points to a chart
marking its symptoms: stomachache, severe cramps,
sores that won't heal, sudden broken bones,
insomnia, unexplained rashes, impotence.
Her mixtures are sought in cities as far
as Murcia and Barcelona—one thousand pesetas
for one bag. I ask if she has a mixture that *will*
inflict the evil eye on someone of my choosing.
I buy two thousand worth, with thoughts of sprinkling
a pinch on the flaps of the self-addressed
stamped envelopes that magazine editors have to lick
to send back my rejected poems.

FOR MY FRIEND WHO COMPLAINS HE CAN'T DANCE AND HAS A SEVERE CASE OF WRITER'S BLOCK

Then, take this tambourine
inside the sheep barn,

listen to the anaconda's intestines,
the shark's walking stick,

learn the river insect's secret
neon calligraphy,
swim through Frida Khalo's hair
and come out smelling like orchids,

lift your appetite
towards the certified blue turtle,
feast on Garcia Lorca's leather shoes
and taste the sun, the worms of Andalusia,

don't hesitate in front of a donut,
a ferris wheel, the crab nebula,

excavate diamond-eyed demons,
Chaucer's liver, Minoan helmets,

paste Anne Sexton's face on a $1,000 bill
and purchase a dozen metaphors,

beware of the absolute scorpion,
the iguana with the limping leg,

permit indwelling, white words around the eyes,
the confrontation of windows,

never feed your towel to the alligator,
he will eat you and eat you and eat you.

Paul Beatty

STALL ME OUT

why you   no rhythm

afraid of women asexual pseudo intellectual
bald mt. fuji shaped head

       no booty havin   big nose
   size 13 feet   pigeon toed crook footed

taco bell burrito supreme eatin
       day dreamin

            no jump shot   bant dunk

comic book readin
nutrition needin

knock kneed sap sucker
non drivin

         anti fashion
   constantly depressed clumsy no money mutherfucker

        take your weak ass poems
        and go back to los angeles

Raymond Filip

MOTORMOUTH

Motor mouth motor mouth
North East West South
Putt putt zoom zoom
Ride a broom
Spank my tank
With Canadian crude
Traffic tied up
Like a Fallopian tube
Bumper to bumper
Burper to burper
Don't scratch my chrome
Don't sit on my throne
Drop the hammer
Watch your grammar
Free parts and labor
Gonna donate my organs
To the JP Morgans
2 wheel 4 wheel
8 wheel 18
Faster faster
Radar can't touch her
Run that cop
Right up a treetop
Roll that troll
Inside the toll booth
Rollercoaster round
Highlands lowlands
1 lane 2 lane
4 lane astral plane
White lines minus signs
Wheels whine like Windigo
White knuckles gold buckles
Truckloads of honeysuckle
Kissin' in a sitzpin
Dancin' on a hairpin
Let the rush gush
100 smiles per hour

Livin' lovin'
Run out the clock
Livin' lovin'
Run out the clock
Livin' lovin'
Run out the clock

Robert Allen

From VOYAGE TO THE ENCATADAS
II GALAPAGOS TED: HIS PERILS

59

ash. / — *come and go, talking* of Atlantis in a tongue fat with lying, You
won't get to Hollywood, Ted. To the bisque bred, you'll find we eat
our young and our successes, both live and in the scandal
sheets, before and after they're dead. / GALAPAGOS TURTLE

GIVES BIRTH TO ELVIS'S
HEAD / MIA & WOODY SACRIFICE YOUNGEST CHILD IN SATANIC
RITE / ALIEN WROTE DYLAN'S LYRICS / NEW HUBBY FOR LIZ?
Galapagos Ted—yes, that same lounge lizard implied
in the oceanic tryst! First human in Eden! Out of the blue! God
shakes

60

his fist, whacks off his own head with a scimitar. The shell game! (not
Elvis at all, though the slicked-back hair, center-parted, brings Rudy
Vallee to mind) singing just for you, jacktars, at the Hotel
Gobernador, with complimentary

prawn cocktails for all, outside beneath a peach of a moon—
but Ted's running off with himself. He always does, snoozing half up
the beach, evolution's untimely etched box leaking its secrets.
Secrets! He cannot

run swiftly like the hare / cut through the air like a swallow
swashbuckle like Errol or dance like Astaire. *Only poor flesh in a gilded
pot / Teddy's my name and I like it a lot*—"Ladies

61

and Gentleman, the Hotel Gobernador is proud to present, straight
from The Isles of Ash where he hatched out of his egg! That heavenly
hoofer and heartthrob—not just another empty shell or hollow
Armani suit—the antediluvian

vaudevillian, the one, the only, Grandview Ted!
                                    Gringo, drifting
the length of this beach as you drifted the length of the world. Shells
lie everywhere, yellow and pink inside, whorled and opal, winding to
the point of nothing

where storms from the ocean, like songs from a single note, rise to cloud
the sun. Shell beaches are rare on the Galapagos, where Beelzebub's
own black moat rings everything with ash. *Los Encatadas:* the enchanted

62

lands. Drifting islands move like outlaws, restless on the sea, kept from
harm's way by a tidal intelligence sensed by its first sailors, whose
charts were useless, since the islands side-stepped every voyager

who aimed his glass at them. Ted wrote them as tap-dancing turtles in the
show he staged for them, so they'd sing lost Popeye songs to the Broadway
carriage trade, till given
the vaudeville shepherd's hook the minute they tap-danced
on the maps. Be lost, lost islands, is Ted's incantation, but they are
lost with him, each a map of the other, a blue-edged, tear-dewed

63

map. The bestiary starts here: simple germ limbering and growing eternal,
changing in the tide, following Ted's score—*the map has gone, how can we
grow old, grandma's tears have made the barbecue cold* ... Sing and dance,

mazurkas of suitability, sonnets of survival, dead-end elegies for some. Our
turtle Ted doesn't know where he is in the litany, hanging on the breast
of the moongoddess, all growed up, floating in the tide grass singing hymns

learned from the Osmonds, buoyed by the salt to near divinity. But the lot
of the sea-going shell-clad ardent amphibian is not what it's cracked
up to be, not given his dreams of the legitimate stage, and this new canny fear

64

of oblivion. Clack! Clack! It's the new lost carol of turtles fucking, like
sleek heavy machinery, yellow diesel cats brought to eat the islands
down to their roots, never mind the lacelike shimmy of new life

in the pond. Clack! Clack! Our engines are warm, but we will refrain
from coitus as it curbs our desire to colonize. Say bud, this place will look nice
condo-ized! We'll truck in sand, fence off a safe stretch of beach, machine

gun the guerrillas, put bank machines in every king-sized bed— / *kiss
our fingers while we grind our heels, / dance your dance while we transform
jungles to malls, your raw germ to our own kind / while indians, savages,*

65

*communists, tap-dancing turtles with stage-struck eyes, the long ladder of
creatures climbing out of the sea, all give way to the thousand year real estate r
eich. CONDOS UBER ALLES , writes a PR snake /* Exit Ted, up right /
pursued by cream pies. *(Follow*

Ted's adventures in succeeding numbers / ADVERTISEMENT

Richard Harrison

LOVE AND THE HOCKEY POOL

1. Draft Day

Among the ten of us who sit together and draft players by name I
know only Robert because once you and he were lovers. Now you are
friends: there he is. I want it to be as if we had known each other
from the days of table hockey when each of us was complete and
right with himself as instinct. When the games begin, my pick
Bourque goes down with a shoulder, and Ricci, my horse for Rookie
of the Year, the kid from my adopted home town junior team, he
breaks a hand trying to grab a slapshot. Robert calls me up and leaves
a message: *Your team SUCKS!* he says and laughs and we become close.
But when Messier, his main man, falls to the ice and cannot rise

without his team-mates' help, the iron box of his face unhinged, *oh no oh no* going through his mind, his leg curled like a baby's, I feel no 'there-but-for-the-grace,' only the gain of my own leg on the scoresheet; now we are closer.

2. Talking Trade

I'm trying to trade with Robert whose defence is weak, who has a couple of big guns and I might get one. I must keep in mind the men who disappoint me—even as now I imagine myself seen through the eyes of the loves I've abandoned—them I will let go. I nurtured their photographs, smelled the numbers of each day's ink, my fingers black with print. I own them by name alone, and for trading, that alone is enough.

3. The Consummation

And when the trading's done, each says I got the better deal and holds his new man dearer having won the big talk afternoon of wooing and lies. When evening comes, the highlight films replay assists and goals, we smile or rise with anticipation or delight at scenes filmed long ago though we know no human face is waiting there, nor body needs our love.

4. Ice

About the surface. Counting. Hard-edged things. Like ice and pennies; in the face-off circle, a skate cuts *R loves L, R loves L.* The beginning of the story is the theory of jealousy, the game about everything except the goals and assists, the colorful, public men we pass between us, your name unspoken. This is the meaning of victory —a puck sliding over ice into the bag of cords that holds a man to his duty—that I should be the one, the winner, how I come to love him, hate him, the mirror your love brings to my face.

Richard Tayson

REMEMBERING THE MAN WHO MOLESTED ME

His mouth opens and closes like a hinged
shell, his tongue studded with red
barnacles, the way river stone is
encrusted with tiny mollusk shells,
sucking protein. I smell
whiskey, his eyes hover toward
me, the way spotlights float under
water, his hands
huge as black flippers. His blood
beats against his wrist pressed
to my belly as he goes for
my nipple, his hands
like great webbed feet of an animal
rising from the pond's dark
bottom. He chews my
nipple like seaweed, gnawed rubber,
and I rise above the water, am suddenly
the omnipotent god watching over all
the children. Before his fingernails tear
my inner membranes, before
he grabs my hair and yanks
my head and shoves
his swollen purple-veined penis
head to the back of my throat
and I gag on the sperm of my father's best
friend, I take over: I fill
my mouth with fish
hooks, loop fishing line
around my neck, stuff
lead sinkers into my ass, cover
my head and hairless sex with yellow
pond flowers, I sink
down past the protean
insects and gold
fish, down
to the pond's bottom—I save myself, drift
down, feel my skin compose with fish

bone and bacteria, the black
silt and polliwogs' bellies, I say
you may now have this child.

SACRED ANUS

You are putting your finger on the place
    never spoken,
I am remembering the baby in his crib,
    I am the baby
seeing the face of my motherfather, hearing
    the voice say
nice boys don't touch, your finger at my most
    private place.

I am letting your finger dip in and dip out,
    I am feeling
your breath on my thigh, then I am my thigh
    with your left hand holding,
I am your left hand, your finger, I am my anus
    opening and closing
around your finger, sea shell with the salt sea
    sifting in.

I am living in a place of air and blinds flapping,
    where men are not hurting
each other, I am feeling your first and second
    fingers slip in,
your thumb on the seam connecting my anus
    to my scrotum,
I am trying to say what even our rich language
    has no word for.

I am feeling your tongue along the place
    people call a crack,
though it's not a crack but a half-moon touching
    a half-moon, I am
the moon floating in thick placenta sky, you are
    slipping in and out
of me, the way high tide moves across the beach
    then retreats.

I am remembering Walt Whitman's twenty-eight
   young men whose bellies
swell to the sun, I am the twenty-eight young men
   lying on their backs,
you are the fifty-six hands exploring, three fingers
   then the cock
that is not fucking me but is the music
   my body's a string for.

Stan Rogal

VOWELS

I breathe the same air Rimbaud breathed.
Don't I.
Breathe.
Like, those pretty painted vowels
Want to go on forever, man.
But the breath runs out of legs.
Faithless as this.
Why.
Or a consonant making the scene
With its shaved head &
   bulging leathers
Kicked shit out of poor
Insubstantial
You.
Trumpeting harsh with strange
Silent
Oh.
The violet light of his eyes.
Gone crazy in this black wood, man.
Gone crazy.
Gone.
Oh.
The violent, oh,
Night
Of his
Thighs.

Steven Heighton

ELEGY AS A MESSAGE LEFT ON AN
ANSWERING MACHINE

Hello, you've reached 542-0306. I'm unable to answer the phone just now,
but just leave a message after the beep and I'll be sure to return your call.
   Goodbye for now.
Won't bother waiting up for you
to get back to me on this one. Waste of time.
My dime
in a bar by the water, your factory-new

answering machine is—like anything bereaved—still
full of your words, the waves
of your voice, the nervous laugh that gave us,
sometimes, "cause" to laugh. And which we now miss. Well,

human nature. I say Fuck my own. I own
up: this stinks. Too late
to erase all the crap, a watergate
of gossip, off-hand words, no time to phone—
in those last minute changes, additions, to say
what we find it so impossible to say—
I find. So cut all this *can't*
come to the phone right now cant, I don't

buy it. I figure you're in there somewhere, still
screening your calls, you
secretive bastard, pick up the phone right now, if you
would hear a friend. Don't stall,

don't, like me. Thinking
there's time, there's still time enough, or rather
not thinking enough. Now look, I'm not sure whether
the executors will be disconnecting

you—your line—tomorrow (nurses, almost, pulling closed
the green curtains & tearing
out of your torso the drips & plugs & electrodes
to leave you drifting

with that astronaut in the film
who squirms awhile, signals some last, frantic word
then spins away into the void)—
that's why I'm here. Sky's clear tonight, by the way, calm

the wind, the water. Not sure really
why I called—
gesture of a drunk old
friend and ally.

Anyway, it was pretty good
for a second or two, to
get through,
Tom,

goodbye.

Steven Ross Smith

BREN GUN GIRL. 1941

       she is
assembling a weapon
          stroking smooth metal
she is independent
       alone
she thinks of soldiers
         left hand on the gun barrel

a cigarette in her right hand
smoke drifts beside her face
past bandanna-held hair
       she is
in the factory / standing
        behind the boys at war

       she is flesh & blood
she is quality control

she is an image
industrial &
sultry
a prop optioned
for propaganda

she is code that speaks
more than intended
code dispatched
to foreshadow
the other breaking war

From THE BOOK OF EMMETT

FLUTTERING. 4.

jazzy salvage. go to the razed place. the unpremeditated midden.
midway there make a turn for the verse. then back. to the dark
museum of unforeseen speaking. houses wrecked or for sale to
distract. cash and borrow. crash overhead will draw you to it. your
baby's cry. wails beyond these margins. go. burrow into another hot
one. vegetable syntax. so hot. the difference between tomato and
potato growing. light and dark. what task for poetry. such overburden
antidote to the techno-market. marked in words in Paz' *Voice* book.
wait. beware the agent hustle. cradle an instrument. pause. stay lean.
hear the cast-off home. blowing octaves through us.

FLUTTERING. 8.

Blaise (cat, after Cendrars) returns in early morning. walks (that cat walk, cat
breathing) across a neighborhood (eight blocks) into the waking poem. her
own transSiberian. full of de Nerval longing. but more determined. how
achieved? with mapping? or steps ex tempore? she has awakened feral
memory. but the toddling Emmett boy, more compelling, has allergies.
blocked baby breath. impulse and particle unseen. but direct. infecting.
incomprehensible. Cendrars riding his own train to invent surrealism.
nourished himself with flames. flames so distant this problematic morn.
something not linking. green envelope. brown paper. mismatch. the flame
again. dander to sensitive lungs. cleared now. though smoke is everywhere.

North Ireland. Chechnya. Montana. where is the aura in this soot? not keyed
in today. key left in the gypsophelia. baby cries. footsteps on stairs. in the brain
stem, feral, reptilian, a blazing restlessness agitates the limbs.

FLUTTERING. 9.

stairs. forgetting the stairs comes to haunt. no not the stairs. the
difference, the open door at the top. go Freudian symbolic. *discovery
leading to unconscious.* all mind. never mind. what's thudding in the
chest is not a symbol. you were preoccupied with perforations,
manuscript and tearing. my god! he's whimpering at the door. you
leap. address yourself as idiot. clutch. beside the saint of air's tumble.
shoulder shut. thud. thanks to all deities invoked. everything moving
forward stopped to lean on the doorframe and cry. stare. your head
swims. knockout stars in your eyes. the saints sitting on your shoul-
der at sight's periphery. a word was framed in your thoughts last
night, one letter making all the difference. (your friends were carving
fish). difference like a tiny hinge. almost invisible. swings. which way?
you forget everything you've read or know. forgetting in the whimper
of hinge movements. time hung. fate swung toward you without any
words. without any letter that could make a difference. just a tiny
body. all the difference.

Timothy Liu

THE SIZE OF IT

I knew the length of an average penis
    was five to seven inches, a fact
I learned upstairs in the stacks marked 610
    or Q, not down in the basement
where I knelt behind a toilet stall, waiting
    for eight-and-a-half inches or more
to fill my mouth with a deeper truth. The heart
    grows smaller, like a cut rose drying

in the sun. Back then I was only fourteen,
     with four-and-three-quarters inches
at full erection. I began equating
     Asian with inadequate, unable
to compete with others in the locker room
     after an icy swim (a shriveled
bud between my fingers as I tried to shake
     some semblance of life back into it).
Three times a day I jacked off faithfully, yet
     nothing would enlarge my future, not
ads for vacuum pumps, nor ancient herbs. Other
     men had to compensate, one billion
Chinese measured against what? Some said my cock
     had a classical shape, and I longed
for the ruins of Greece. Others took it up
     the ass, reassuring in their way,
yet nothing helped me much on my knees at night
     praying one more inch would make me whole.

Wayne Keon

HIGH TRAVELLIN

no shaman
denied that
high up winter
is long

been
almost two
years in the snow now

nd i
never met any
one along the ridge

not many come this way

just the eagle
nd raven

soarin
nd cryin
soarin
nd cryin
soarin
nd cryin

on all that
blue nd
wind

TO TEOTIHAUCAN

in teotihaucan
there's a
temple

for praying

where you wore
a plume and
a gown

made of quetzal
all bronze
green

and silver

with red on your
mouth and at
dawn

there's moonlight
fastened to
feathers

there's sun

on the breath
of your
hand
and you walk by
the pillar and
toltecs

where jaguar
soldiers
began

i've staggered
behind
the
procession

and followed you
all that i
can

to teotihaucan
power
and

beauty

dragging my heart
in the
sand

to a temple
of conch
shells

and petals

to the temple
where you
had

to lie down

where the sun
and the moon

were

created

where gods
and love
had

to die

where gods and
your love
had to
die

MEDIA BYRONS

Anne Elliott

WHEN I RETURNED FROM MY MOTHER'S FUNERAL, HE SAID I WAS TOO REBELLIOUS

I drive her to her daily radiation appointment and between snoozes against the window she says:

Before I go, let me give you some advice. Even a gentle man requires a place to stick his anger, and you are not that container.

Her bald body is fifty-six years old, and contains cells which multiply in fast, angry clumps and wrap themselves around bone balls and sockets. She walks stiff for the deep ache in her hip; I walk impatient beside her, toting her bag of pills and pillow for sitting. Her bald body is fifty-six years old, and contains a latin list of drugs too toxic to flush after she is gone, that body contains a growing thing in her brain which makes her mouth droop on one side, and a growing thing in her lung which makes her face cough red and wake us in the night, and that body shrinks under the weight of all it contains shrinks too fast thirty pounds lost, now forty, how can I make her food taste like eating? And

now she lies in her last bed and morphine mouth can no longer form words and she growls like a bear and I ask what is wrong and she growls and I say are you angry and she nods faintly and I stroke her wispy head because tube-tied hands feel nothing and I lean into her face because coma eyes see little and she growls like a baby like a bear and her eyes still the same shape same color as mine know that I understand the reason for growling: this body has always been a container has always been a quiet container for cancerous rage and now she has no choice but to leave it

I sort through her things, return to New York, and absurd how he wants me to wear a better dress so his mother will like me and *why don't you greet me with*

romance and warmth and open legs like the pretty girl who left and if you really loved me
you'd sleep facing me you would not face the wall and cry, and tell me the truth Anne admit
it you've been sleeping with someone else and why don't you tell me why you really went to
California and

she is fifty-six years old and dead and I won't leave this body yet, but I will leave
this bed and

I am crying rage walking to the Hudson and even a gentle man needs a place to
stick his anger and

I am not that container

RECIPES

Take the gall of a cat and hen's fat, mixing them together. Put this on your
eyes and you will see things which are invisible to others.

Take the sweat of an opera singer and the taste of a garlic pickle. Put this on
your forehead and you will be entitled to anything you desire.

Take the cheese of a week-old pizza and the rattle of a broken refrigerator.
Put this in your pocketbook and it will fill with money.

Take the glass of a tenth story window and the air sucked through a har-
monica. Place this under your feet and you will have a better perspective.

Take a hair of Lolita and a tooth of Quasimodo. Wear this around your neck
and you will understand love.

Take the words of a sociopath and thirty nine blue crayons. Stick these up
your asshole and you will create a world class masterpiece.

Take a yoyo string and wrap it around the Mississippi River. Wear this in your
watch pocket and you will know the date and hour of your death.

SHE THOUGHT STARVATION WAS SOMEHOW HOLY

SHE THOUGHT STARVATION WAS SOMEHOW HOLY BY SLOWLY
DYING SHE COULD MAKE   DESIRE DISAPPEAR
GRIEF COLLECTED LIKE BUTTS IN HER ASHTRAY NEVER THROWN
AWAY JUST PILING UP   BUILDING A QUIET STENCH OF SAD
NUTRITION IS MILK IN A CONSTANT COFFEE CUP AND SUGAR IN
    PAPER PACKETS
GRANULATED GRITTY LIKE WORDS AND LAUGHS SPOKEN FROM A
MOUTH THAT
        NEVER OPENS

SHE THOUGHT STARVATION WAS SOMEHOW HOLY BY SLOWLY
DYING SHE COULD MAKE   DESIRE DISAPPEAR
SHE COULD ERASE HIS STAIN FROM ITS SPOT ON HER BED
SHE COULD ERASE THE SPOT THAT RETURNED AND STAYED WET IN
    HIS ABSENCE
SHE COULD ERASE THE SPOT THAT IGNORED SOAP AND RE-
SPONDED ONLY TO THE   SCRUB OF RIBS AGAINST COTTON

SHE THOUGHT STARVATION WAS SOMEHOW HOLY BY SLOWLY
DYING SHE COULD MAKE   DESIRE DISAPPEAR
HIS SPIRIT HAD STORED ITSELF LIKE SOME MAD DRUG IN CELLS OF
    FAT AND MUSCLE
NOW THERE WAS TIME TO BURN NOW THERE WAS TIME TO BURN
NOW THERE WAS TIME TO BURN THOSE CELLS ONE BY ONE SO
FLASHBACKS WOULD NOT SURPRISE HER
        SOMETIME NEXT YEAR

SHE THOUGHT STARVATION WAS SOMEHOW HOLY BY SLOWLY
DYING SHE COULD MAKE   DESIRE DISAPPEAR
SHE COULD CRY ALL THAT FAT OUT HER EYES
SHE COULD CRY ALL THAT FAT OUT HER EYES WHEN SHE
        THOUGHT NO ONE WAS   WATCHING
SHE COULD CRY ALL THAT FAT OUT HER EYES AND LET IT RUN
DOWN HER BODY   IRRIGATE THE DIRT THAT WOULD
                BURY HER

Beau Sia

A LITTLE KNOWN TRUTH ABOUT
FINANCIAL SUCCESS

when I get the money, i'm gonna pitch the first ball in the world series, and
i'm gonna buy the stanley cup, and i'm gonna sit so close to andre agassi at
wimbledon that i'll be able to stab him over and over again in-between sets
(and i'll get away with it), and i'm gonna make jabba the hutt a quarterback,
and i'm gonna be the towel boy for the laker girls, and i'm gonna force pro
wrestlers to wrestle, and i'm gonna parachute off of manhattan skyscrapers,
because I want to impress the simple of mind.

when I get the money, churches, lakes, museums, malls, shoes, power tools,
crayon colors, and chinese people will all be named after me.

when I get the money, i'll have pudding pops in madagascar with uma thurman
and spock, and me and tarantino are gonna buy the bones of bruce lee and put
them in a movie called, "the bones of bruce lee are alive!," and i'm gonna
burn doogie howser's stupid diary, and i'm gonna have punky brewster in a
nightgown reading me bedtime stories, and i'm gonna buy expensive crystal,
because it's expensive.

when I get the money, i'm gonna be the model american, and white suprema-
cists will admit their inferiority to me in mandarin chinese, and barney will be
maimed, and michael bolton will be assassinated, and everyone will be denied
uttering the words "alanis morrisette" in a public place, and bands like the
rolling stones, led zeppelin, and the eagles, whom I formerly thought were all
dead, will just be put into retirement.

when I get the money, i'm gonna have a microchip in my head, so that I can
say, "I have a microchip in my head," and i'm gonna make alyssa milano a star
again, and i'm gonna teach children how to fly, and punk rock girls all over the
world will have their sid & nancy shirts say, "sid & beau," and the cast of
friends will be exiled to B-movie hell, and my face will be on every condom's
receptacle tip, and mel torme is gonna rap "ice ice baby" to me while I shower,
and i'm gonna kill the offspring, before there are any more of them.

when I get the money, i'm gonna have a tibetan monastery in my backyard,
and i'm gonna make every muslim learn breakdancing, and i'm gonna set fire
to the protestants, and i'm gonna make priests wear l.a. gear, and i'm gonna

give rabbi's cadillacs with big, furry interiors, and i'm gonna give wiccans a broom and a pointy hat and put them in my screen production of cats, only it will be called witches, and i'm gonna go to jerusalem and build mini-malls that only sell nativity scenes, and i'm gonna make mormons work comedy clubs while on missions for god, and i'm gonna start a grape kool-aid drinking religion where everyone knows what might happen, but drink up anyway and end up happy that they didn't die from cyanide poisoning.

when I get the money, i'm gonna publish 382 pg. books with nothing but my name on the cover, and people will buy them, and i'm gonna have benefit concerts where I sing everyone else's songs really badly, and i'm gonna eat barbecued smurf everyday, and i'm gonna reveal to the world that mr. rogers is really delta burke in disguise, and i'm gonna get an incurable cancer and cure it by applying a salve made out of the breast tissue of gloria estefan.

when I get the money, i'm gonna buy all of the baby kittens in the world, eagerly awaiting the second coming of alf.

when I get the money, i'm gonna roam the galaxy in a star destroyer piloted by bill cosby and danny zucco, in search of movie roles for michael j. fox.

when I get the money, the actors from the breakfast club are going to come over and watch the movie with me and they'll have to listen to me say repeatedly, "wow! I really thought your careers would take off after that!"

when I get the money, i'm gonna throw my weight around,
when I get the money, i'm gonna use people,
when I get the money, i'm gonna own mtv,

and sure, money can't buy you love,
but love
can't
buy you
shit.

Ben Porter Lewis

WAYFARER DUMMIES

I drove my car across this country, I even chased windmills through Kansas
because somebody told me to leave
I picked up this hitchhiker in Nevada, he was a lizard standing on a rock with
his thumb pointed in the air
we told each other stories, swapping anecdotes like wayfarer dummies
I told him someone once said it was our thumbs that made us different from
apes or primates and that he should be thankful that my hands worked well
enough that I could drive this car
he shrugged like a skinny atlas holding the weight of something I could not
put my finger on
I said you know about those monkies, they couldn't hitch a ride if they
wanted to
he didn't get it, remember the thumbs i said, never mind enjoy your cigarette
i told him, thinking the whole time if he didn't have fingers he'd have a hard
time smoking
I don't feel bad it was he who was stuck in Nevada desert until I came
along—like black Moses get me out of this desert or something
I don't know but he looked like a sunburned and dehydrated Dead Head,
here have some water, I don't use sunscreen
he said he came from the Dead shows in Vegas—should of been there,
I said didn't Jerry die a few years ago, he said I know, never trip on acid in
the desert unless you have a plan, caravan, or something, I said dammit this
is a station wagon not a camel,
he laughed looked beyond the shadows of my face and out the window, nice
landscape he tells me, yeah I
haven't seen much sand since ben hur, besides don't all these rocks look
alike, no, they're special rocks
he tells me, I glance at the crystals around his neck, I figure he was the
resident expert, maybe he was involved in reefer madness
I don't know, something i read about in high times
relationships are spatial but if you're a pot head you can't tell the difference
then I wondered which one of us was tripping, maybe he was a mirage, an
illusion, you get those in the desert you know
but he was so real I could smell him and his patchouli driving me crazy
how far to Los Angeles he asked, dying in the heat of the desert lizard lounge
cactus plant migraines running up and down my head
I put on my ultra-violet mirauder looking sunglasses, lit a cigarette,

rolled down the window, and stared down the road
I didn't have the heart to tell him he goes as far as the next stop,
besides two dummies can't occupy the same space at the same time.

Buffy Bonanza

AUTONEUROTICA

It's a difficult thing
desire in an MTV era
when masturbation is an oft heard word
like sorrow or fire

but they're wrong
Masturbation is defined by Webster's dictionary as
the manipulation of genitals—not specifically one's own.

and back where I'm from we just call that a Saturday night

it's auto-erotica they mean
for they do it alone
the easy slip of hand from chin
past belly and beyond

It's there that the images appear in staccato flashes
but it's not enough to have one person
splayed in my minds eyes,
I'm thinking about the mouth of one person, the hands of another till I am
ripping each lover I've ever had or ever wanted (and they are legion)
and sewing them together
like Dr. Frankenstein's monster with
two billion breasts
a million cocks and
a million venus swells
I'm channeling surfing desire like it's a bad TV night
convinced I'll go blind and hair will sprout on my hands, my vibrator, my
pillow
and just when I get

to the point when I think I can hit
the target, where I can let the world dissolve into one blinding flash...

my attention wanders, I've always had a short attention span.
I start thinking about Jennie Garth's new haircut on 90210 or Friends or all
that great TV I miss 'cos I am never home on Thursday night and I've never
bothered to learn how to program my VCR and
where was I?

Ah yes.
Momma always told me
If you want anyone to love you
you gotta learn
to love yourself.

So, I'll keep trying,
distilling my desire into
tiny points of fire that will eventually
sear my flesh

'Cos Momma always told me
If you want anyone to love you
you gonna first gotta learn
to love yourself.

And with each and every one of you as my witness,
I swear—
I'm learning.

Carl Hanni

NOT MAKING IT IN MEXICO

We were drinking
in Oscar's Cantina
during the World Series
when the worst
mariachi band in Mexico

walked in the door.
They were bad,
really bad.
And they were drunk,
really drunk.
So drunk they didn't
notice the two gringos
huddled at the bar
drinking shots of mescal
and too many cervezas,
one wild redhead
in combat boots
and me, tall, skinny
and fuzzy around the edges.
Finally, game over
the locals got curious.
"Who are you?"
they asked,
"WHO ARE YOU?"
"Un poeta"
we said,
"NOSOTROS SOMOS POETA!
We are poets!"
we slurred through
our 20 words of Spanish.
Poetry, beer, hotel—
that's all we knew.
Holding each other up,
we sauntered back
to our cheap hotel,
quoting each other's lines
with mescal exaggeration.
South of the border
under the shadow
of a cathedral
under a harvest moon
under a single sheet
too drunk to sleep
too drunk to fuck
too drunk to make it
in Mexico.

Carl Hancock Rux

RED VELVET DRESS LULLABY

First he was a boy...
                and then he was a man...
                        and...
mispronounced profanities
of little football head boys knocked him down and scarred him for life,
        because he played with little Barbie Doll girls...
        combed their hair
        and played in a gentle world of painlessness...
he allowed them to baptize him with faggot and sissy
and names of ridicule...
        branding him with words of mockery,
and he kept them as his own...
        hid them secretly between his first and his last name...
        between his pride and his...
        shame...

First he was a boy...
                and then he was a man...
                        and...

Marilyn Monroe spoke to him from the pages of old magazines
        and the frames of old films,
        she said
        Laugh at yourself boy! Before the world laughs at you—
And so he slipped his feet into his mother's heels...
        stared at the distortion of his face in her vanity mirror...
        lips painted
        Crimson Rose No. 32...
And he prayed to be blonde
        and beautiful
        and glorified when he opened his eyes...
        prayed to laugh at his own reflection...

First he was a boy...
                and then he was a man...
                        and...

every now and then someone would notice the rhythm...
every now and then...someone would notice
    the rhythm in his voice...
    and the dance in his...
    walk...
and call him by his middle name...
     shame...
so he
lay his head on the world and said

    CRUCIFY ME

it's all right
it's all right
it's all right

He closes his eyes
and he can see further back than he ever has...
he can remember the first time
someone ever touched him
It was a man of thirty-4

He was just a boy of
four
he remembers the little red dress that man made him wear,
it was a little red velvet dress that came from his sister's doll
    and socialized him into self-hatred.

    He remembers
            spinning and
    twirling
              and
    twirling
              and
    spinning

    hands on him
    handling him

and even though he promised not to tell
oh yes
he promised not to tell

oh my I
promise
still
every time he feels shame
every time he's called a name...
he's just twirling in that little red velvet dress...
    yes
    he's a boy
        in a
            red velvet...

First he was a boy and then I was a man...no...first he was a man and
then I was a boy...no...first he was a man and then I was a boy...first
I...was mispronounced...hands on me handling me...thirty
four...4...Marilyn Monroe...blonde and beautiful and glorified...Crimson Rose No.32...hands on me handling me...and I promised not to
tell...oh my I...promised...still

first I was a boy...
and...now...
I...am...a...

man.

Catherine Kidd

From I-SOCKET

    This keyboard is not plugged into any machine.
It is not a piano, it is not a typewriter, it is just a piece of hardware with finger-keys on it. But it is the only writing utensil left in this empty apartment—no
pens or pencils exist here even—there's only a plastic tarpaulin on the floor, and
tape around the window frames and floorboards, and 15 gallons of KILZ basecoat,
and 10 gallons of Dutch Boy interior satin latex (colour number 27Y3, colour
name Morning Oatmeal) and Avram, and me, and an airless paint sprayer.
    I found the keyboard in one of the kitchen cabinets and set it up on the
humidifier in the corner, with a chair. I am typing these words on a keyboard
which is not hooked up to any machine—if they turn out to have any significance,

no one will know it, nothing is being recorded. Avram asks me what I am doing and I tell him I am writing about writing on a keyboard which is not hooked up to anything. Avi says this sounds beautiful, and pointless. I keep typing, regardless, if only for the vascular motion of it.

I am not wearing my clothes.

I am wearing clothes, but they are not mine—they don't belong to anyone in the same way that this empty apartment doesn't belong to anyone, unless both are mine while I am in them (I am typing this, I am typing quickly). These jeans and this shirt were repossessed from a Goodwill bag—the clothes had belonged to Avi's ex-wife and thus they don't seem to fit me so well. It is Avi who says they don't fit me, or don't suit me, perhaps this has to do with the fact that he has seen them for so long on a different body. They are connected to Lisette's body, in his mind.

(She's not that unlike me, the times that I've seen her, we both have short torsos and long reddish hair, and are both melancholic, and both tend to stare at fixed points for long periods of time, with our quick-slow eyes, hers blue and mine brown. I am not the reason she and Avi don't live here anymore, I am honestly not. But she's not that unlike me, except that her movements are brisker when I am around, like a fluttering bedsheet, but perhaps this is me moving slower.)

I have now stuck the cord of the keyboard down the front of my jeans / Lisette's jeans / the jeans I am presently wearing. Customarily I don't wear things under my clothes, so I can feel the metal plug just grazing the upper regions of my pubic hair. See—Avi had seen the cord lying there on the plastic covered floor like a faucet left running and had suggested I plug it in somewhere.

So I stuffed it into my jeans, navel-level at first but it wouldn't stay put so I stuffed it down further and there it sits like a cramp. (I'm typing this, my hands are moving, I'm typing this into space).

Removing the mask, Avi smokes a cigarette now and I brush my hand through the floating smoke and it disperses (smoke drifts out open windows, when windows are open, and it exists whether or not you can see it).

The airless paint sprayer seems to fit with the intergalactic motif of Avi's Vader respirator mask and the white plastic sheen over everything and the countless paint speckles like stars. The paint sprayer stands waiting in the center of the room, white and exo-skeletal like an Imperial Sandwalker. Avi's boots echo in the void as he paces around with power cords in his arms. I can see him through the slats of the ladder leading up to the loft, through slats and plastic tarp. This is a movie set. The light is strange. When Avi is finished all this, the interior walls will be covered with latex Morning Oatmeal—it will be complete —it will justify itself. Meanwhile, my disconnected words dissolve into space. I could get up and go buy a pen, if the idea occurred to me, but then again I seem to have left my notebook somewhere. Normally I would never leave my notebook somewhere, in real life.

Avi is hooked up to the Imperial Sandwalker and is testing out the spray on the corridor walls (I keep typing). When the noise stops and Avi is smoking again, I tell him about a Hindi film I once saw, a certain scene in a brewery or a waterworks or some other industrial building with huge phallic pipes hanging down all over the place. I tell him about these very sublimated erotic scenes, where the hero never actually kisses the heroine but there are several suggestive near-misses and close-ups of lip-gloss. In the film with the dangling pipes, the heroine dances on a workbench or something with a troop of a dozen men dancing around her in a sort of sexy back-and-forth dialogue of dance. The men's shoes going clackety-clak and the heroine's shoes going clickety-click, with her head tossing back in a gasp. She wears a white sari and dances, her half-bare arms and bangles over her head, and suddenly the pipes bust out and spray frothy whitewater all over the place. Very subtle. The sari is drenched like her shiny black hair, making it practically see-through, almost but not quite. It was the paint-gun which reminded me of these scenes—Avi keeps calling it a gun but it looks to me more like the nozzle of a garden hose.

Spent. Once the new tenants move in, there will be little proof that anything has been created here and that things aren't the same as they were before, just a lingering paint-smell and slick walls. Nothing much comes of painting a wall from white to off-white or off-white to off-off-white, but another blank space to fill up with something (I'm typing this). I ask Avi if I should write down all the those phone numbers scribbled on the wall where the phone used to be just in case someone needs them, either he or Lisette, before they get lost under layers of paint. *Write them down where, and what with?* Avi says, grinning, and I type that down too on these dismembered keys—the cord still stuffed into my jeans / Lisette's jeans / these jeans that I'm presently wearing. I could type all those numbers and maybe absorb them in utero like astronaut food and maybe recall them tomorrow by massaging my belly.

But this assumes a certain direction of flow—that the information flows up from the keys through the cord and into my body, instead of the other way round—that is, from my body through the cord into the keys. This assumes that the vascular motion of typing itself transfers information into my body that wasn't there before, or was only there as a bundle of cells.

The flow of the sprayer seems to have got blocked by something, apparently. The machine chokes and spews paint in a brief little fan in the air, splattering down on the plastic. "Goddamn piece of shit machine," mutters Avi, he lumbers about finding instruments to dismantle the nozzle and find out what's backing up the flow. He's cursing Rent-A-Tool, rehearsing a sarcastic speech to leave on the 24-hour Rent-A-Tool answering-service about how he should have mentioned needing a machine that actually sprayed the paint *outward*, duh, onto the *walls*, instead of back into the belly of the beast and creating a fucking explosion.

(The plastic-covered room is silent now. I have stopped typing entirely because nothing is more annoying to someone who's supposed to be working but can't than the sound of someone who is busily working. But I'm not sure I can even call it work, this typing into space, I'm not sure I want to call it work. It's a thing which I do with my hands. In the end, the walls will still be pale and blank. Whatever shade of pale you choose to call it.) The room is humming again—like a light saber—with the paint-flow going the right-way now, and the corridor walls turning from white to off-white strip by strip. The phone numbers and the names attached to them have disappeared, and Avi looks like an Imperial stormtrooper, with the Vader-respirator mask and the goggles now shiny and white. The odor of paint is intoxicating, I can scarcely smell myself but I keep nervously moving my hands like a madwoman typing myself into oblivion. I seem to have fooled myself utterly, fooled my mad-typing veins to such an extent that I'm even hitting the delete key when I make a mistake, back-spacing, erasing words which weren't even there in the first place. Unless they were there in the first place and I'm just typing-tapping into them like a secretarial clairvoyant.

Listen. I'm pretending for now that the flow goes like this: not from the machine into me like astronaut-food, but starting inside, concentrated like a white dwarf and forcing its way out, from the hip, from the chaotic current in the veins. It's a vascular sort of thing, it's compulsive, my fingers moving regardless of the silence they drift toward. This may be enough. The walls are becoming blank, a certain shade of blank called Morning Oatmeal, the smell is illegible. I type into space, and here in my hands, if it's necessary, is proof.

I mean here, in the blue-on-red light saber veins of my hands is the proof.

C.D. Jones

COMING OF AGE

V. Woolfe, Oprah Winfrey, Catherine Mansfield, Francis Farmer,
Marilyn Monroe, Karen Carpenter, Sylvia Fraser, Maya Angelou,
Linda Lovelace, Kelli McGillis, Billie Holiday,

Incest   Anorexia   Rape

Dig
Pat down
Dig
Pat down

In my memory he was very big.
Clean white boy's t-shirt.

Dig
Pat down
Seven or eight maybe years old
Dig
to my five and he knew
everything.
Pat down
How to buy popsicles at the corner store
where the best trees were to climb.
Dig.
Where Dad hid the extra change.
Pat down.
He was my first love hero
Apollo
Dig.
He knew to warn me
"If you tell, you'll get the beating.
It's your fault. Mom knows that."

As I lay in the shaded room
summer heat from his arm
dripping down over my cheek.
Pat down.

Later, I forgot. Everything.
Dig.
Until he came home one day,
drunk
his sixteen year old manhood poised
like the gun
Dig.
That goes off forever
in my mind.

Because after I shot him,
I buried him.

Cheryl Boyce Taylor

WIND

For Audre Lorde

That November day
came a bright wind
a brazen bride you walked upright
salmon azaleas in your hair

Now you are gone i mourn not
i fill my mouth
with butterflies
ride the northern wind

A fleeting fragrance—
i dab you behind my ear
spritz between my breast loaves

I am stuffed
bursting like an opera cow
with your words

When i am heavy with loss
you descend upon me
larger than evening
my tongue uncoils

You rise the weight of a tulip petal
riding the white November wind.

PLENTY TIME PASS FAST, FAS DEY SO

1.

i used to kno when mango ripe
an ready to pick
i used to wait for guava
to turn from a hard green ball

when it yellow and creamy ripe wid sun
i'd drag a chair from de gallery
stand up on it an full meh mouth
wid de sweet meat right from de tree
now dat was livin

ah used to kno
if meh grandmudder left hip hurtin
rain comin
an if she right hand damp
it go be sun in de mornin
rain after lunch

dem days chiren would sit out in hot sun
for hours me din kno notin bout tannin lotion
in we house when it come time for goin out
if yu skin did real dark an pretty like mine
man dey shinin it up wid coconut oil
so everybody for miles could see yu comin

an dem nasty ole men
dey seein yu first
dey crocodile eye on yu lil breast
yu eh even kno yu hav yet
an if yu lil chubby huh
de grin gettin more wider
is like de bigger de better
de more de merrier
ting was nice tho

2.
dem days pas fast fast so
we leave an com New York
well   if yu see me up here
in dese people country

ah hav four lock on me door
ah runnin three job ah still cahn see
whey de money goin

Queens geh hard hard
ah pick up me fas self

an move to Chelsea
Chelsea was a place for Sunday brunch
all you can eat and drink for $ 13.95
gay modern post post modern and retro

"You don't have $ 2500 finders fee?
sorry honey—this water closet will be gone
by midday"

Chelsea was a place for hard white cocks
stirring pain my black pussy could never fathom
hard boots open shirt pierced nipple
and a lil doggy collar fastened to de cock ring
i got tired of walking behind flat ass
weighted down with money
de damn Gucci back pack bumping
carelessly in meh face

who fader know this one fader
who kno dat one fader
who runnin de Exxon corporation
dat one is a lesbian avenger
who will proudly use daddy's
gold card to make bail

i'm tired of this fucking, privileged,
politicallycorrectfakedfuckingfreedom
Harlem is still a tourist attraction—

3.
if yu see me in dis place
time pas fas fas fas so
i eh ha time to study rain
never mind sun
meh left hip hurtin
but it eh predictin notin

i want to hold my friend Letta's hand

at water's edge
transcribe the news waves tell
i want to braid Olga's hair into a tree
fuse her roots backbackback into black soil

i want to play dominoes with Donna and Linda
make soup for Keith when he's sick
draw a bush bath till Billy's fever breaksbreaks
i want my family back

i want to sit and rock you
have my hips predict your coming
sit and rock you back to a time
when we sought respite in each other's breath
i want my family back

i am blown away
in the loose dust that is this city
this house of confusion
these rooms of deceit
we have come to know intimately

i want my family back
in your absence I am Havana
speaking Spanish to Port Au Prince
i am Papiamento speaking Wolof to Curaçao
the shrill spaces your withdrawn hands
leave in my body carries dull knives
and cracking trees

at this bewitching hour
i hold out my hands to you
somehow these empty nights
seem the right size for making homes

my tongue is heavy with its own lacks
i hold out my life to you
cause dese days dese days
duz pass fast   fast so fast
            so fast so   fasfas so—

Daniel Roop

HANDING OUT POETRY

Handing out condoms
is like giving people
a license to have sex.

Handing out genitals
is like giving people
a license to wear condoms
and therefore have sex.

God
what were you thinking?

Handing out fingers
is like giving people
a license to pick up condoms
and open them and put them on
their genitals, assuming they
have a license for their genitals,
and therefore have sex.

Handing out eyes
is like giving people
a license to look and see
and register Cool shirt or
Nice hair or I'd like to have sex
with him or her or both,
and therefore have sex.

Handing out ears
is like giving people
a license to hear
and making them want to hear
beautiful things, like Marvin Gaye
in the background, and another
person saying, Uh,
and therefore have sex.

Handing out vocal cords
is like giving people
a license to speak, and say,
Nice weather we're having,
or So, do you wanna have sex?
and therefore have sex.

Handing out feet
is like giving people
a license to wear socks
which look like condoms
to remind them of sex
and make them want to have sex
and therefore have sex.

Handing out brains
is apparently not like
giving you a license to think.

Handing out knees
is like giving people
a license to pray,
to go down on those knees
and praise their maker
for every beautiful thing
they have been handed,
to reach past themselves and say
Oh god, which might remind them
of sex, and make them want to have sex
and therefore have sex.

Maybe you have sex. It's not so bad.
Maybe you don't. That's okay, too.
Maybe you were in love when you wrote
your editorial, and maybe you will
have a child someday. Maybe that child
will grow up hungering for human touch
like we all do, and will be surrounded
by disease like we all are. Maybe
that child will fold and crumble
under the only four letter word
that makes me shiver, the one that took

my cousin, turned him into a raspy scalloped
rib cage with lesions and a ventilator and no family
visiting, and could take anyone in this room.

Handing out condoms
is not the final answer.

But

Handing out lies
to children
is cowardly.

Handing out silence
is
the worst form of murder.

Handing out knowledge
is
handing out life.

Handing out life
is
like giving people a license
to change and grow
and change and grow
and change.

DJ Renegade

SUBTERRANEAN NIGHT-COLORED MAGUS
(3 MOODS IN THE MODE OF MILES)

Subterranean means underground
    deep, profound
Miles was one deep brother
    deep as a mine shaft
      decrescendoing to the motherlode
      blue blowing undersongs

Miles was a tenor trumpet
    ten or eleven levels deeper
    than the next cat
    painting all up under the canvas
    making it bleed All Blues
    out the other side
Blowing subterranean solos
    underground rhythmic resistance
    visual virtuoso
    battling musical mafiosos
    burrowing under they skin
Miles, son of a dentist doing rootwork
    with a hoodoo horn hollering Bebop toasts
He was Petey Wheatstraw
    Satchmo's son-in-law
    a Signifying Junkie jumping cold turkey
    out the Lion's mouth
    Shine below the deck of the Titanic
    blueing up the boilers
Miles could blue like Bird
    fright like Trane
    early like Bird
    night like Trane
    wing like Bird
    rail like Trane
Rumbling underground.

Nightcolor is blacker
    than a million miles of fresh asphalt
Miles was a deep black brother
    black and fluid as floating smoke
    black as the sky round midnight
    black as a tire turning for miles ahead
    black kettle stewing a Bitch's Brew
    so black, he was Kind of Blue
Miles, slick as black ice
    cool as snow
    sweet as black cherries
On the Downbeat like a blackjack
    a black jackhammer
    black Jack Johnson
    black jack of all trumpeting trades

Miles, Jack of Spades
    was our Ace cuz he played
    nightcolors
Deepblack, tripleback
    shinyblack,
    cinderblack
    ashyblack,
    quarterblack
    multi-meta-megablack
All shades of Miles
    shifting harmonic gears
    in his chromatic Ferrari
Blowing Blue Moods
    with his black turned
    to the audience
    speaking cooly
    in the colors of the night.

Magi are priests
    spell-wailing wizards
Miles was deep, black and magic
    conjuring in the key of We
    Magus, Magus? ask minders
    of the metronome
    Miles is secular they say
    but we know you spiritual
    a soloing sorcerer with ESP
Lord have mercy
    you Rev. Miles totally testifyin
    from the Book of the Blues
    blowing muted magic
    as chapter and verse
Making a joyful noise
    unto the Lord
    and nobody else hip enough
    to dig the scene
You Magi Miles with crazy styles
    even sported a Tutu
Miles, 1.6 sacred klicks of cool
    5,280 feet doing
    the east Saint Boogie
    moody as any Monk

you were Live and Evil
   but In a Silent Way
your holy brown hands
      scribbling neon-blue notes
       throwing Milestones through
       the stained glass windows of Jazz
       so deeply, so darkly
Such magic.

FATHER, SON AND THE WHOLLY GHOST

We meet only
in the alleys of memory
our broken smiles
littering the ground.
Although we wear the same name,
identical scars,
you can't remember
what day I was born.
Anger spills
down the side
of my face.
This is all you have taught me:
needles are hollower
than lies,
leave bigger holes in families
than arms.
Now a prisoner in death's camp
you grow thinner every day
until I can count your T-cells
on one hand.
the phone rings
Mama pleads
Please buy a dark suit to wear
I tell her
I wear black every day
all day
anyway.

MAMA AFTER MIDNIGHT

Last week
    at a chardonay and cheddar
    poetry reading
A powdered nose sniffed
    Ghettos are not beautiful.
Yes, ghettos chew children
    between concrete teeth
Throw women against walls
    piss-stained with poverty
And swallow men whole
    in swift gulps
But a question bloomed
    in the furrows of my brain
Do folks snorting
    Ghettos are not beautiful
    understand
That it don't rain
    in the ghetto
That it rains
    on the ghetto
That those born without designer umbrellas
    gotta learn how to walk wet
    and dream about being dry
That minus the luxury
of judging life by price tags
Love becomes
    a necessity
Peep this
    it's Christmas Eve
    and St. Clair Village
    lays under the heavy silence of snow,
icy air whirls at the windows
    its fingernails feeling for cracks.
Mama's in the bathroom
    with a tubful of warm water
    and a can of Comet cleanser.
Every day of the last four months
    has found her at Thrift Store
fussing while picking
    through piles of secondhand toys

like they were bananas for
her babies' lunchboxes.
Now the envious eyes of santa's elves
   watch her thin hands
      scrub a tiny truck until it glows.
After drying each item
   with the soft tongue of a towel
      she starts down the hall,
pauses outside the bedroom door
   marveling at our
      shallow sleeping breaths
then treks to the glashing tree
   to lay her presents
      like precious eggs.
In the morning we'll awaken
   in a burst
and rush into the living room
   like runningbacks
      to pull shiny toys
      from under the tree
never knowing
   the difference.
I ain't never been to college
      don't know the boiling point of blood
     the sincerity test for sweat
     or the atomic weight of tears
But I do know
   if there ain't no beauty in ghettos
My mother never scrubbed us
    never hugged us
    never smiled.

Evert Eden

MANDELA

so this is why I've been
in New York all this time
to stand at the UN

and vote for a man
Rolihlahla Nelson Mandela
his life cut by twenty-seven and a half years
yet he said, I'm not bitter
I'm not bitter?
    up here in the north
we could sure learn from his south
here the smaller the brain
the bigger the mouth
    you liked New York, Nelson
but I gotta warn you
we poopscoop our dogshit
and giftwrap our bullshit
we're all prisoners in a dark sitcom
some talk revolution
but the closest they get
is to call Doctor King
an Uncle Tom
    praise-sing Rolihlahla
Nelson Mandela
your mother Nosekeni
your eldest son Thembi
they too went underground
prison-bound
unable to go to their funeral
where did you go?
the last walk to hell
a deep descent
but you came back
your back unbent
you knew a nation
marched from Lagos to London
Beijing to Boston
Moscow to Cuba
Makgatho, Maziwe
Zenani and Zindiwe
how proud for them yeah
that you were *their* tata
    my father was proud
when you went to jail
he, a ten-foot crackpipe
I couldn't inhale

his idea of father
came straight from hell
he touched me only
to beat the shit out of me
and when he finished
he beat the shit as well
    all those years I made up
two fathers for me
the one I could smell
whiskey-fart near
the other gone
island-bound, gagged
Nelson, he ain't here
    I liked having one father who was missing
he made up for the one
who was too much there
but far from my fatherland
on the isle of Manhattan
where the hype high-fives
to maroela-tree size
you get to spot self-deception
it wears a funny freen hat
check it out
the cold smile of fact
Nelson, I can never dig my tata
the way I love you
but marooned in my whiteness
how long? very long
in my self-imposed exile
I know one thing that's true
the father who is my father
is my father
and the father who is not
is not
is you
    amandla!—power
awethu!—is ours
the price of freedom has been paid in
blood, in pain, in tears, in rage
hey, dad, I count the scars
you wrote on me
I price the resentment

I kept forever on simmer
I total up the rage
I ate each New York night for dinner
but now today
as I make my cross
with Rolihlahla I say
sweet freedom at last
    I'm not bitter

BIG BREASTS

I detest big breasts
I'm not talking about those milkless udders
on Arnold Schwarzenegger
or the flopped-out titties flapping from the hairy chests
of old men on the beach
like emaciated rats hanging from barbed wire

I'm talking about those Playboy antheaps
those Penthouse dungbundles
those alabaster orbs of high-blown high-flown high-tech highlights
those airbrushed planets
that look like they've spun in from another solar system
to land on soft launching pads
I hate 'em

nobody's born with them
the Department of Agriculture can't grow them
they're made
handmade
manhandmade
for manhandmaidens

I think I've given up on breasts entirely
the last public breasts I liked were Anita Ekberg's
La Dolce Vita
Fellini
1904 or something

what kind of an adult comes from a baby that sucks silicone?
lawyers?

I detest big breasts
as for big butts
aha! that's the size of truth

Edwin Torres

I 5 MINUTES

eein the tradition
of The YEAR Of The WHO-man
of Black HIIIS-story MONTH
of secretarial's WEEK
of Earth DAY
of ANY individualistically challenged group
to which THEES accent
can find a home to, I give you...

"HISPANIC CITIZEN MINUTE"
Everything you could possibly want to know
about The Hispanic Citizen...
in one minute!

The famous sponsor for this infraction shall be
"Citizen Watches—You know what to do!"

Well, well...it looks like our time is up!

Thees has been
"HISPANIC CITIZEN MINUTE"
Everything you could possibly want to know
about The Hispanic Citizen...
in one minute!

We now r-r-r-return you
to your r-r-r-regularly scheduled
op-press-sors

CATCHING THE RISE IN THE PALM OF MY HAND

We have mountains in our eyes
and when I look at you I climb.
Mountains gather to decide my fate
but grander spirits like us—decide.

I see no one blue you are, me...I'm just
another pebble on the shore to you. An' you
don't even know I'm here...I realize
things of such power don't need
to acknowledge existence—let alone me.
If I'm the one who sees you're here, then
who sees me when I'm with you?
Against my words, I fade to your slopes
recede against the backdrop—of what you are.

Mountain doesn't say
Mountain says *Me*.
Today your ocean is kind, something
rare—I've been told. But I know you're just
resting for the real show.

Far off peaks pull me through the closer alleys.
The ribbon of my world exists for reflection, aerial perspective
paints distance through layers of clarity, walk out
across the waters and save me. Leave me
ice volcano, sprout sickle vomit far
from a gathering shore—THIS is the gatherer
of too much, heaven of all.

Gather the restless chambers.
Fold equinox into tide and season, cycle
ignorance from *this* pebble...and iron out
the wrinkles in your past. Quilted gatherer on a
frostbit climb, blued fingertips on a mountain glove.

Wiggle sense to keep warm.
Leave the boots to keep clean.
Continue your walk
along the rocky beach...

: :

Volcanoes surround,
and emit pink e-mail, at
sunset, overgorged landsupper!

How does everyone get pieces of us to claim?
How do I give out the chemical that fuses
a room of ears into one pacific overswell of grand enlightenment:
in the form of necessary evil, in the guise
off a serendipity eavesdrop, in the too-tight sweatsuit
of need, who hangs onto my withered coattails?

Potter of mass land excavate & valve, where do I hold on
to the throw-out while sailing on this wind
I've created, how spit comes back
at the end of the tongue, at a salivation's interval
at the minuscule grip I call myself.

In this hold, I'm cast out
like a fishnet of withery me, a hopeless ranger
awaiting devil-freedom, harmonica in tow, evil
is a song to the local mutes—an easy happenstance
of opposite heavens, frozen in the wake of an eagle's soar
in the spit of a timely capture, or just a hell
in this heart, a slow decimation—as kindness has a mask
for all eagles who feed their young before themselves...CRIEEE,
CRAEEEE, CROEEE.

WITH HEART SKY DROWNING

Black swan swirl
With heart blood diamond
With black heart
Glove black swan finger
With blue pool surface
With shining blue skim with
Skin red heart black flutter, swan
Crumpled with birds attacking air
With sky littered, with jet birds flawing
Over nest, white nest crumpled
From where swan swims, with

Wrinkled eggs, with shining brush
Eggs with black swan babes
Swan black trumpet
Drowning with song

horehound stillpoint

ALL RIGHT I'M OKAY, YOU'RE OKAY, EVERYBODY IS OKAY,
NOTHING HUMAN IS ALIEN AND ALL THAT, FINE, BUT
THERE ARE STILL A FEW PEOPLE I WOULD LIKE TO SEE
TAKE A LONG HIKE OFF A SHORT PIER

i'm queer because i was born left-handed but society forced
me to be right-handed, so when I started trying to play ball,
everybody said: what a queer, ya throw like a girl, ya big sissy,
big queer, and this was back when queer was a bad word

i'm queer because my parents rented out rooms to college-attending women,
so between the ages of 1 and 5, i had approximately 8 mothers at any
given time and they all wanted to see how their lipstick would look on me

i'm queer because of that fun little gleam in god's eye—or—
because the devil has to win sometimes

i'm queer because i was born in Columbus, Ohio, where a lot
of weird new products and services first get tested

i'm queer because in my last lifetime i was a hefty russian
peasant woman working this farm with a butt-ugly husband who
landed me with enough rough-house brats to start another
revolution and i wanted something really different this time

i'm queer because some rank pedophile jumped on top of me
when i was just a wee thing and the fact that i don't remember
that happening only proves how deeply scarred i am

i'm queer because someone has to balance the statistics

i'm queer because it's normal to be queer
it's normal for a forty-two-year-old man to wear tie-dye
and ride his bike all over town while he hums: "now i wanna be your dog"

it's normal for someone to be called a poet just for getting
up and talking about what a tongue-twisting, titty-chewing,
ass-kissing, dick-licking, ankle-grabbing slut he is

it's normal to meet up with half a dozen ex-boyfriends, ex-
lovers, or whatever, and want to pull your hair out wondering
which ones will survive the year

it's normal to live in a city where grief blankets the air
like fog in the sunset

it's normal to run away to an s & m circus and find yourself
all dolled up in cherry red spandex bondage gear with leather
restraints and steel locks, being led around at the end of a
3' chain mail leash by your strong-arm master (and there are
pictures available upon request)

it's normal for a guy to reach his second orgasm in 15 minutes
cause one man is going down on him while another is working
his nipples and a third—praise the lord, nobody knew it
would be like this—the third is pissing all over his ass

well now people say i go too far
i know people didn't ask to hear about this
i know but i don't care

cause i live in what is supposed to be the most liberal city
in america, the golden gate asylum, freaktown, usa, the last
refuge for the weird and the wounded, so it surprises me when,
even in the poetry scene of san francisco, a macho wordsmith
tells me my sperm is being wasted if it's not aimed at ovaries

it galls me when a featured poets says he'd rather put a bullet to his
temple than discover he enjoys sucking dick

it hurts when people fold their arms and turn their backs
just cause they're hearing about boys in bed

it makes me worry all the more about what is happening out
there in the rest of america
cause i know what they're saying

they're saying i'm queer because of testosterone levels
i'm queer because of a thing in my brain
i'm queer because of a thing in my mouth
i'm queer because i like it

i remember when queer was a bad word
seems like just yesterday

REINCARNATION WOES

in my other life, i am a ninja villain with daggers for eyes, spikes
for nipples, and nunchucks i can work with my buttcheeks

in my other life, i am such a lowdown filthy slut, L7 kicked
me out of the band, babes in toyland kicked me out of the band,
courtney love is grossed out by my hair and makeup, and madonna
is stealing my shit, left and right

in my other life, i can eat mcdonald's without throwing up, i can
eat cheese without developing kidney stones, i can drink tap water
without getting diarrhea, i've never had an std because my body is
a maseratti

in my other life, i am a black man with so much to say, lady liberty
gets down on her knees and hands me the torch, the liberty bell
cracks open wider than wide, and the mississippi delta queen can't
wait to kiss my beautiful african-american ass

in my other life, i wear tiny lace panties and turn all the boys on,
oh, wait, that's actually this lifetime

in my other life, i'm a slick chick who can do the splits and i do
them at rock n roll shows, in restaurants, hotels, on the street,
cause i want to make sure that everybody knows my pussy is
athletic pussy, it's not tired pussy, floppy pussy, or ragged pussy;
no, she's working pussy, she's *serving*, she's blade runner pussy,

the terminator's terminator, thelma and louise, drew barrymore,
magnolia thunderpussy, pussy galore, mrs. peel, and catherine
deneuve, oh yeah, let me say that one again, catherine deneuve

forget everything i said
in my other life, i am *catherine deneuve*
i am somebody else, anyway
and i look so much better than this

in my other life, i love myself as much as michael said he loved me,
as much as eric said he loved me, and greg and mark and carol and
dianne, and all my friends and lovers and all your friends and
lovers are still alive and well, and the whole world is just
          completely   different

in my other life, i talk about flesh in such a way that it becomes
transparent, i talk about walls and they disappear, when i bring the
void into the room, it falls like a veil so the blissful awareness that
is *who i am* and *who you are* becomes so present, so immediate, so
perfectly known, that everyone slaps his/her forehead and goes:
god

oh, in my other life, the youth of the modern world have no reason
to be bitter and cynical, and poetry isn't used to get laughs, and
engelbert humperdinck never happened, and the eighties never
happened, and reagan was never president, and the religious right
never learned how to get politically active, and david bowie never
went straight, and ellen never even had to come out, and dennis rodman
is my boyfriend, and devo still sells millions of records, and my
father was a nice guy (very mellow, really), and bosnia, rwanda and
iran are lovely places to visit and the people there visit here just as
often because everybody is filthy rich and hung like a horse and
they all want to kiss me and hug me and fuck me and love me and
cuddle me and lick me and save me, save me from my desires, save
me from my fears, save from these reincarnation woes

in my other life, i'm you, you're me, and the galaxy spins

Ian Ferrier

YOU WANT ME

I was a witness to those last years of my life
I slept in doorways off the Main
and prowled St. Catherine in a raincoat of desire
feeling whores and growling like a dog.

My teeth turned purple and I got ugly
I blew cigars at babies passing by
and held a yellowed hand out to the moms
        and college girls and pointed to my pants.

Winters I lay on subway ventilation grates
and sometimes when I slept I saw the molten core of things
flare up between the bars and then blow out.
I watched the snow fall down in words and then in
        sentences and drifts.
Buried I felt the rumble of the trucks going by
my ear fell off   I spat at cops and organized the stars

Awake I heard the liquid sound of tires in the slush.

My world   My picture
I signed my name to it in snowbanks
    with the only kind of pen
I carry in my shorts.
Ha Ha! Man I got mean… !
skinny and butt ugly
howling at searchlights
leaning against the well-dressed clientèle
        in narrow aisles in grocery stores
squeezing sausages till they burst.

Winter of '95 my boots broke open and I lost two toes.
Slowly I was being dismantled
thoughts falling apart
Memories stuck with packing tape
boxes breaking IN front of my eyes
The strangest times:

A summer day in February
trees and flowers in the snow.
30 below and a girl who held my hand in '84
    and didn't charge a dime.

Hell I said "Honey don't reach out to me.
The only things I know for sure I figured for myself.
So what is it you're looking for?
Do you want me?
DO YOU WANT ME!!!!?"

EXPLODING HEAD MAN

We'd just started talking when the scent of your body
exploded the top off my head

And I went blind searching for you
some taste of you among the starlight falling on my
thoughts

below the moon's face cracked like pearls or lucite
in the spellbound sky

God It was hot
I thought the lightning would shatter the world:
the ragged, star-clothed edges wheeling
    cracking on the rocks

machinery that woke those constellations
circling in the water high above my head
the gold fish approaching the sun
glittering in my thoughts
the water blasting through my sleep
like Van Gogh's river

So you create the shreds of evidence of this crime
and paint them all to detonate
the time bomb of your lipstick slashed
vermilion on my face

and in that chalk outline where we both lie down
I am exploding headman
holding the fuse that blows the universe machine
till space and time spill out and freeze
and fill the nothing with a million tangled
molecules of you and me and it and what and how
and us and thee and why and now

Joe Blades

CONTINUATION (OF SERVICES RENDERED BY THE FALMOUTH LIFEBOATS OF THE ROYAL NATIONAL LIFEBOAT INSTITUTION)

gave help
saved boat and nine
gave help
gave help

gave help
rescued
took out doctor and
landed a body

took out doctor and
landed a sick man
took out doctor and
landed a sick man

stood by vessel

gave help
saved vessel and one
gave help

landed a sick skindiver
saved boat and five
landed two (and dog)
gave help

escorted helicopter
took out doctor and
escorted vessel
stood by vessels

gave help
saved two boats and
landed thirteen
gave help
gave help
gave help
stood by vessel

gave help
gave help
saved boat and two

gave help

Justin Chin

EX-BOYFRIENDS NAMED MICHAEL

My mother is concerned that I haven't met a nice boy to settle down with. She keeps asking me if I met the right guy yet.

Well, Mom, there've been some nice guys who just didn't work out, some guys that have broken my heart, and there've been ex-boyfriends named Michael.

Ex-boyfriend named Michael #1 was a sheer mistake, but we make such delightful mistakes when we are young. You're supposed to learn from your mistakes, but heck...

Ex-boyfriend named Michael #2. I've washed him right out of my colon.

Just for once, I'd like to date a man and not his therapist.

Ex-boyfriend named Michael #3 said I had communication problems, and I said, "Oh, go fuck yourself asshole." What I should have said was, "Honey, I am trying to understand your feelings of frustration at our seemingly inept articulations of our emotions, but I do have some unresolved feelings of anger towards you, so please go fuck yourself, asshole."

But maybe there's the off chance he's right. I have never been that great at communicating. Ex-boyfriend named Michael #4: I should have known better the first time we met and went back to his apartment to fuck. His idea of fuck music was Dan Fogelberg's *Greatest Hits*. I asked him to change the CD, and he changed it to the only thing that could have been worse: *Neil Diamond Live at Madison Square Garden*.

Coming to America, indeed.

But I stuck with him and every fuck at his place was sheer hell. I tried telling him that his taste in music sucked and that I could seriously help him, but somehow I lacked the communication skills to do just that. But then I thought I loved him, and then I was young enough and foolish enough to believe that love can overcome Linda Ronstadt.

It cannot.

But love did not stop me from throwing his Yanni CDs behind the bookcase nor did it stop me from torching his *Ballads of Madison County* CD on the gas stove. Oh, what a beautiful blaze it was! He swore the CD was a gift but like all ex-boyfriends named Michael he was a lying dog. Now I'm getting ahead of myself here, that's about creatively destroying ex-boyfriends' property, not about ex-boyfriends named Michael.

Ex-boyfriend named Michael #5 was suffering from a severe case of yellow fever and dumped me for some little Taiwanese guy, fresh off the damn boat. Two weeks in the Yoo-Ass and the little pissant faggot manages to find his way to Cafe Hairdo, ready to be picked up by his American Dream of Homosexual Romance. I can just see him sitting there, legs crossed, working his non-threatening little Third World charm, offering to share his table and newspaper. I can just see them now: sharing haircare products, making mutual consensual decisions about dinner, movie, sex and their emotional well-beings. I can see them sitting on the sofa with the dictionary in their laps trying to figure out the difficult words in Barabara De Angelis' *Making Love Work* video seminar, and thinking about adopting a fox terrier named Honey. I can see them having deep, deep discussions about which one of them has a better butt:

"You do."
"You do."
"No, you do."
"Stop it! You do."
"Yours is tight and tanned."

"But yours is pert and angry."

What a pair of goddamn fucking freaks. I would just like to see them in a big car accident crashing into an oncoming truck carrying a shipment of Ginsu kitchen knives.

But hey, I'm not bitter, I'm descriptive. I'm not jaded. I just have too many ex-boyfriends named Michael.

Just once, I'd like to see everything of my life with ex-boyfriends named Michael laid out on a fat barge sent off to the landfill of affection. I'll watch the barge ferry it's way through the flotsam of therapy and crabs, dishsoap & bad sex, shared shirts & worry, devotion & drugs, pissed-off nights & legless drunken revelry.

I'll wave goodbye and I'll be fine.

Kélina Gotman

GLOBULAR MUD

the Discoverers prepped for their twelfth sojourn of the day—their twelfth VENTURE deep into the murky waters of Sarbandia—and mickey knew that this was it. this was the glory. fate. regency. that he had sought for five hundred and thirty kazillion years. he adjusted the mask about his nose. marky, at the other end of the tube, carefully watched mickey's approach. marky too had sought glory. fate. regency. for five hundred and thirty kazillion years. in fact, marky had sought glory. fate. regency. for five hundred and thirty three kazillion years. this was a fight to the death. mickey approached the box. he lifted his mask from atop his nose and looked inside. sweet sweet Sarbandia. globular Sarbandia. my very own—Sarbandia. marky stepped aside the box too.
mickey took a deep breath and dove in. he was always the first to dive in, even though he was the junior navigator. marky adjusted his lens. both knew that today, more than any other day, mickey HAD to find the Gurp. both knew it with a certainty stronger than steel, and mickey clenched his fist, like steel. this was a fight to the death. marky dove in.

the Discoverers were never to find the Gurp. countless Forgs, Sops, Biddjes and Hams emerged from the depths of murky Sarbandia, but never the Gurp. still, mickey died a superhero, forty seven bazillion years later. marky, no less a superhero, died five years after that. both knew, however, that their quest had not ended and that it never would.

Kevin Sampsell

ULYSSES

I remember entering the hotel lobby
and seeing those New York boys
sitting close together on a couch
by the soda and candy machines.
They were leering at me,
leaning forward,
as if trying to look in my pockets
or find the borderline of my underwear
as highlighted by my tight ass jeans.
They listened as I talked to the clerk
and they laughed so I could hear them
and said something about northwest boys
being "fine".
I joined them on the couch
and tried asking them what they thought
about the festival we were all attending.
I got no straight answers.
Their speech was filled with innuendoes.
The one sitting next to me was an eccentric
Jewish boy with a safari hat and khaki shorts.
I let him lightly brush
his hairy legs against mine.
His name was Ulysses.

That night Ulysses bought me
a drink as we listened to a Top-40
cover band in the lounge
full of small-town types and fake leather booths.
Old ladies asked us if we wanted to dance
but we declined.
He bought me drink after drink.

Later, in his room
I paid him
back
with my mouth.

The next morning he wouldn't shut up.
"I really liked that dick in the mouth routine"
he said.
He did not use the phrase "giving head"
because he thought it conjured disturbing images;
as if
watching a blanket bob up and down
with a stranger's teeth and claws inside
made him feel at ease.

Ulysses and his heckling lechers
kept their post night after night
on the lobby couch
harassing the clerk and every young man
who walked nearby.

On the fourth and last day of my stay
Ulysses and a friend
were easily swayed into a
three-body free-style massage
in my room.
We spent the night quietly
touching and moving.
Their voices turned low in the dark
and serious. Loving.
We curled into balls after cumming
on the pillows,
hands,
and necks.
We rested with the sheets off
as the sun started to appear.
The wake up call two hours away.
Our glowing bodies.

ANSWERING MACHINE LOVE

This is not an obscene phone call
not for you and I anyhow
not for your hair curling
to the sound of the inflection

in my moaning
  and my breath losing its stride
and twisting your nipples in my teeth
  my lungs heaving through the
      tiny speakers
        and into your ear
        my tongue kissing it...
Will you listen to this
over and over
even when I am there?
  I am slipping it on now
    over my head tightly
my Batman mask
      you are purring
long and hard now
    I feel the vibrations
        my kitty, my pussy,
        my cat, my woman.
We are the king and queen
of Gotham city and
    even though you are not here
I am there
(or a part of me is)
  Sometime soon while I am out
      I expect to come
                  home
  and find
(a part of) you

JACK NANCE

he regrets angels
who can eat   anything   and
        not die   like old films

RIKKI LAKE

Drowning in milkshake
              plowing through beef with lockjaw
my breasts full of guts

DAVID DUKE

His constant nightmare
  is a young white girl buying
    huge watermelons

M. Doughty

IN THE MIND OF THE MIND

His mind is an angry place. When he is drunk, and can't explain himself, he says his
mind is broken. Then he smacks his head repeatedly with the ball of his hand. Everybody laughs.

his mind is something that is very angry with him.

His mind is an angry sea of colors and references. his body bobs alone in it. his mind
is an America for jingles and mottoes. proud detergent names and happy cartoon
animals with bow ties. they flock to him on ships. they labor on the assembly lines,
screwing and drilling on the components of his dreams. they come out in the morning, smudged with soot.

his dreams are complex and ridiculous, Hong Kong epics of bullets and swords.
Flying punches. Homely women in princess drag. Their reaching arms are draped with jewels jewels. he slays her enemies but he never screws her. His mind is indifferent to fucking, though he pleads with it. A white arm emerges from behind the door and
hangs a Do Not Disturb sign on the gilded knob. Everytime. Then the credits roll,
and his mind bills itself as best boy, electrician, cinematographer, gaffer, technician,
Man In Hotel Lobby Number Two. everytime. Every Time.

His mind is a jealous mind, always campaigning for his attention with garish
colors
and melodies. Waving its hands in front of his face to obscure the exterior
influences.
Even as those influences are welcomed inside and incorporated into the
process of seduction.

And those influences that refuse the invitation become the object of
murderous
thoughts. Because the mind has only thoughts for hands, a murderous thought
is in
the mind the equal of murder. And the job becomes selling the pitch to its
corporeal
accomplice. But the sin is done.

Because the mind hates what is too big to swallow.

I'LL BE YOUR BABY DOLL, I'LL BE YOUR SEVEN DAY FOOL

Tonight the train is a curveball
sloping towards portions of
Darkest Brooklyn; some house unlit,
like a blank face, where I assume
you sit unsatisfied in a cubical room.

ROOTLESS

We roamed across Texas in a rented car,
buzzing with aimlessness, squinting
in the dull, hard light.
The greenery shooting past us slowly hardened,
turning into desert, burning away like a menthol into space.
We stopped on a gravel flatland
to piss and smoke, wandering off
to the powerlines at the edges
of our eyes' grasp. Onward.

By the junction, up the panhandle,
you slept, mumbling a pulp of words

to an unseen companion.
The air curling out of your nose,
droning into your mouth
like a kiss reversed on itself.
Your eyes flashed open and threw down
a bleary glance at the white dashes
and shut again. I could smell you.
My head bent, straining through the whoosh,
to listen. The baby words fell from your lips,
and I sifted them for music,
trying to hear the meaning
in a sucking sound.

FOR CHARLOTTE, UNLISTED

Her room is still; a bed, a desk, and the one word Easy on typing paper taped to the
wall. This is eight years later, still dreaming that room this night, alone, the hand
drifting down—a gasp is gasped but the room still sits around me in its own July; the
air there like walking underwater or through olive oil in a pan; the sheets quick to
the skin like icing, her wide hips forcing my skinniness against the wall.

I fall to the carpet and drift off, the soul traveling to a nightclub behind a door deep
in Sleeptown, and it's her, eight years later, same eyes and hands and every-thing,
taking tickets.

The hour? I ask. How much? She gives the same answer as last time: No.
There. No.
More to the left. The back. Anywhere. Again. Please.

Mary Elizabeth Grace

SHE

she came fast and hard to this life's dream
she came fast and hard to this life's death

some would say it was time
some would say it was passing

some would say
I would say

it had to do with such things as

a certain shade of lilacs could make her a
born again believer
she would stand in front of the mirror
hold her left breast laughing say
this nipple
is the mouth of a madwoman yawning
she read too much
talked too soft
stared at him as if
he was the one with the brilliance

it had to do with such things as

how they can break open
how they can break free

for her
there was no time there was no passing

everything came as still-life
no boast of death
no boast of dream

I knew her a little

SEPTEMBER NEVER COMING

I asked you to cut me flowers from the soon-to-be-September fields.
I asked, because I thought it would please.

Instead, you brought me the head of a dead man
spoke of the greatest gift being to teach one
of another's grief.

I asked you to bring me a pale pink dress.
I asked because of need.

An attempt at beauty,
something to cover these bones
that, still assembled in this order,
make my body.

Instead, you brought me the bowl part of a broken cup
to catch the dripping of my blood.

Mercedes Baines

CLIT SING ALONG

Ahhhhhhh!!
That song that song
makes me makes me
dizzy dizzy
phone ring please
ring
    (mind switch off for a moment
    so I don't obsess for a few minutes)
tricks
I don't know any more
ways to trick myself out of this business
some kind of modern disease
Skin against skin

sweat sliding on sweat
sweet breath lips barely touch the skin make the hair erect
wet tongue
  (simple tactile stimulation
  maybe my mind will get over it
  but my clit sings a song that
  makes my head swim and makes me shift in my seat
  as I listen to you)
I am trying to listen !
but the song is moving through me hip hopping the running man and
roger rabbit bounce in my groin
how many ways can I say I just want to fuck and hold hands later?

THE LAST TIME I SAW YOU

The last time I saw you
and you wanted to touch me at the same time
we were talking on the drive
and you said something/ what was it?
You laughed
I remember you laughed
and you had a piece of food caught between your teeth.
You got embarrassed.
But hey, at least I told you.
What did you say?
I can't remember.
Shit, I hate that.
The last time I saw you and you wanted to touch me at the same
time....
what was it you said?
You laughed/ I remember you laughed?—you had a green piece of
something between your teeth....
and I wondered who you had dinner with....
I was going to ask
but decided I didn't want to know.
What did you say...?
The main thing is you saw me
and wanted to touch me at the same time
and I remember feeling this pain in my chest
right between my breasts.

I had to take a step back and you said something and laughed and
all I saw was that stuff between your teeth
and I knew she had probably made dinner for you.
And then I started feeling stupid for feeling possessive.
But I knew you wanted to touch me.
What was it you said…
anyway
you saw me and wanted to touch me at the same time
and
I didn't let you…
I couldn't let you.

Minister Faust

REGGAE IS

So, mi wuz a young maan
When mi wirk fid di gubment
An mi wirk wid a girl
Ah—mi mean a young Whitewoman
She wuz nice, an so wuz mi
So wi bigin fi tok bout tings, yu see
Di kaanvahsayshaan moved an shifted, drifted an lifted
Close to mi heart
Di subject called REGGAEMUSIC
Si mi tot—ere muss be an intelligent woman
She may be White—but she's arright
So mi say—What yu like bout Reggaemusic?
She say a mi:
I like reggae cuz it's nice in di mornin
It so soff and sweet, an mek mi feel waarm an
It goes so nice wit mi maarnin kaaffee
Like a fresh-baked croissant wid jam as a toppeen

NU naat impress.

She say a mi:
I like reggaemusic cuz it's soft an pretty

Like a drive inna country or Sunday inna city
It relocks di girls an relocks di boys
An don't mek dem upset like dat rapmusic noise.
Mi NAAT impress.

She say a mi:
I like di klaasicks in reggae—
Mi tink: Finally!
Mi say: *Who yu like?*
She say:
Ziggy Marley!

So mi tink she juss ignrnt an she naa know no betta
So mi give er a tape an mi say: *See yu layta*

Well di music wuznt Ziggy nor wuz it di Blondie
Nor dem Red, Red Whine bastuds dem call UB-40
Mi tink, give er sum strengt an vitality
Sum reggae wit passion an spirit
Some poetry, sum beauty
So mi give er LINTON KWESI JOHNSON AN DI DUB BAND
Music wit sum KICK

Well

She come back to mi
She say:
I don like dis ere musick
It talk too much politik
Soun too communistick.

MI NOT IMPRESS. CUZ MI KNOW DAT DI PROBLEM'S DAT
IT'S TOO REALISTIC!

Mi want fi say:
Dis ere reggae music might be socialistic
Or ighly Africentric an kram tick wit politic
But whaat yu like an yu hear wit your dam Labatt's beer
An your blonde Kalifornya krowd wit DAY-GLO so LOUD
An your sippin kappacheeno an fresh bokkle of vino
An your Vuarnet & Benneton's & Perrier & Polo
An your Marsaydeez-Bends an your new BMW.

DAT'S NOT REGGAEMUSIC—DAT SHIT MEK MI SICK!
Reggaemusic is bombs... reggaemusic is burnin
Reggaemusic is HOT HOT SUNSET on eyelaans of yearnin
Of cries in di night in Babylon of concrete
Of streets filled wit rage in dis age of di cage
Of Blaack fists pumped skyward ... of cries of BLAACK POWER!
Of arteries hearts pumpin out anger
In an hour so sour an wretched an wrongful unrighteous
That might juss spill over
Pass woovers an tweeters
An into di muscles in pain an restrained in di AUDIENCE LISTNIN
Vibratin an waitin fi signal be given
In bodies packed tight on di dancefloor once more as dey were on slave ship...
Reggaemusic's di cry dat went out on dat slave ship
Reggaemusic's di langwidge wuz used on dat slave ship
Wedder Ibo Yoruba Mandinka or Hausa
Reggaemusic's di cry dat kaamyunikaytid
Di rage an di pain an di hate an di suffrin
Reggaemusic's di beat of dem souljahs in chains
Reggaemusic's di music di langwidge di cadence wid which
Dem unchained slaves wud slash deer slaver's NECKS
Reggaemusic's Nat Turner an Touissant L'Ouverture
Reggaemusic is Brixton Kingston an Watts
Africville Sharpeuille Accra an HOT
HOT HEADS AN HOT FISTS AN A CRY COME FROM HELL
OF A PEOPLE BOKKLED UP LIKE A MOLOTOV COCKTAIL

Reggae rnusic aint quaint an aint witty or pretty
REGGAEMUSIC'S DI INFERNO COME BURN DUNG YUH CITY

An all a dis to her mi had wanted fi say

But she naat impress.
She'd wokked on away.

Nancy Dembowski

LIFE ON VENUS AVENUE

Ran out of gas.
Stuck with a broke radio and two kids fighting in the back.
Make it to Rachelle's,
she is watching Life of Venus' Avenue.
We decide to drive to High Park.
Loading the trunk, Latino in sunglasses
posts himself to the mailbox in front of the Donut Cove,
arms and legs cross he's enjoying the view.
Park looks like a back-home cemetery.
My daughter stands in line for the slide,
chickens out at the last minute.
A woman—rhinestones, painted fingernails, no sunglasses,
calls out to my girl who's hanging with one hand.
Her voice sounds like a poem.
Not Whitman or Plath,
but one of those poems that push the line,
one of those poems nobody prints unless the writer is famous,
sound too much a speech.
I love them in secret,
like the New York sound of her voice.
I'm brought back to rappers and ghetto blasters,
a drunk in the next apartment begging,
"Come to me baby, come to me."
She flies down happy.
The diner's littered with geriatrics;
twelve bucks buys drinks and to-die-for muffins with a slice of carrot
for decoration.
I head home to ten different ingredients, new and improved, and the
good old American blues.

Noel Franklin

BLOOD QUANTUM
(UPON PURCHASING THE LATEST BOOKS OF SHERMAN ALEXIE
AND MARGARET ATWOOD ON THE SAME DAY)

what does a half half breed (woman) mean?
what does a half half breed mean to you?
if i had seltzer water running through my veins
it would be no worse
maybe better
evian could sell my ass on television
and i'd lose rights to my name, my face, my worldly fortune
as it is i don't have the right to my own losses
the short smirk at the poetry reading
the tall great uncle
100 percent eastern band cherokee
shellshocked from the battle of iwo jima, WWII
slobbering in the basement of my childhood
where all memories pool
where the toad i caught that dirtied my hands died
where i first tasted blood pressed from tissue between fingers
and teeth
it is here i need to take you
with a lamp and laser pointer pen
to point out the man with broad forehead and dark skin
southern drawl crying
"lucielle!"
to his sister
curled over the bed
having incorrectly done the washing and drying
"lucielle...
lucielle..."
she is not there to administer the medicine
i back away

no one said the word "cherokee"
(the words "filthy mexican" as i was pushed beneath the lake)
no one said the word "indian"
until it was too late
15 days after the eastern band closed their rolls

i find the internet cherokee web site
and weep tears that water, still, the dreams
of taking a motorcycle all the way to the carolina's
falling over on the inside of the reservation line
begging somebody to take me home!
i wonder who would do the kicking and laughing
at the white girl who didn't know the way

meanwhile, back at the homestead on 5th street
in mishawaka, indiana
a man
with eyes sharp enough to shoot far beyond any expectation
the photographer of the family
chews the skin off his second knuckle
and speaks the language of toddlers
though he has cleared the age of 80
and she is there
dark, wrinkled, round face
a perm to keep the hair from growing straight
to hide the potential for long, dark braids
lucielle
now needs someone to call to
someone to raise her
like she raised her brother
like she raised her kids
like she raised the kids of my generation
and i choose to stay here
instead of going back to return the favor
because i am afraid
of her misunderstandings
of my father's hands
afraid of the day when he does come back
hating his blood enough
to try and cut the indian right out of me
(again)
hating his blood
how did this come to be
lucielle?

somewhere
in margaret atwood's universe
the goddess athena table dances for a living

while, just 10 blocks away from me
the dark skinned woman sells herself for a 5th of forgetting
because there is no going home
and this is the treatment she received, there, anyway
'cept, at home, there was no sweet hush-money money
honey, won't you come out tonight
buffalo girl
come out

lucielle
if there is a healing word in the world
sometimes, i believe, it will be you who speaks it
but then i remember
the death of your mother
how she reverted to a language
that, as a child, scared me
how she lost all our names
in the white of the nursing home
so very far away from where she had come from
with no spirit honored
no ritual for her passing
just tubes
and an attendant
making 5.50 an hour
to separate the dead from the asleep
my reservation grown ex-boyfriend
had a grandmother who died in much the same way
is it any wonder
lucielle
lucielle
lucielle
won't you talk to me lucielle?
but i do remember
how you revered god and man
brought us to the trailer park church every sunday
it didn't matter that you grew beans, corn and squash
(the three sisters crops)
or that you had your own honors
your cyclical thinking
i remember the church
and the death of your mother
and your sons fist

delivering the wrath of his god
and i realize
i'll sell myself for a 5th of forgetting
before we see eye to eye
lucielle

what does a half half breed (woman) mean?
what does a half half breed mean to you?
the short smirk at the poetry reading
makes me realize i steal the night to say anything
and still i do

LONG DISTANCE EX

my heart clings to you
like a child clutching a box of sugar cereal
"put that down," i say
"it's not good for you"
but it screams and cries when i wrestle you away
and runs back to your aisle
before i am halfway across the store

in actuality
i am halfway to canada
and it is my head that tumbles towards you
southward down the highway
and i must admit
my body looks smaller from 400 miles away
still standing in seattle

speaking it's red, headless language
into 8 separate phone lines
incommunicado
a gurgling desire

if you were a local call
i'd be making you all day

Phlip Arima

JANE — WAITING FOR THE LIGHT TO CHANGE —

at the corner where cigarette filters cover the pavement
and little girls stoop to look through car windows
a woman smoothes her hair back over her ear
and waits for the light to change

she doesn't say a thing
as it goes from red to green and red again
then stepping out into the traffic her shrieks begin

worthless fucking slut bitch   you don't deserve to live
take this   and this   and this   and this

as the cars honk and swerve the hand returns
to slap her face and turn the skin a swollen mauve
rip a lip so blood begins to flow

worthless fucking slut bitch   you don't deserve to live

the watchers seek each other out in eyes dry against the cold
see prophesy caught and denied as the woman
reaches the other side

she smoothes her hair back over her ear
and waits for the light
to change.

BE QUIET

There's something different about the house. The kitchen looks the same.
And the bathroom still smells like the can that sprays. But something has
    changed.

I was watching television, playing with my toys, when outside I heard the boys
    from next door.

One was Darry, my friend. I went out to see what they were doing. When I
    came in,
all my toys were put away, but no one was mad at me.

There's something different about the house. The stuff I'm not suppose to
    touch
in the back room is still leaning up against the wall. There's laundry on the
    washer
and some beside it on the floor. But something, I don't know what, has
    changed.

After dinner, when Daddy went out, he didn't slam the door. Mommy and I,
    we read a book.
Halfway through the story the phone rang. Mommy talked in a normal voice
    and I even think
I heard her laughing.

There's something different about the house. All the lights still turn on and
    off.
And the candies in the dinning room haven't been burned. But something has
    changed.

I'm going to go to sleep now, but you have to stay awake. I'm going to sit you
    here,
right beside my pillow. It's your job to watch and see what bad things happen.

Ritah Parrish

THE RULES

ATTENTION!
I will list off the rules
You are to live by one time
And one time only!
If you fail to follow them
You will be punished!
If you fail to pay attention
You will be sorry!

THESE ARE THE RULES!

Number One
When your mother is chasing your father
Through the house
With a pan full of grease
In an effort to kill him
You will remain seated at the table
And quietly finish your Cream of Wheat.

Number Two
When your mother tells you that
You have ruined her life
Whether you believe her or not
Whether you agree with her
Assessment of the situation or not
Whether you understand what the hell
She is talking about or not
You will apologize, drop your drawers
And take your medicine.

Number Three
When your father drinks Budweiser and decides to
Roast pumpkin seeds with salsa on them in the oven
At an inappropriately high temperature
Nearly burning down the house
You will eat them and say to him
"These are the best damn roasted pumpkin seeds
With salsa on them that I have ever tasted!"

Number Four
When your mother comes home drunk,
Pulls you out of bed by your hair
And tells you that you are a whore
You will forget that you are a virgin.
You will call upon D.H. Lawrence to help you.
You will concoct a believable story
Drop to your knees and say the Rosary.

Number Five
When your teachers ask you
How you got those bruises

You will tell them that you are in the midst of a growth spurt,
That your limbs have become unwieldy
And you are no longer able to control them
Which causes you to fall down a lot.

Number Six
When your sweet little grandma asks you
Why you continue to pee your pants
Even though you are nine years old
And ought to know better
You will say that it is because
You don't love Jesus enough
And beg the Holy Spirit to heal you.

THESE ARE THE RULES!

You will follow them to the letter
Until you are eighteen years of age
At which time you will be released into the world
And realize that you are screwed.

You will become addicted to cigarettes.
You will drink too much beer.
You will whore yourself.
You will take anti-depressant drugs
Prescribed to you by a licensed therapist.

You will suffer nightmares
And have a number of trust issues.
You will wonder why you are unable to give and receive love.
At which time you will realize that
Your will has been broken
That the excellent training you have received
Has turned you from a caring, feeling human being
Into a lean, mean fighting machine!

THESE ARE THE RULES!

At ease, soldier.

Robert Priest

ELVIS/BACCHUS ITERATIONS

Elvis Bacchus, Elvis Bacchus
has no-one else ever noticed the similarity
between these two names?
Indeed say Bacchus 22 times using those precedents
of consonant decay over time
(as described by archaeologist
Colin Renfrew)
and Bacchus *is* Elvis.

Listen:

Bacchus Bacchus Bacus Bakis Bekis
Mekis Mawkiss Nawkis Nawbis Nawlbis
Nelbish Nelfish Nelfish Snelfish Stelfish
cellfish elfish elfis—Elvis!

Elvis is Bacchus
Elvis in his prime
and Elvis in his decline
Dead on the crapper
with a body full of drugs
Elvis is Bacchus
and Bacchus
is
us.

From PARALLELVIS UNIVERSES
THE DEATH OF ELVIS I

Elvis sat down on the toilet as big as Buddha
it was the anniversary of his mother's death
Elvis strained and his face went a little red
he thought of his mother dying that day
he had lost certain rights
he had become mythic in the mind
you lose so much when that happens

Elvis strained again. He could feel something
moving in his center.
Something really big
Excited he pushed harder
He pushed and grunted
It was coming! It was coming!
Elvis strained until the purple veins stood out like
tree roots in his beet red neck
and then it came
bigger than Mt. Sinai it came
bigger than the first orgasm
like a deathstar spiral
the big black bolt shot through him
and Elvis keeled over
and groaned
a big fat man on the toilet
the sound of that last fart still reverberating
amidst the gasping
the crying.
like anyman dying

VOTE SHIT

Its just a big dogshit
someone left smiling
at the sky
but vote for this piece of shit.
Because it is the only socialist.
Because there is 7 percent compassion in the shit
and that makes shit tops.
Because you get a nice photo of a piece of shit in a suit and tie
and shit looks good
But shit is different.
Shit won't lie.
It is justsome species of feces
but it will not cut social programs.
It won't offer the gag to the weakest in their screaming
as it cuts their throats
for all of us.
We are gonna keep conscience with shit.

Because Shit can do it.
Because we deserve shit.
because shit is what you want
when you don't know what it is
You really want

WHEN YOU CALL SOMEONE DICKHEAD

When you call someone Dickhead
you refer to the glans penis—the frenulum
the super sensitive male penis tip
an almost supernatural part of the anatomy
almost a brain
almost a lung
almost another hanging heart

When you call someone Dickhead
you insult the wizened face
of who knows what hung
ancestor
in this vivid
wrinkle
this lifeboat
on the big tug

When You say Dickhead
drop the inverse reverence
you are bestowing a well earned title
This grandest of all grandissments
should be reserved for those whom
we respect the most
Popes, premiers, heavy metal singers—
are Dickheads
because we are fair
because we respect the penis

rob mclennan

dukes of hazard monologue

fr r.m. vaughan

         & who remembers daisy duke,
the pretty underside. surviving archetypes
   of character, beauty, charm.
old references beyond date in poems

           & daisys thin braless smile,
raging in reruns on afternoon cable,
    bo & luke duke & police cars crashing,
               good old
boys thru hazardous counties on the run.

as southern belle orange
        turns at the corner of a tired thumb,
    changing channels back
& remembering television daydreams,
          lunchboxes & t-shirts

        daisy duke
in short white shorts that showed
     just not enough
   & blue blouse, daisys running breasts
           from house to pick-up, smiling.

sure. I remember daisy duke.
as uncle jesse never left anywhere
     w/out his checkerboard,

left on a light for the last to get home.

Sean Thomas Dougherty

I'M LOOKING FOR LORCA IN YOUR LETTERS

*For my friend Catherine O'Brien
and in memory of my great-uncle Leon Bailey
who was murdered by the NYC Police Department*

Searching behind each word for a small
Andalusian eyecase, a bag of gypsy bones,
A song—of green shawls & mountains,
Of black shirted legions & goat herders
Climbing into the clouds where the sun
Sifts through mist & rosaries crumble
Like cake in the hands of the rich—
I'm looking for Lorca in your letters,
For that small laugh he's said to have
Given, for the psalms in his pockets,
The blue marble he stole from the Gypsy King
To give to the boy he once met in *la plaza*
With eyes of *azul* & emerald, how he vowed
He'd seen Christ in the walk of a man
In a workshirt with unshaven cheeks,
How he held the face in his hands like water—
So deep he drank the tongue of a nation trilled
Like cicadas in heat, & the clicking of boots
Like castanets down a hallway where the orders
Were given & the firing-squad took aim
In the shade of a hill in the summer of 1936—
I'm looking for Lorca in your letters, for the man
Who refused to fight, for the old woman
Who sat on the steps of a night much like this one
And counted the threads in her shawl, & sang a strange
Song like a wail for the dead in October when the men
Gather to discuss the weather, the coming weather & count
Their stores, & the corn husks lay bare in the fields
Before the smoke & fire begins—
I'm looking for Lorca in your letters, for the rain
On the Brooklyn Bridge & Hart Crane diving
Off the ship & rising cherubic—the papyrus of myth
Like Mayakovsky's last poem found next to his breast,

Before the bullet pierced his brain he believed
In the flags above trains of black bread & steel,
In the arms of the people uprisen like a field
Of wheat in the wind—
I'm looking for Lorca in your letters,
For men waiting on corners for work, brushing
The dust from their faces with hats, straw hats,
Picking their teeth & talking of heat, waiting
For the man with the truck to arrive & ask them
For a day of their lives to bend their backs
For money for meal for their wives to bake flat
Tortillas for children who stare—
I'm looking for Lorca in your letters,
For the names of the disappeared, for the names
Of the strikers who died, for the names
Of the organizers, for the names of the unwanted,
The outcast, for the name of the man in the mill
Who carried the cloth to the woman he loved
Who spoke her name aloud after work in the church
He would marry, for the name of the last song
Played on the trumpet stored in a corner away
From the radiator blowing off steam
By the window of a third floor apartment
In Harlem on 125th street where the cops
Broke the door down & shot without warning
And a young man slumped like Vachel on the bed
Before Lorca was dead before he even walked the streets
Of New York City....

Sky Gilbert

ROMANTIC POSSIBILITIES OF THE TELEPHONE

If you think I ever went and put you on speed-dial
you are sadly mistaken
A boy has to last longer than three months
and suck my dick really well
which you didn't
Boy am I glad I put your name at the back of my phonebook

It's EASILY erasable
there beside guys from Wisconsin and San Francisco who I haven't called for
months
and it doesn't take up too much space
(thank god!)
I might not even erase it!
The fact that you were able to find fifteen minutes on your
fucking break
to call and break up
was not lost on me
I tried to hurry
Wouldn't want you to waste some half baked croissant
honey
and there's nothing like cold coffee
Did you put down the phone and sigh
"Oh my God he's SO neurotic!"
to one of your co-workers
at that fucking telemarketing place?
They're all a bunch of drunks and has-beens who work there anyways
I didn't enjoy being invited to their stupid parties
I only pretended that vulgar woman was exciting
No, telemarketers are not fascinating
contrary to your twenty-three year old pseudo-artistic romanticization of
them
And there's only one fucking thing I will miss
one fucking thing
and it will take awhile
to get over
Turning the phone off at night
will not be easy
There is perhaps nothing sadder
after all
than a phone you expect nothing of
There it sits
still as vinegar
I guess I'll watch a late movie
Who is Betty Hutton anyway?

Taylor Mali

LABELING KEYS

Though not a secretive man,
my father understood combination locks and keys.
I tell you, the man had a love affair with brass.
You have to have seen how quickly one key
begins to look like another-
> *I'll never forget that this is the key to the front door—*
> *I'll never forget that this is the key to your house—*
> *I'll never forget that this is the key to the tool shed—*
> *I'll never forget that this is the key to. . .*
> *What the fuck is this the key to?*

Excuse me.
> *To what the fuck is this the key?*
>> —to appreciate a well-marked key.

It's the same angel that made him label and date
butcher-paper-wrapped
leftovers in the refrigerator along with suggestions
for their possible use
(MARCH 3. TURKEY SCRAPS. YUMMY TREATS FOR THE D.O.G.?),
secured with (count 'em) one, two rubber bands,
one for snugness, one for symmetry.

But there's an art to labeling keys:
The one you keep to your neighbors' house across the street
must not say, "Neighbor's house across the street:
In Maine for all of May."
Similarly, SILVER CABINET, GUN RACK, BURGLAR ALARM,
SPARE SET OF KEYS TO SAAB:
these are labels you will not see at our house.
Instead my father wrote in his own argot,
a cryptographic language of oblique reference.
the key to the burglar alarm is SIREN'S SONG,
The gun rack, THAT INFERNAL RACKET,
the neighbor's house across the street
is now the FARM IN KANSAS.
VICTOR was the Volvo, HENRY, the Honda,
GABRIELLA, the Saabatini.

A security of the mind, no doubt, and not so much
precluding burglary as providing challenges
to the industrious burglar.,
as well as evincing from my brother and me
much in the way of loving parody:
NOT THE KEY TO THE SIDE DOOR. OH NO!
DESTITUTE NEIGHBOR'S HOVEL FAR—FAR AWAY FROM HERE.
BOATHOUSE IN BAY OF FUNDY.

But among the neatly labeled keys (some to cars
we no longer have, like POTEMKIN and GERALD, the Ford)
is a brass ring of assorted expatriates
called KEYS TO UNKNOWN PLACES.
Little metal orphans, they have lost their locks; or rather,
their locks have all lost them, misplaced them all in the same place, on the
same ring,
which is a sadness that no boltcutter can cure.
Even the key that simply says HARTFORD—
somewhere there's a door, a box
a closet full of secrets locked—
and the only thing I know about it
is that it probably is *not* in Hartford.
I keep them all, jingling and jangling,
turning tumblers in my heart.
For who knows when I might *not be* in Hartford again?
And who here knows nothing of the magic that escapes
every time a key that should unlock a door does?

SWITCHING SIDES

I'm writing the poem that will change the world,
and it's Lilly Wilson at my office door.
Lilly Wilson, the recovering like addict,
the worst I've ever seen.
So bad the whole eighth grade
used to call her Like Lily Like Wilson.

Until I declared my class a like-free zone
and she could not speak for days.
And when she did, it was to say,

Mr. Mali, this is . . . so hard.
Now I have to . . . think before I . . . say anything.

It's for your own good, Lily. Even if you don't, like . . .
it.

I'm writing the poem that will change the world
while Lily writes a research paper about how gays
should not be allowed to adopt children.
I'm writing the poem that will change the world,
and it's Lily Wilson at my office door.
She's having trouble finding sources,
or rather ones that back her up:

> *They all argue in favor*
> *of what I thought I was against.*

And it took all four years of college,
three years of graduate school,
and every incidental teaching experience I have ever had
to let out only, So what are you going to do Lily?

> *I can't believe I'm saying this,*
> *but I think I'd like . . . to switch sides.*

And I want to do more than just believe it,
but to enjoy it.
And that changing your mind is the best way
to make sure that you still have one.
Or even that minds are like parachutes:
that it doesn't matter how you pack them
so long as they open at the right time.
O God, Lily, I want to say
You make me feel like a teacher
and who could ask to feel more than that?
I want to say all this, but only manage,
Lily, I am, like so impressed.

So I finally taught someone something,
namely, how to change their mind.
And learned in the process that if I ever change the world
it will be one eighth grader at a time.

Tish Benson

NO PARTS SPARED
for Sabaah

woke up today
surprised myself
stray bullets poppin inside me like radiated icicles
dreamin this was
The Day
body would finally
loosen up enough so real me
could go on about my business
flesh and bones holdin on with a python's clutch
like i aint got stuff to do without being weighed down
in this 100 pound cemented suit
lead bound feet
hands dipped in acid rain
naw this aint no travlin boat i'm in
a war hit ship
hazard waste infested
pesticide injected
my spirit struggles against a spiked iron lung
belly full of molten crabs
and a pack of rabid dogs scratching my throat
so its nearin
grim reapers scythe huvers overhead
gonna whipp me away
and i aint scared no mo
pain finally beat up fear in the battle of the fittest
pistol whipped tripple overtime
just a matter of a few more notes plucked
from rotted janglin teeth before i get to tie on my travlin shoes
so for now
i lay here paying homage to volcanoes forming on my thighs
bile leaking out my ears
hair like wintered leaves
though it hurts to blink
i click my lids diggin the sounds of rusted plates
though motion opens
howlins gate

i slow rock conjurin up the wolfs cakkle
i keep my nose tilted
but still quicksand spurts out
covering snot stained sheets with rancid goop
my greatest feat is turning pain into a game
im in costume when i see
worms digging through my face
marking territory with tar n feces
bald is trendy as bone protrudes through fish skin
0% body fat is the American Dream
in between theres the wind rushing thru to disembowel
make me fess up to crimes i aint commit
i withstand the call to walk on clouds
bludgen myself with a hatchet
or put my name on Kevorkians things to do list
now when glass travels through my veins
i give laughter new names
i tally time on my bed post with the venom that oozes out my pores
acceptin vice's grip with arms wide open
making games out of pain
comparing it to pleasure
FACT: i have moaned the exact same sounds when i've had lust swirl inside me
as i now do engulfed by stagnant cesspools of fermented mud
acceptance is pure
purity is uncontaminated
and because i have accepted my body rotting before my eyes
i have become well...wholesome...regenerated
and now that i've become whole again in spite of
my insides clawing me to extinction
i concentrate more on the living
i hear pain from calloused hearts whose owners
disown their razor embedded memories
thinking forgetting is akin to blunted realities
souls like these reach out for me now
wounded plexus finding comfort in the born again
i place my ear against scabs
listen to bleeding sores
i stroke the stuff folks blind themselves to
whisper lullybys to matted yarns
                              watch the unnarling
i stroke as ulcerated cores

                              become clear again

whisper lullybys

                        healing begins

i stroke   whisper

The Healing Begins

Wayde Compton

COME TO

I found
the sound
of smoke
the surround
system
louder than dope
massive in the hull
of the shadow
of bliss

can I get a witness?
can I get a street name?
can I get a foothold?
fly in the flour
sugar in the shit
blood blurred
can I get
more than a metre
more than a mention
more than a boom
and a crack
a few verses
of guttural slackness?
scratching, scarring the record
the word the work
the ache
the fetish
of courage

of those cussing out the world?
check the attack on that beat
it's happening
enough to scissor through your soul
make you stomp your foot through the floor
and tear yourself in half
check that jungle roll
that drum and bass loop
like the sound of a cycle
leaning versus the curve
of race music
dig that muse implacable
kickin west coast samples fractal
the genre of squander
the puzzle of our caressing capture
our broken strobe gaze
routes of each new school traced
along the trail of dispersal's ark
london kingston toronto new york
to vancouver
synapse of aurature
ambient to trance
ambivalent to entrance
decks of dance
branded and banded
in the darkness of our masks
the cant
of gun talk
when the muzzle mouths its chant
electronica oracular
like the moon of lobe
globe of interface
space of sound
system of trick
truncation of trope
tape of manipulation
lull
and lullaby
of the ecstatic

BAND

in the late fifties there were so few black people in vancouver, my father used
to get into night clubs without paying the cover by posing as a member of the
band at the back door. it was assumed by the white doorman that if you were
black, you were obviously a musician

in this ghost town any spade
can con his way
into any night club
just by *being* black
and at the back door claiming
I'm with the band

just like that
any nigger can con his way
like slippin between the spokes
of the wheel of fortune
known as the west
where claims are staked
names untaken
second starts given
pasts forgiven
between the spokes of the wheel
of where
we be livin

drinkin in
the landscape
these mountains are something else, bro
and something else
is good enough
drinkin in the land of
not opportunity
but at best, belief
at worst, desperation

but doors open for us at night
when the lights collapse on the crackers
and the sun fucks up
their empire's cons-
piracy

we breathe
respire
deep

inside smoke-filled lounges
and lungs
of the western recesses
and excesses
where race carnivals take place
under cover charges
and of darkness

the paramount
the penthouse
the orpheum
the taj mahal
the cave
the commodore
the colonial
where cash crashes down doors
and crackers act-
ually inter-
act
with niggers slingin slack cash
on a saturday night slick
as our music flickers
through the turnstiles
of theatres
and booze cans
and after hours joints
and night clubs
the hub of
darktown
at strathcona's corners
all the way down
to the intersection of hastings and main

no negro could really entertain
fantasies of fortune
how could any even great pretender
get his white hopes up
about luck
in love

or happenstance
drunk
before the band
that plays our music good enough?
it's enough
that the circuit spins the big acts north enough
to vancouver
across the border
(always an iffy prospect
like diggin for gold
or other shades
of negro)
blue notes fall
like leaves across roots
that speculate their darkling way
into the truth

and the fog rolls in
past the docks
and the cop shop
and the steam clock
and takes its time
to intoxicate our section of the city inside
inside,
blues
just
slays
souls
just so damn much cooler
than vancouver asphalt, tar
and feather blues
like truest birds
called home to roost

you

can get into
any night club
in vancouver
just by *being* black
and at the back door claiming
I'm with the band

IN/FUSION

Alex Boutros

From BABY BOY BLUES

the taste for breath has you stung
so make haste and clear the liquid from each lung
and it has begun—a twenty year vibration of the tongue.
a compilation of sound
that comes to surround your station in life.
a variation on strife.
you take the best and ignore the rest
and try to avoid the harvest
of hate,
but wait

there be the open mouth gape of curiosity to satiate
the heart wrench stench of each atrocity to narrate
before it's too late
and the roll of fate dies on lips
frozen by a chosen path—20 years, you do the math.

it's in the stars by far, a charred astrology
and so in the interests of a chronology
we be spinning back to the beginning
examining the underpinning of your birth,
determining worth on the girth of a tale
for sale to the highest bidder.
a litter of mirth and mystery swirl in the gale of a history
scattered with shattered intention, invention, dissension,
not to mention

presumption, assumption,
your gumption as insurmountable as your tale is credible
barely legible in this spider light
where i sit
barely lit,
after the first hit, immersed in the worst of it
watching you breathing in the dark
the plot seething with the marks i make
for heaven and hell's sake, everything's at stake
watching you breathing in the dark
the plot seething with the marks
of weaving, leaving, grieving,
pen wielding,
pleading for a different ending
i'm spending time mending broken rhyme.

Alexis O'Hara

NIPPLE'S HINDSIGHT REVENGE

Ironically,
That very morn
I had been feeling kinda torn
Wondring if I shoulda worn
A bra beneath my shirt   geez girl getta grip...
Later
Lifting heavy objects helping out a friend
When down the street comes a truck loaded with three men
The old-enough-to-know-better one
Is trying to impress
With vocal prowess
Smart guy, kinda snide, cracking lines about ... my hair?
"Hey Rooster boy, tell me where you come from
Mars or something?"
I'm not really noticing too busy focusing
On trying to get the fukn futon in the car
I turn around, already feelin' surly
And genius guy realizes that I am a gurl, eek

Some leering and jeering then the best one of all...
(they call these cat calls though they usually come from pigs)
"HEY NIPPLES!"
      I am not grinnin my head is spinnin and I'm not
Swallowing I keep swallowing I keep swallowing more than I can take
My fists are clenching gut is wrenching and I refuse to make it seem
Like I can deal, like I can't feel
The crushing weight, the stinking bait
Your lousy worm of a line
I am not fine.
How dare you look at me like I'm a steaming steak?
Like I'm a loaf of bread like I am chocolate cake?
You try to eat me with your eyes
You'll see
You will despise the taste I leave in your mouth
You'll be sick for days
Throwing up your stomach lining always moaning always whining
Wondering how you came to be that way?
      Well
You plant a seed of loathing in me
And whaddaya know: A fukn tree
And it will fall and crush your skull
A glorious sound round and dull   resonating no more hesitating
Your brains will be splattered
And really you should be flattered
That I have just spent this much time
Twisting up a twisted rhyme
About some sorry piece of trash like you.

Anne Stone

SALINE 90

The only spontaneous thing he ever did was combust. All those small intima-
tions he might have made over a life-time condensed into a single flaming gesture.
Leaving nothing more than a dark hump slouched on a bed inside of a hospital
room.

Leaving me to dream of large lumber yards at night, large lumbering yards, yard sticks—which are a species of ruler and are meant to measure something, anything, the sky or the ground or the table top it lies on. Or the ruler just folds back, the way that skin folds back from the edge of a burn, the way a measuring tape folds in and in, like the tail of a snail, and measures itself. Or the thinnest strip of air pressed down close upon it, pressed down close upon him now, tearing at exposed nerves like the gritty lick of garnet paper or some animal's tongue. *I know it isn't licking you cause it likes you.*

Used to drive you crazy you said, all that talking I did, like my brain was laid out in millimetre demarcations and was forced to give the minutest measures of itself, continually. That there were no abstractions, you said, in my talk. Just the bare raw facts that fill time [spilling out].

But you were thinking them too. Thinking them so hard that flames sprouted just under your skin. Though your body, even now, tries to lay those scars on me. The way the burns concentrate themselves around your chest. Where I laid my hand. You can see where my hand protected you, just the same, can trace the outline of my palm. Can trace where the hot of it sealed the point of contact, so that they had to take me with you, had to keep me beside you in the ambulance, had to cut my hand away from the blasted ruin of your chest, revealing the perfect imprint of my palm. Which is all the fire left of you, for me.

It took my hair.

It swallowed my hair, because my flaming red hair was indistinguishable from the fire. When the flames snuffed themselves out and withdrew back into your body, it couldn't remember where it began and where it ended, so it took my hair. A bushel of it, laid like a swallow's nest around your heart.

But first, it took your eyes.

A billion years ago, something of you scuttled from the saline bath of creation without particulate orbs to guide your ascent. But a seeing flesh. Perspective came to you then from the soles of your feet and fingertips and tongue, and why end there? your gullet and stomach and the curl of your intestine coiled in on itself, to measure you and the world and find them somehow the same.

When skin is cut, they tell me, and then pressed together, it seals. Like the press of words on a flower, those ad hoc entries we made in the dictionary under "love." The rose you gave me, bleeding—a rust colored stain on opposite pages—so that the flower was fused to the words on the page. I could read that flower now, turn *fulcrum* and *fugue* between my fingertips as I sit outside your hospital room waiting for them to hoist your remains from the saline tub.

When skin is cut, and then pressed together, it seals. Which explains all the talking I ever did, just keeping my mouth in constant motion because otherwise like a raw wound, it might cleave to itself, leaving only a line where the slash of lips once were.

But all this talking is for your sex, which, aside from your buttocks and the soles of your feet was the only part of you the fire spared. Staring up at me, in one-eyed expectation, erect almost constantly.

So that this whole conversation is something I'm having with your penis. Your "John Hancock" you called it, like it could endorse cheques, finalize contracts, leave some vast genetic signature upon this world. It never shared in your self-emulative act of love, and even now, stares at me with something like indifference.

The sudden fusing of touch led me to believe that I should open myself to you, that it was your final wish to elide my flesh with yours. That if I could spread my legs wide enough, I could simply engulf you, I could open my sex and house you and you would cleave to the walls of my belly and grow there—like a tumor. All except for your sex, which being perfectly contained in itself already would remain an independent city-state, staring out of my vagina like some telescopic creature in search of new universes to conquer, dreaming blue prints for rocket-ships, calculating lunar distances, threatening to erupt at once into a hyperbole which would rock my world.

The outline of your body still smolders in the lazy boy in the centre of our living room, which isn't really living anymore, though the title still hangs, as the rouge dust hangs from the wings of certain lunar moths, beating themselves blind against the red glow of the window the night you, me and the lazy boy went up in smoke.

They tell me that the most difficult thing to rebuild is the eyelids. That even glass eyes need lids. That skin grafted from pigs and laid over you like a poorly made quilt can be overlooked, but unblinking eyes / like an oracle's / staring into some fixed point in space must be interrupted. That the gaze cannot exist without the shutter action of relief.

So that, even now, as your body struggles to accept this pigskin quilt, it's the lids that they worry over. Sewing labial flaps over your eyes, teasing the edges [*here* and *here*] to ease your glass-socket gaze. But wounds erupt along the seam lines, and these newfangled lids of yours threaten to heal shut.

I lose the word for seamstress, as my fingers find that small bladed hook that will tear even the most carefully laid stitch. I will free you of that shutter blindness, so that like a ruler or a measuring tape or some creature that rose from that billion year gone slew, you will coil in and measure yourself and me from the gullet and tongue and the soles of your feet and find us somehow together, the same, the same.

Carol Rosenfeld

DYKE-OTOMY

there are two nuns on the cover of ON OUR BACKS
when I was little I used to wear my mother's black half slip
on my head as a veil
maybe that's why
as I listen to the S&M dykes
I have an urge to confess

I like white bread
      The Sound of Music is my favorite movie
            I use water imagery in my poems
                  fruit too, sometimes
                        when choosing a dildo, my maxim is:
                              "Less is more"

Yes, I did order wrist restraints
from the Good Vibrations catalog
but they were on sale
and besides
I can't find a woman
who will put the damn things on me
my dates just want to know
"Do you like children?"

eighteen year old college-drop out
living at home working as a receptionist
taking a poetry workshop at the Y
one night the leader mentioned a book
called *The Story of O*

I wrote down the title and author
and the following Saturday
I went to the fiction section
in a small suburban bookstore
and looked under the author's name
but *The Story of O* wasn't there
so I went to the sales desk
and asked if they had carried it
the man looked it up
LEERED at me
and said "That has to be specially ordered"
so I said "That's fine, please do, thank you very much"
and the next week when I picked it up
I thought, "Wow this must be an intellectual book—
there's no illustration on the cover"
so I took it home
yes, I took *The Story of O* home
to my parents' house
with the piano in the living room
and I started to read it

and my mind said, "OH!"
but my body said, "YEAH!"

right before I came out I visited my friend Steven
he asked me if I wanted to see a side of gay life I hadn't seen
and took me that Sunday afternoon to the San Francisco Eagle
where a leatherman with the eyes and air of a wizard
took my hand and said,
"If you see anyone you'd like to meet, you must tell me and
I'll be sure to introduce you"
I wondered if he knew something about myself that I didn't
and hoped I wouldn't need to use the bathroom

Steven explained to me
that he came out as a gay man,
then he came out into leather
then he came out into S&M
it took me thirty-eight years to come out as a lesbian
if I'm going to come out into s-something else
I'd better do it soon
before I get too old to remember my safe word

Cheryl B.

YOU ARE NOT THE HETERO DIVA

Your insanity permeates your entire body
you have no soul
your pap smear tested positive for prozac.

Like the Wicked Witch,
you came from the West.
Los Angeles to be exact and one year after meeting you,
I revel in the thought of you covered in shit and
you are in the deepest moat ever dug
but your liquid makeup does not move,
your lipliner does not move.

Behind your skewed and scattered empty blue eyes
lays a never-ending catfight between Linda Blair and Sybil.

You are a genital wart imbedded and festering deep within the vagina
of womanhood.

You feign serious women's political health issues to get attention,
to get us to feel bad,
to get us to feel lucky about our piddly lives as compared to yours.

Then we found out you don't have breast cancer,
you have breast implants.
You've never worked for Coppolla.
You don't know Wim Wenders, you can't even spell his name right.
Your birth mother is not a famous Hollywood screenwriter because
you're not even adopted.

It was lie after embellishment after augmentation.

Having a conversation with you was like taking the trolley around the land
of make believe over and over again.

And when I came home early that night to find you boiling away the chicken
gravy and looking like you had snorted one-hundred lines of cocaine,
I asked you what was wrong as if it was any of my business and I remembered

to take along the empty bottles of prescription drugs and motrin that you had abused for so long and had finally gone overboard and in the triage room of the hospital you told the nurse you were twenty-five when you had us all convinced that you were twenty-two.

Where does it end Kristy?

I was your friend,
I cared about you,
I put up with your doll of the valley bullshit.

We were going to make a film about being young and female in America, remember?

But now I'm not even sure if you're human, you fucked me over so bad I didn't know what hit me.

You fucked over Richard and Tom and a cast of thousands that were to play in your game of High Drama Queen no longer.

You give fag hags a bad name.

You are not gay man trapped inside a straight woman's body.

You are not the Hetero Diva.

You collect gay friends like you're curating some kinda freak show to become the bohemian intellectual you've always wanted to be.

You're one of those lezbophobic bitches who thinks that any lesbian or bi-sexual woman is just dying to fuck you.

I wouldn't touch your lithium happy snatch with a ten-foot pole.

And you ruined my summer.

You ruined the summer of 1994.

It was humid and hot and your twisted brain was ripe for the picking and you shoved me on sixth avenue and I felt like grinding your heavily made-up face into the brick siding of the Here theater and ripping your fake tits off because you told me I was insane.

But I don't get violent, I write poetry and I read the poems in public places
and I don't hold back.

Her name is Kristy Kooms and she lives in my old apartment on First Avenue
by St. Marks Place and she was my theatrical collaborator and together we
were going to do wonderful things.

And you should walk by her building and look up to the third floor window
and you'll see her there staring down, staring blankly, she's the one with the
really fucked up eyes but don't get sucked in, don't feel sorry for her.

Never trust a crazy bitch from Los Angeles, never let Kristy know your
weakness.

And now we group in bitch sessions and ponder is she insane or just mundane?

Is she human or evil muppet?

Can we ever trust anyone ever again?

And we find solace in the fact that someday we may tap dance on her grave.
We'll bring it on home on her grave.
We'll do the motherfucking Charleston on her grave.

You are not the Hetero Diva.
Nobody calls me a fucking dyke cunt.
You stole my roomate's lipliners.

We must excise this malicious aura, we must go on.......

Christian Langworthy

HOW COULD I INTERPRET THE EVENTS OF MY YOUTH, EVENTS I DO NOT REMEMBER EXCEPT IN DREAMS

Because I was a newly adopted
        child from another country,
(a prostitute's son in a Vietnamese

city bristling with rifles
and as a result of my mother's truancy
    from motherhood I was given
to nuns and locked within the confines
    of missionary walls)
I crossed the South Chinese Sea
    and Pacific in three days
(barely surviving anti-aircraft fire)
    aboard an eight prop-engine plane.
I came to this country
    to a nine-inch carpet of snow
and a sure welcome by strangers
    engaged with the possibilities of parenthood.

My new beginning consisted of firsts:
    first experienced snowfall in America—
(how it was magic in a fairy tale land)
    first toilet flushings,
(at the airport, when I flushed every
    toilet in the men's room to my new
father's delight)
    and another notable first—
the first cartoon I ever saw on Saturday
    morning: Bugs Bunny and Elmer Fudd,
and how there were no wounded or dead
    from the flying bullets,
and I laughed so hard I cried
    though I did not understand their language then.

As the years of my second life progressed,
    my adopted parents tried to be
a good father and mother and to the cinema
    we went, and I saw the children's epics:
Snow White and the Seven Dwarves
    and Sleeping Beauty; at home my mother read
fairy tales to me, tales like Rumpelstiltskin,
    and I learned
the false beauty of the wicked witch,
    the castle besieged by thorns,
the terror of the kidnapped son.
    I could have told them I'd seen these tales
before, but I was too young to know the difference.

Crystal Williams

IN SEARCH OF AUNT JEMIMA

I have sailed the south rivers of China and prayed to hillside Buddhas.
I have lived in Salamanca, Cuernavaca, Misawa, and Madrid.I have stood upon
the anointed sands of Egypt and found my soul in their grains. I am a global
earth child who is still excluded from conversations on vacation hot-spots.

I have read more fiction, non-fiction, biographies, poetry, magazines,
essays, and bullshit than imaginable, possible, or even practical. I am
beyond well read and am somewhat of a bibliophile. Still, I'm gawked at by
white girls on subways who want to know why and how I'm reading T.S. Elliot.

I have shopped Hong Kong and Bangkok out and sent them to replenish their
stock in heat so hot the trees were looking for shade—I was the hottest thing
around. Still, I'm followed in corner stores, grocery stores, any store.

I can issue you insults in German, Spanish, and some Japanese.
Still, I'm greeted by wannabe-hip white boys in half-assed ghettoese.

I've been 250pounds, 150 pounds and have lived and loved every pound in
between. I am still restricted by Nell Carter images of me.

I've eaten rabbit in Rome, paella in Barcelona, couscous in Morocco, and
am seated at the worst table by mentally challenged maitre'ds who think
my big ass is there for coffee.

I am still passed up by cabs
passed over for jobs
ignored by politicians
guilty before innocent
Black before human.

I am still expected to know Snoop Dog's latest hit
Mike's latest scandal
to believe in O.J.'s innocence.
And I am still expected to walk white babies
up and down 92nd street as I nurse them, sing a hymn and dance a jig.

Sorry, not this sista, sista-girl, miss boo, miss it, miss thang, honey,
honey-child, girl, girlfriend.

See, I am not your militant right-on sista wearing dysikis and 'fros with
my fist in the air spouting Black Power while smoking weed, burning
incense and making love to Shaka—formally known as Tyrone.

I am not your high-yellow saditty college girl flaunting Gucci bags and
Armani suits driving an alabaster colored Beemer with tinted windows and
A.K.A. symbols rimming my license plate.

I am not your three-babies-by-fifteen, green dragon lady press on nails
welfare fraud ghetto Ho whose rambunctious ass is stuffed into too tight
lycra with a lollipop hanging out the side of my mouf and a piece of hair
caught in a rubberband stuck to the top of my head.

I am not your timberland, tommy hilfiger, 10K hollow-hoop wearin
gansta rappin
crack dealin
blunt smokin
bandanna wearin
Bitch named Poochie.

And I am not your always supportive, constantly smiling, black-face
sounding board for your obsessive whining about those democrats and
decreased nra support.

I am not your conscious clearer.

I am not your convenient Black friend.

Notyourprototypenotyourselloutcause
massa and the big house is too good.

I am not your Aunt Jemima.

In my (8957) days of Black Womanhood I have learned this:
Be careful of what you say
of what you think
of what you do
because you never know who you're talking to.

David Jager

WORDS

When I was born
the doctor raised me up in one broad hand
raised a lexicon in the other
and slapped my mouth full of words
I've been trying to get rid of
ever since.
Sitting in my high chair
as an infant
I spat up alphabet blocks—
words crawled into my ear
and never left
Bright words, strange words, subtle words, ugly words
words that combined in incantations and spells
that put me in that corner of my room
or the office of the principal
sharp words, foreign words, comic words, sacred words:
I put my head through a book and gave birth to myself through words
touched the flesh of gods knitted together from words
became infected by and addicted to words—
At night I'd write out my body in words
that in the morning were blood bone hair and flesh made from words
peered at nothing through a window of words
tried hanging myself from a noose of words—
As I grow older the cycle accelerates
words flutter away from me like dead leaves
leaving me bare
causing my roots to go deeper
into words:
I fall down in words
drown in dreams of words
wake up gasping for words
shower in fragments of words
my tongue is a paper scrap flapping
in a gust of words
I eat words
shit words

fight my wars with words
dress my wounds with words
bury my dead with words—
You walk into a room and I paint your eyes
your body, your face with words
charm and cajole you with words
entice you home with words
slide you into a bed of words
so that we fight. grapple, pant, scream
and reach
for that final unspeakable word

or maybe silence

Just silence

CADILLAC BOMB

Cadillac Bomb
Baby
Cadillac Bomb
With razor fin shriek and
Ominous chrome
Rumbling down the midnight strip
Cadillac Bomb
Motored black shadow hearse
Bending light
Around the fender
Piston muscled panther grace and
WIDE
Back seat lust

Cadillac
Bomb
Baby

Death Waits

SCREENPLAY IDEA

It all takes place on a submarine
deep under the surface of the water
something is wrong with the engines, stranded
drifting every which way the currents take them

Before the opening credits a murder takes place
roll opening credits as an inquiry is instigated to find the culprit
an impromptu trial in the little room with the periscope
they have a suspect, select a jury, the trial commences
but no sooner have they begun to prosecute
than a second murder occurs
suggesting that possibly they have arrested the wrong man

So a new witch hunt begins
everyone suspecting everyone else
long, hazardous shots of the entire crew
running en masse from one end of the vessel to the other
a stampede of violent, panicked sailors
fleeing from the could-be-anyone murderer
while chasing after him at the same time
a second trial is begun, a second sailor
into the make-shift witness box
being drilled by some hot-shot rookie

And then, wouldn't you know it
a third murder takes place
this time all hell breaks loose
everyone has guns and no one is trustworthy
what's more, they are running out of oxygen
portals are opened, three sailors drown
in the watery onslaught
the ship is taking on water
three shootings take place, one after the other
all unfortunate accidents: two dead, one wounded
your time could come any moment, watch your back
the corridors take on all the subterranean menace
of Hitchcock's worst nightmare, the one where he drowns
and there's nobody to save him

Then, without warning, the killer is revealed to the camera
and to no one else—finally we know who did it
it is the person we least suspected and he is already dead
as the accidental killings continue to continue
and the submarine drifts deeper down
into the blood-soaked oblivion
of the sacred but unknowable depths

Donal Power

PORNO

he's making pornography
tonight on his living room floor
conducting a flesh epic of *Ben Hur* scale:
an aria of locusts beaten out
on an army of typewriters
as a friend might have said once;
this is how the rain carries-on
when stirred with ladles of lightning
he's making lonely love to the alchemical
rhythms of locust wings, chattering on pavement
the back of his skull, biblical buttocks
to the cool tongues of wood
someone's genius made to interweave

a cigarette runs down in the glass bowl
ignites a forsaken matchstick
and his fingers brush black mosses
pull his cock up, up into the Morse
of locust rain
an opal of semen balanced
on the tip.
thunderbolt smashes through
the reels of storm—it is the pleasure of
all the lovers in the world
wound together like onion
skins and shot from a sapphire cannon

makes his ass tighten sudden
plunging up pelvis, his harpist hands and penis
deeper into the epic infrastructure
clicking alphabets, cannonblasts
wet lacework wings

the audience, a drenched hedgehog
tiny under a bush outside
waits without a word
in the exact place where some moments before
a sumptuous leaf and a hedgehog mouth
became one

EXCAVATIONS

I heard the archaeologists confess today
those old Mayans weren't quite fragile builders, stargazers
but super-rude megalomaniacs, decapitation fetishists
How nobly they hacked and bashed their empires
into encyclopedias and packaged tours
Very unsettling
like rising this morning to uncover another silver filament
clanking in my scalp
or just when I could unravel next to you naked and unafraid
finding my services no longer required

at this hour, only me and gnatholithic Governor Ragbone
arguing his cup clear out of the Tim Hortons.
Must've seen the same show.
The all-night geezer knows this sour mugful
celestial temple glyphs finally unclothed
"then we offed the Zamboni-makers,
the Pouting Folk, the pygmy Mimes..."

The announcer explained the Maya soon ran out of strangers
and pureed their friends to pass the time
the camera blinked sideways, and I caught it
a small structure encoded
in the flesh of the primeval jungle
four stone posts and your duvet

Elena Georgiou

A WEEK IN THE LIFE OF THE
ETHNICALLY INDETERMINATE

Monday
Sitting in McDonald's on 103rd & 3rd
I notice a couple staring at me
and hear them say *Indian*
they walk towards me
the woman has white skin
blonde hair, blue eyes
the man has ebony skin
black hair, brown eyes
excuse me, says the woman
we were wondering
where you were from
yeah, says the man
because you look like
our people
I look at the whiteness
and the blackness
wondering who their people are
we're Puerto Rican, they say
and walk away

Tuesday
Walking to the store
in Crown Heights I see
an African-American man
sitting behind a table
selling incense and oils
he calls out sister, hey sister,
baby and then makes a noise
like he's calling a cat
I don't respond
on the way back
from the store
he calls out mira, mira,
hey baby,
in any language,

English, Feline or Spanish
I don't respond

Wednesday
I am buying lunch
at the falafel stand
on 68th and Lex
and the man serving me asks,
you from Morocco?
no, I say, Cyprus
where's Cyprus, he asks
above Egypt
to the left of Israel
and below Turkey
oh, he says looking blank
how much for the falafel, I ask
for you three dollars
for Americans three fifty
I go to pay and another man
stares hard into my face
and says, are you a Jewish chick
no, I say, just leave me alone
I know who you are, he screams
I know who you are
you're just a nigger from Harlem
passing for white
with a phony accent
nigger, he repeats
as I walk away

Thursday
My boss calls me up
I have a funny question
to ask you, he says
when you fill out forms
what do you write for ethnicity
I check *other*, I say
Well, I have to fill out this form
and it doesn't have *other*
we look really bad on paper
all the positions of power are white
and all the support staff are black
could you be Asian?

Friday
I am with my Indian immigration lawyer
do you mind if I ask you
a personal question, he says
go ahead, I say thinking
he is going to ask me
how I've reached my mid thirties
and have never been married
But, instead, he says
I know you're a Cypriot
from London
but do you have
any Indian blood in you
there are so many
mixed marriages these days
and you look like the offspring

Saturday
I am at a conference
and a European-American woman
looks at me excitedly
as though she's just won a prize
Oh, I know where you're from, she says
my daughter-in-law is an Indian
with a British accent too
I'm not Indian I say
continuing to not see me
she concentrates on
hiding her anger
for not winning the trophy
in her self-imposed
"guess the ethnicity" competition
and then she walks away

Sunday
I go to lunch at the home of a friend
whose family are Africans of the diaspora
they don't ask me where I'm from
later my friend tells me
they've decided you are
a biracial Jamaican

Later on, Sunday evening
I'm at a poetry reading
and an African-American woman
crosses the room
to ask me this question,
are you the colonized
or the colonizer?
what do you think, I ask
you could be both, she responds
and walks away

LESSONS IN HONESTY

I
We were two women
sitting on a bed
and I said
if I could have one wish
I wish I could sing
with a voice that made people cry
and I felt
what I said was
a rare ruby.

And she said
I can't tell you what I wish
because just saying it
makes me want to cry
but I pushed her
to say the words
and she said
I wish my sister could walk.

And in the silence
I felt selfish
in her selflessness,
mean in her generosity,
decadent in her sensitivity.
Wrapping her in my arms
we cried together
rocking as tears
mixed with mucus.

And in this moment
I felt moved to kiss her
eyelids, nose, chin
and keep kissing her
until the soothing rocking
changed rhythm
and moved into a grind.

And in this moment
I felt what I thought
was a masculine kind of hunger
but worst of all
the surfacing
of a moment
not shared
turning me
into an unanchored buoy
drifting guiltily
out to sea.

2
We were two women
sitting on a couch
and I said
I think there is no truth so bad
it can hurt as much as a lie
and I meant what I said
right to my marrow.

And she said
I can't tell you what I think
because just saying it
will incriminate me
but I pushed her
to say the words
and she said
lying
is the easiest thing in the world.
And in the silence
my body tightened
with distrust,
shivered with unease,
hardened for protection.

And in this moment
I wanted to take back

every truth
I ever told her
and wondered how many
of her truths
had been lies.

And from that moment
I monitored her movements,
words, remembering
the conversations of others
saying she's not to be trusted.

And from that moment
she said nothing
and did nothing
suspect
turning me
into an unanchored buoy
drifting warily
out to sea.

3
We were two women
sitting in a diner
and she said
if you could have one wish
what would it be?

And I said
I can't tell you what I wish
because just saying it
makes me want to cry
but she pushed me
to say the words
so I wrote them on a napkin.

I wish I could make love
for one night
with someone I loved
and who was in love with me.

And in the silence
I felt vulnerable
in my honesty,
needy in my revelation,
tears in my eyes.

And in this moment
I watched words
crumple in my fist
using the napkin
to wipe away
public tears
I wanted to escape
feeling angry at her
for forcing me
into a truth
I wanted
to avoid.

And she
in a moment
not shared
turned me
into an unanchored buoy
drifting defenseless
out to sea.

4
We were the same two women
sitting in the same diner
and I said—its your turn
what would you wish,
be honest.

And she said
I was wondering
if we could ever have a relationship.

And in the silence
I was shocked by her wish,
disappointed in her honesty,
cheated by the question.

And in this moment
of discomfort I suddenly
understood the words
to that silly song
by Nancy & Frank Sinatra saying
and didn't I go and spoil it all
by saying something stupid.

And in this moment
not shared
I turned her
into an unanchored buoy
drifting embarrassed
out to sea.

Emily S. Downing

WAR MOVIES: MEN IN ARMOR IN ARMS

this is about the bravery I see in you long for sometimes so hard
like metal and you are

a cold room cold war beaten black and white film junkie
a prisoner of wars on television and
I have never seen such a chaos of soldiers as those in you
in each direction they are hunted hunting hunched and hush now

waiting for instructions
(it's not you but if it was) you trying to flatten uncrease these
maps with your palm on the kitchen table you would know always just
how hard to press hard enough now hard enough they don't make
anymore heroes just like that one just like that they would smile
at you up at you in the last scene of this war movie your father
leaning back in the chair heavy knowing nods at the screen says,
yes, says, such bravery, says, I am so proud (his voice coming from
all directions)

bullets of rain on your thin frame rib cage and each shoulder
pressed against the brick now the wall is leaning into you the
world rocking and shifting its weight slowly a woman swaying walks
and is singing when the world rocks sea gently you have to be
strong standing straight keep the edges steady on nights full of
water and wind you are a mast a master of anything of holding and
of holding on

hunted hunting hunched and hush now waiting for the next old time
war time man to come on tv the carved black and white jaw line
dignity the way you press your own jaw together refusing to cry
this never happens to you the victory the simplest endings sunsets
shot down cigarettes and keep standing you feel sometimes as though
you were bleeding too strong to hurt to feel around for wounds keep
standing when the movie is over the screen will go dead blank like
the soldier's mind the one with no name who fell down you do not
want to watch that one the fade out the soft hushing sound of the
tv in static it is saying no where is anyone moving is glory is
anything on

and you will be the last man standing

waiting for when they will come softly final frame from every where
need you know you your name even rest hands on your back your back
is strong now strong enough

though there is no war on today

Golda Fried

THE DINER

BREAKFAST you ease your way in
like a knife through a jelly donut
saying hi to the manager as if he were your dad
I feel like I'm in your house
as you wipe off the crumbs on the table
with your sleeve

you smear my daze
as she takes the menus away
something comes scrambled

today the subway smells like donuts

LUNCH there's a circle of pink rubber
dish gloves
around our booth

my toes are like pie dough on the edge of a subway track
you say lift your stomach
I lift my stomach
you say give me your tongue
our stomachs touch
I burst open the washroom stall door
before we get caught
you make fingernail moons through the paint on the sides

look at the guy covering his girlfriend with cigarette mist
like this morning's newsprint
and look at her getting some home-made apple pie
gulping it down
in wafer-thin sucks

I'm always asking what kind of diner it is
you say, you don't have to memorize the menu until you work here
and you don't want to work here

the manager has "his girls" running around
one's pregnant
one's frown taints the whole place something foul
like glazed doughnuts under a steamed-up plastic display case
I am tossed one with coffee

she flems, *mugs of morning make me rag*
makes my fingers crawl into the icing

you hand me a napkin to write on
you say, write something that you could put
on the underside of the blinds
go on

you demonstrate
and words come for you like creases on a tent
but I can't do it—

DINNER and spatula coming down hard on beef patty
squashing it all out of shape
my mascara feels like oil

we're too distracted to eat
the waitress leans against the counter,
waiting for the fall of a toothpick

you rip the blinds down like newspaper and leave
like a final cut
the jelly seeps through all thick and red
my hands reaching out to the napkin dispenser
and I'm using the napkins,
I am

DUSK in a naugahyde booth near the back
every minute someone moves a shaker one table over
as they clean up

I can see you walking in with a shoulder stacked high
full of takeout
just to get kicked out   I write on egg shells

STICKY AISLES

in the summer of bicycle paraphernalia
we're at a movie theatre

I'm skipping stairs on the escalator up
thinking about souls in candy wrappers
a garbage bin full of everyone else's claws
the comfy chairs in the lobby

at home I have
dead hair over the bathtub
not in your fist

you draw up coke from the enclosed cup
never expecting the movie to be better than this

the movie going by like sunglasses

I'll tell you about how she passed me
her breath like a screen of cookies

the theatre seats
butterflies, while we're here

THE POETESS IN LATE AFTERNOON UNDERWEAR

angels on earth habitate in glass jars, she says this in her late afternoon
underwear. they like both the hardness and the fragility of the outer shell. they
breathe on the glass to remind you they have the smear of light, then turn into
their feathers. (and you can't shake them out like pills) everytime I reach for a
cotton ball, I scoop out more and more night into day. her glass jars are neatly
lined on a wooden plank. I have to drown in sleep now, she says. we were just
getting to her poetry. how she encases her poems in plastic sheets. I'll show
you where to get the plastic sheets, she says, then backs away greasy with
fingerprints. I was just thinking of coffee, I saw it spilling all over the plastic
but the words would be protected, I mean, I thought that's what the plastic
was for, the coffee spilling over *because of the poetry.* I wake up looking through
the window.

she is floating on the sidewalk laughing her head off for some guy, the laugh
stuck completely in her throat.

Guillermo Castro

BALLOONS FROM HELL

rubber-masked demons get themselves
invited to any party
blue-green children burst in mid-air
accidents bring no compassion

weeping mothers, *lloronas*, go away!
you are not needed here

for I will sweep the floor myself
collect fallen faces twisting

like eels
like whips

sew the pieces together
disguise seams as smiles

fatten their emptiness
watch them rise

horrible suns
bound to a fanged sky

FASCIST MANIFESTO
After Stephen Dobyns

The fascist midget within me
wants either sex on top or to get blown
and will come in seconds.
The fascist midget within me
lives for the Spanish Inquisition
with improved torture devices.
You have way too many books.
Burn them. And those dirty movies as well.
My fascist midget wants you,
tall, bright people, to put out
your cigarettes in your neighbor's cheek,
wants you to eat one meal a day
in damp houses, only after prayers.
The fascist midget cheats
the unemployed, the homeless, the meek,
the badly dressed into submission and,
if fitting, back to their countries of origin.
It's more tanks we need, not more "thanks,"
my fascist midget yaps
in the fascist midget meeting

where we all goose step around the room.
We need the dead quieter
and the living even more so.

SHIP OF FOOLS
To Stanley, an ex-landlord

We're in the same boat, you say.
But you hold first class tickets.

Heather O'Neill

INSOMNIA

we're at a dance club, costume ball of the urban empire
and this is where we like to go
I climb up the back fire stairs with
this older guy
I can see my boyfriend looking for me down below
wasting his time, he looks like an idiot even though I love him
the dancers are swinging from the ceilings
on their ambulance silver swings, shiny as medical tools
I'm just kidding with this guy because he was
        flashing his money
as though I had never seen a peacock before
my dad wouldn't let me wear peacock feathers because he said they were
                              bad luck
this curly haired outsider is lonely to the point of being dragged
        around by me
anyway I lose him going along the rat labyrinth to the can
I must have really big holes in my pockets
the bathrooms are pink, as icing, as a bridal shower
I slide off the metal doors
there's a boy wearing a sailor cap and his ass hops so high

behind him he reminds me of a puppet
he talks to everyone. Even me behind the stall walls.
I like any kind of company even bad.
Throwing up is comfortable for me tonight
It feels like I just straightened my tie

and I'm going to feel really good so that I will be satiated and have
        to sleep in another world
Because sleep, what's that been to me lately?
I could be taking a shower, I couldn't sleep
        stand out under the dance lights that are like rectangular hail stones
        exploding pink flamingo airplanes
and I can't even blink

my boyfriend nods to a girl's purse
o fuck me fuck me it's fucking easy. there she leaves it down again
am I a saint? do I believe in karma?
I will have to bank on there being no tomorrow
in the non-existent country, Quebec
what can I do about morality when
I should be feeling guilty about having a good time
being poor you have this paranoia you are spending the tax payers
money
            all the time

so here it is and I'm spreading out credit cards like butter
        on my hands
and shit, look, it's American money

American money, I love it
I can't believe it. I never believe the confetti and the New Yorks
        that pop out of these wallets
no matter how much I steal from strangers,
they always have more than me
            what's that about?

it's party's over for me: Cinderella time
the sign outside the club is a great ball glowing with something
        painted on it
blazing white with a little blue booty trim
goodnight to the sign that gets a face lift every two months
        everytime a management gets busted

That lightbulb orifice is so huge
I wonder if ships guide themselves by it or drive right into it,
    mesmerized like rabbits

whatever is crashing at the harbor
my boyfriend takes all the money and puts it in his pocket for safe
keeping,
        he says
and time has a little glitch, takes a curtsey that lasts too long and I see
its privates
I let myself be carried off on a stretcher in bloomers
I'm less interested in the war all of a sudden,
I'll be forever less interested in looking at him,
        because I have doubted what he's about
at home the light in the staircase has sprained a muscle
it must be illegal for the landlord to rent these spaces out
  because the hallway windows have been painted black
there are scratches and chips where the moon bets through
I feel it like a silk umbilical cord inside me
        even though it doesn't help me find the keyhole much

I pull my shoes off and the nylons are all ripped at the toes
my fingers are cigarette brown and my throat is numb
my boyfriend's passed out before me again
jerking off in his sleep

I hang around the window of his 200lbs
but its no good
the danger signs from the power plant
and the river port are buzzing fluorescent sounds, what I imagine a
snail would
        sound like if it could sing,
and I never sleep

WEDDING DRESS

money in your sneakers
cat under the bed I'm allergic to
cigarette stubs in your sink
and shrimp in the freezer
look you are always going to be
        my homeboy aristocrat

but there is no wedding ring rattling in the
    toilet
like a basketball skirting the rim

will I come back for you
well, will you come back for me
here comes morning wrapped around itself
    like a bath towel
lightweight curtains all stained
  with it
thin toes twinkling under the hair net
               sky
shot full of thimble holes
who never knows what I
will think about when a new day
comes around
screwing up the chopstick color
of this shaded bulb evening
screwing up the tranquillity of a swim
    we have been in

I can love, maybe
I'm standing on a suburb train track really
    swinging over the city neighborhood
with a fishing rod out like a gun
I'm hopeful about bait
I keep loading more and more on
winding up my legs
wasting money on clothes even though
    I'm a single mom
but I come back home usually like a stick of glue
  covered in cat hair
and grains of cement

I borrow my sister's wedding dress
a garage style wedding dress
I've turned it off white with one armpit torn out
crass love from a popsicle stand is what I date
and I would bite a knife if I could feel like
    running after it
instead I go waltzing for the doorknobs   wander off downtown
to the slanted dancers out on St. Saint street
    advertising their girls

I wear a plastic bead purse
have the glow of a low rent clothing store

I will sleep beside your building
I will sleep on top of your building
I can even sleep underneath your building
but really really I cannot sleep inside your building
even though you give me flies in candy wrappers
we are scuffling by the door again
and I see the future of your fists
      I am not a private strip show,
    just not private for anyone
there are different princes of love
the cleft nose pigeon picking up a seed from the sidewalk
that's me raising the polluted phlegm in my throat
      to begin a poem that says:
there are different princes of love

I go to find night who stands up in shock with
      nothing but his stockings
night with his army pension
and loose elastic underwear
loose as beer on loveless balconies
the moon is the colour of his old, old
      underwear
night is glad I took time off a man
to come by and see him
he has the magic box of songs of the past
    the de Michelangeli of songs of the past
the Glenn Gould pills of the made up past
he wants me to contribute to them
to give a little alms
and yes something, anything spoken at all
by me now
might be as niggardly and present
    as the kind of love I want.

Jeffery Conway

PRE-APPROVED OFFER TO A POET IN DEBT

There is no money in anything holy —Judy Grahn

"Dear Sir, Congratulations! You're Pre-Approved!"
So you pick up a pen and write $50,000
as "yearly income" and put poet
as "occupation," then laugh
because you're penniless and hate to lie,
but the only hope is another credit
card. Lick the envelope: sticky poison
on your tongue tastes like gold stars
you seldom won in grammar school. An orange
fright wig bobbing in (strangely enough) a green
cab catches your eye on the street—a clown
crying in the back seat, bizarre as a guest on a daytime TV

talk show. He's whisked away in a second. You're reminded of a TV
movie about a serial boy murderer who proved
circus drag is evil—he donned a rented clown
suit & red rubber nose to close-in for the kill. "$5,000
Fine For Tampering With U.S. Mail," the institutional green
letters warn on the lid of the box. Dear poet,
when your parents painted their house orange
a few years ago, you laughed
even though you knew your stars
were doing some funky shit. "I love it," you lied.
Your mother complained of weeds, sprinkled poison
about the yard. Much to your credit,

you didn't say a word—your first credit
application required a co-signer. Like a black and white TV
show, the yard was drained of color. The poison,
much too strong, obliterated all signs of life. Disapproving
neighbors signed a petition—no reason to lie—
and were bluntly rude at a block party. The clownish
house mocked your ill-starred
family until just last month, when your mom sunk $25,000
into a new yard, stuck out her tongue and laughed

at the sour neighbors—her newly laid green
sod a perfect shag rug in the sun. Your mind flashes to a faded orange
terra-cota statuette atop a buffet table. A troubadour poet

wanders around the dining room singing his poems
accompanied by a mandolin player in tights. Later, they are credited
with the success of the party by the hostess who's wrapped in an orange
Givenchy original. She looks like an ancient blonde TV
sitcom star. Before the guests arrived, as you decorated with greens,
she flew into the room like a poison
dart: "If anyone bumps into my statuette," she said with a dry laugh,
"save the piece *not* the person!" You didn't approve
of the way she called you and the other waiters "boys", but at $25
an hour, you were willing to smile and lie.
Meanwhile, the rent is due, so you run like the zombie-stalked star
of *Carnival of Souls* to the ATM with its mechanical clown-

like personality, just as scary as the drive-thru clown
at Jack-in-the-Box in your hometown. Punch in your PIN, 6527 (POET)
and watch the cash advance. You are a star,
not because you were once shot for *Interview*, but because your credit
card upped your limit. Money=success, an obvious lie,
like the one that editor told you while sipping a chilled Orangina:
"The 80's were all about materialism, artists after tons of money;
we want 90's artists who don't care about fame" —logic as insipid as MTV's
Real World actress who plays a "real" actress struggling for approval,
telling the camera how tough it is to make it, how she must keep it green
as she faces rejection and the pain of being an "unknown." You laugh
because her "realness" was usurped the moment she clutched that poison

pen and signed on the dotted line; the moment that poison
lens focused on her "unknown" face, she became a ditzy clown.
You too were duped, throwing your head back and laughing
while that bloodsucking magazine editor praised your poetry,
your honesty. As you walk away from the ATM, green
stuff in hand, thank the trees your face was dropped from that star-
starved rag. Back at home, you're greeted by another pre-approval
letter, this one from Martina Navratilova, pushing Queer Credit
for Gays, Lesbians, Bisexuals, but no transgendered, t.v.'s
or drag queens, please. The *Rainbow Card*, because your strength lies
in buying power. With monthly minimum payments of $338,
you'll get behind Martina's flag of purple, blue, green, yellow and orange.

Dear Sir, You're Pre-Approved! A credit line of $5,000
awaits you, poet, *priest of nothing*, so stop whining, have a laugh.
It's no lie you're queer—but oppressed? Maintain good credit,
behave yourself—no poison pen letters—and you'll be a star
to companies and political parties, those apples & oranges, each green
with greed, indistinguishable from clowns, as unreal as real people on TV.

STARSTRUCK II

I arrive at Gregory Hines' apartment in the West Village at 3:15 P.M. I'm
running late and my tuxedo is in a suit bag slung over my arm. The captain of
the party orders me to change immediately and start setting the buffet table. I
go into the laundry room and shut the door. I take my clothes off and notice a
pair of black Calvin Klein underwear in a green plastic basket on top of the
washing machine. I lock the door then slip the briefs on. I dress in my tuxedo
and go into the kitchen. Gregory Hines is standing there and turns to shake my
hand. I stare at him and smile. I'm thinking, *I've got his underwear on.* He leaves
the room. I get nervous and tell the captain that I forgot something and must
return to the laundry room. He huffs, "Hurry please," and rolls his eyes. Safe
behind the locked door, I strip and remove the underwear, place them strategi-
cally in the green basket. I dress again, return to the buffet table, and begin to
decorate it with lemon leaves.

I'm passing a silver tray of potato pancakes around a crowded living room. I
offer some to a small group of people standing in a corner. A woman turns
around and eyes the tray. It's Jane Curtain. She smiles at me (all upper teeth)
and grabs a pancake. I circle around the room. I notice Jane staring at my tray
when I pass by her again. She turns, smiles (all upper teeth) and grabs another
one. I circle the room once more and she is still staring at my tray. She smiles
at me (all upper teeth) and takes another. "If you keep this up," she says
laughing, "I'll need a twelve step program for latka addiction!" I smile back (all
upper teeth).

I'm standing at the top of a spiral staircase in my tuxedo. The captain of the
party has ordered me to lead the "dessert train"—a procession of waiters,
each carrying a different fancy dessert: trays of sorbet in the shape of different
fruits, profiteroles, chocolate truffles, et cetera. I'm actually O.K. with my
duty, until the captain hands me two three-foot sparklers, lights them, and
snaps, "Make it good." I descend the stairs. The theme from *Rocky* blasts from
hidden speakers. I can't see much because of the intense glow of the sparklers,
but when I march past the head table at the foot of the stairs, I see Henry
Kissinger and his blonde wife. Henry claps once or twice, then goes back to

the conversation he's having with the man sitting next to him. Mrs. Kissinger stares at me apathetically and reaches for her white wine glass. Her left eyelid flutters, then closes shut as she takes a healthy gulp.

I'm cutting chateaubriand at an antiques show. Bored stiff, I look around the room and pretend I'm on a *Wheel of Fortune* buying spree. A woman dressed in black wearing a floppy hat approaches the buffet table and asks (looking past me) for a lean cut. "Sure," I say. "And can you put it on a roll?" she asks with her head turned away. "Sure," I say. I realize it's Barbara Streisand. I start to slice a sourdough roll. "Don't cut yourself." "Don't worry," I say, "I cut the tip of my thumb off once—I'm real careful now." I hold up my left thumb for her inspection. She stares expressionless at my scar. I smile and resume cutting the meat which is oozing blood onto the carving board. I look at Barbra, who is staring at my knife. "How's that?" I ask, holding up a thin, dripping piece. "Fine," she says, FINALLY looking directly at me from behind her red-tinted sunglasses.

I report to the twenty-fifth floor of an upper East Side tower. I ring the bell to the apartment. A voice from behind the door yells out, "Please use the servant's entrance down the hall." I walk down the plush corridor and a small door flies open. A woman in a bathrobe and slippers with a hair net, no make-up and big glasses is standing there. "Hi," I say, "I'm with the caterers." She mumbles something about me being the first to arrive and leads me into the dining room where we begin to sort patterns of silver. After a few minutes I ask, "Will Mrs. Merrill be down soon?" The woman looks at me blankly. "I'm Dina Merrill." "Oh," I stammer, "of course." She tells me curtly that I may put my belongings upstairs in the maid's room. The hallway leading upstairs is plastered with framed magazine covers from the fifties. Some blonde woman is pictured on each cover. One of the captions reads "Exciting Dina Merrill!" *Oh shit,* I think, *she must be someone.* I put my bag down on the maid's bed and start back towards the kitchen. The last photo at the end of the hallway shows Dina on a beach in a yellow bikini. She's bending over to pick up a shell and her boobs are just about to fall out of her top. She has a weird expression on her face—as if she's saying, "Whatever you do, don't spank me." I enter the kitchen and see a note on the table: "Please sort plates. Upstairs to change— D.M." I look into the glass cabinets—a total mess, too many patterns to sort. The intercom phone rings and I answer. The catering van has arrived, I'm asked to go down and unload. I pick up a pen and write on the same piece of paper: "D.M., Sorry—have to unload. Will sort later—J.C."

Joan Rivers has volunteered to work as a maid at this (Dina Merrill's) party— a catered dinner auctioned off for some charity. She and I twirl through the crowded apartment and pass fussy hors d'oeuvres. Mario Buatta, of interior design fame, has volunteered to be the butler. Joan is funny—passing smoked salmon on toast points, making jokes. Mario goes a little far. He has a bag full of gag toys (hand buzzers, woopi cushions, chattering teeth) and spends the whole evening annoying the guests. Dina Merrill keeps fake-laughing as Mario pulls prank after prank. I hear Joan say to another guest, "That man is so immature—obnoxious—he needs to give it a rest." Alone in the kitchen with Joan replenishing our trays, I say "She's a mess." Joan looks at me intensely. "The hostess?" she asks. "Well," I say, "her too, but I meant Mario."

Beverly Sills and her elderly husband are sitting in the living room with Dr. Ruth and a couple of other people I don't recognize. I pass a tray of lobster vol au vons. As I near the couch, I smell something unpleasant and figure Beverly Sills' husband is either incontinent or has just passed gas. I pretend not to notice, yet can't help but giggle a bit when Dr. Ruth stands up and says, "Yes, but I must mingle" and exits the room with the other guests. Beverly stays dutifully at her husband's side on the sofa.

The catering company I work for has been hired to do a summer dinner party at Anchorman Bill Buetel's house in the Hamptons. When we arrive at Bill's home, his wife, Adair, makes everyone a drink. The chef unpacks the sirloin he'll be cooking and Bill exclaims to Adair, "Honey, just look at that piece of meat!" When the guests arrive there is a sudden downpour and the party moves inside. Adair spends most of the time in the kitchen with the waitstaff, drinking vodka and smoking cigarettes. She had made such a fuss about the plenitude of crystal ashtrays placed throughout the house that I'm surprised to see her plopped on a kitchen stool, drink in hand, flicking her ashes into an empty Planter's Peanuts can. Later, as the guests begin to say good-bye, Adair decides that the waitstaff should spend the night. I've just seen *The Comfort Of Strangers* and I have no intentions of staying to be murdered. Adair coaxes us with things like "Ya'all can skinny dip in the pool," and "Ya'all can watch TV," and "Ya'all can sleep in the guest rooms." I discover that the guest bathroom has a clear skylight and the hallway upstairs has a window that overlooks the guest bathroom and that with the right twist of neck, one could see everything in the bathroom from upstairs! I convince the other waiters to run for their lives. We pack up the catering truck quickly while Bill and Adair stand on the front porch begging us to stay.

I'm standing behind a pink marble bar and I've drank more cocktails than I've actually made for customers. A heavy woman approaches me and croaks, "What's a girl got to do for a martini around here?" She complains about the service, says the waiter has disappeared. The voice gives her away—it's Brenda Vaccaro. "You're all so young," she snaps. "This place is just like Twenty-one in

New York—you're all just boys." I ask her politely what kind of gin she would prefer. She rolls her eyes and says with condescension, "I don't care, whichever you think is best." I spin around and grab a bottle of Bootles. "Have you tried this one?" I ask. She squints at the label. "Bootles?" "Yes, Bootles," I say imperviously, "a gin I can trust and so can you."

I'm crossing 11th Street at University. I see a woman with red hair coming my way. I stop in the middle of the intersection—I can't believe it, Donna Ponterato. "Donna!" I scream. "Donna Ponterato! What are you doing in New York?" The woman stares at me. "I'm not Donna," she says nicely. "Yes you are," I say, "remember me? It's Jeffery from L.A." The lady smiles. "I'm not Donna Ponterato." I look at this woman's chest, which isn't as big as Donna's (although it's pretty big). The woman raises her eyebrows when I look up at her. "No," I say, "you're not Donna Ponterato." I keep walking and when I reach the curb I realize it's Susan Sarandon.

I'm at a small art opening in West Hollywood. The artist, Joni Mitchell, is showing recent work and giving away free LPs of her new album, "Dog Eat Dog." I'm not real clear on who Joni Mitchell is, but it's a Thursday night and the white wine is free. I wander around the room and view the canvases that are smeared with red and black paint. There's a blonde woman dressed in black standing in a corner. Someone is talking to her. She doesn't say anything, just stands there and nods silently. I notice she's staring across the room at me. She looks kind of bored so I walk over and stand near her. She glances at me, nods one more time at the man in front of her, then turns in my direction. "Hi," I say, "Do you like the artwork?" The woman keeps staring at me—no, at my New Wave hair: Bleached blond, permed on top, shaved to the skull on one side. "It's very, um, black and red!" I say with a laugh. The woman looks at me and nods. She puts her hand out and says coldly, "Nice to meet you." "Jeffery." I say. "Joni." she says, then turns away.

I'm passing a tray of drinks in a very modern upper East Side penthouse. There's this hunky guy standing in the middle of the room. I keep looking at him, but he won't look back. I'm bored, so I decide to make it a challenge. I go into the kitchen and get a fresh tray of white wine. I pass by the hunk and offer him a glass. "No, thank you," he says, glancing at me. I go into the kitchen and refill my tray with Perrier. I pass the hunk again. "Perrier?" I ask coyly. He looks at me and says, "No, thanks." "Are you sure?" He's having a conversation with a blonde woman who is gushing, "I just love your work." I interrupt, staring at the hunk, "Can I get you *anything* to drink?" "Well," he says looking at me, "if it will make you happy, I'll have a Diet Coke." I glance at the blonde, who is glaring at me. "I'll have a glass of Champagne," she announces. "Sorry," I

shrug. "We only have sparkling wine." "What's that?" she snips. "If you don't
know the difference between sparkling wine and Champagne, dear, you most
likely won't be able to taste the difference, so I'll bring one straight away." In
the kitchen, one of the other waiters asks me if I'm trying to pick up the hunk.
"Oh please," I say. "You know who it is, don't you—Alec Baldwin." "Who?" I
ask. "Alec Baldwin, idiot, the actor." "Oh please," I say as I spin out of the
kitchen with my tray. I've never heard of Alec Baldwin and I'm a little irritated
that Hollywood has its hooks in him. I go over to the blonde and hand her the
sparkling wine. "Here your are, dear." Alec has turned his back on her and he's
now talking to Joanne Woodward. "Here," I say, passing him the Diet Coke.
"Oh, thank you," he smiles. "We'd like to get some more drinks," he says,
motioning to Joanne and some other woman. I turn my back and pick up some
empty glasses from a marble cocktail table. "Excuse me..." he calls. I pretend
not to hear him and whisper under my breath "Oh please" as I weave my way
to the other end of the penthouse.

THE ALBUM THAT CHANGED MY LIFE

> *Music pours over the sense*
> *and in a funny way*
> *music sees more than I.*
> *I mean it remembers better...*
> —Anne Sexton

The first album I owned was Billy Joel's
The Stranger, and I hated it. Kathy
Dunlap, a big redhead I knew from church
youth group, gave it to me for Christmas in
1979. I had little
interest in music—born in the 60s,
I was always between movements. Disco
didn't move me, but "Cars" by Gary Numan
did. It was 1980—
it took time for New Wave to reach the suburbs.
In bed one night, listening to my clock-radio,
I heard "Here in my car, I feel safest
of all, I can lock all my doors, it's the
only way to live, in cars..." I was starved.
Entranced by Gary's eerie, nasal voice,
I couldn't sleep till I bought his album,
The Pleasure Principle, which was only

available on cassette, at the Licorice Pizza
downtown. The one tape player at home
was in Mom's brand-new Olds Cutlass Supreme.
No one was allowed in her car, so each night
I'd sneak into the dark garage,
quietly open the plush velvet door,
pop in the tape, and listen for hours
at a time, memorizing the words to each song.
I studied the pictures of Gary on the insert.
Within a week I had a crewcut
and was bleaching my hair blond with
a bottle of hydrogen peroxide I found
in the hall closet. I started
to shop at thrift stores, buying only black.
Mom screamed, "Christ, what are you doing
to yourself!" I'd stare blankly and answer
in a monotone, "Am I a photo? I can't remember"—
a line from "My Conversation," one of
my favorite songs on Gary's album.
Soon I discovered K.R.O.Q.,
the "Roq Of The 80s," a New Wave station
in Pasadena that played songs like
"Los Angeles" by X, "Sex Dwarf" by Soft Cell,
"President Am I" by Slow Children,
"Blue Monday" by New Order,
"Only A Lad" by Oingo Boingo,
"Just Can't Get Enough" by Depeche Mode,
"Blind Vision" by Blancmange, "The Love
Cats" by The Cure, "I Want To Be Jackie
Onassis" by Human Sexual Response,
"Are We Not Men" by Devo, "Flavor Crystals"
by The Suburban Lawns, "I Might Like You Better
If We Slept Together" by Romeo Void,
"Damaged Goods" by Gang Of Four,
"Planet Claire" by the B-52s,
"No-Where Girl" by B-Movie, and two
of my favorites by Missing Persons,
"Mental Hopscotch" and "I Like Boys"—
a song I only hummed around the house,
afraid my older brother
would hear the words and peg me a fag.
I turned 16 and my parents bought me

my first car—a 1973
AMC Hornet Sportabout Wagon.
It was bright yellow with a brown plaid
interior. I was humiliated.
The only thing that made it bearable
was the stereo cassette player and
speakers I bought at Radio Shack.
I'd put on my black wrap-around New Wave
sunglasses, push in Gary Numan, and sing
along at the top of my lungs, "Am I
a photo? I can't remember."
I used the hidden trunk in the rear
of my Hornet to stash Bacardi and Seagram's
bottles. This was the one feature about
the Hornet, besides the stereo,
that I missed after I pushed it
off a cliff in Malibu Canyon
a year later. I turned to my friend Worm,
my accomplice, and said, "Was the Hornet
a photo? I can't remember."
With the insurance money I bought a
'67 Mustang that transported
me to dance clubs like Phases
in the San Fernando Valley.
They played all the KROQ hits and
the latest British dance songs.
But there was more than music and clove
cigarette smoke inside the clubs:
His name was Craig, the first
boy who ever came on to me—right in
the middle of Thomas Dolby's "She Blinded
Me With Science," on the dance floor at the
Odyssey in West Hollywood.
He was 17, I was 18.
I told him I was straight—no, bi—but that I
definitely I had a girlfriend (a big lie).
Driving home in my blue Mustang, I threw up
in a light green Tupperware container
which I threw out the window at 70 MPH.
Was it my newly sparked sexuality
or the quart of booze I'd guzzled?
I was aware of my youth.

The dance clubs gave me glimmers of what
I hoped would be. I knew that life after
high school would deliver me to far off,
liberating places. Those nights provoked
what I later came to identify
as a "celebrity feeling," a feeling
that led me to New York City where I
twirled, fell flat in a club while dancing
to an old Nina Hagen song, and finally
learned how to live. New Wave was out,
and there were fewer glamorous clubs
toward the end—mostly dark bars, Death Rock
or The Smiths, and the sheet-rock walls
of my East Village apartment. Today,
it's all about Stevie Nicks. I play her
80s albums over and over, trying
to figure out what it is I missed
the first time around. Her latest single
is "Desert Angel," a moving song
about Operation Desert Storm.
In the video, she spins in a circle and wails,
"This can't be happening. We will always
love you, Desert Angels." Poor Stevie,
sober and shawl-less in the 90s.
Her tapes sit on the shelf next to
my original copy of Gary Numan's
The Pleasure Principle. But where's
Gary? I lost the insert of the cassette case
years ago, yet when the tape goes in
the player and I hear him singing
those ambiguous lyrics over
the drone of synthesizers,
I can picture Gary—
pale skin and black mascara,
so cold and so distant.

"Am I a photo? I can't remember."

Jonathan Goldstein

5000 EJACULATIONS

5000 ejaculations
sit on my shelf above
the fridge
like beer bottles
clacking like false
teeth at night in
the bathroom
(you pad there in gentle
fluff slippers looking
for alka-

seltzers for your sunday
night stomach [who
knows about next
week & the next]
or 5000 ejaculations)

little white gooey
asterixes in
dixie cups

what're you afraid for?

the come shots of
history are mounted
like a moose
head on the kitchen wall

they don't fear

but it's sunday night &
they can't fear

the clock spins on like
an olive tripping down
a spiral staircase

5000 ejaculations cannot save
you one step

my life is mapped out
in 5000 lite brite stars
scratching for the real
orgasm the always
taut nipple
the pre/post coital world

coit-ta-tit-tee-coily-oily
world

all the trees felt
up in lotions & spermy
fingers

so why do 5000 ejaculations tremble?

they, my reindeer,
pull Santa-fat-bastard-
me
through the snow of
all those faces
faces faces
creamy white tits not
a drop of blood or
nipple

5000 ejaculations be/come
5000 pillars raising
my bed up to the ceiling
where my dink rubs out
some Sistine ceiling
image of Adam

5000 ejaculations be/come
5000 arrows stuck
to my tummy
at the end of a hard
night

5000 ejaculations cannot pure
me of 23 dirty
thoughts &
5000 ejaculations be/come
2000 angry kids who want
a reason why
(papa's so on on the couch
all funked & watery)

10000 pee-pees are
10000 times more simple
all in the toilet
10000 flushes lead em
out to the great sewer
universal consciousness
swimming 8 feet under
our feet so:

all you dixie cups square dance
all you spunk rags knot
you lil white white-outs
become the white hot sun
beating me down bald-headed

on a hot new bleached beach.

Julie Crysler

THE FURY

I've got a raging Plymouth Fury,
built the same year I was born.
She's a lot like me, got a vicious streak
that's at least a mile across.
Her body's nothing to write home about
but she was smokin' from the start
and the speed I squeeze from her rusted-out carcass
is the sheer g-force of desire.

The guy in the next lane's got a black Camaro
and I've got my pedal ready to gun.
I eye him up with a nasty sneer,
because unless he's got an airplane engine,
I'll leave him in my dust.
He gives me a slimy wink, the stupid macho pig.
So when he points his finger
like a hell-bent arrowhead
I'm set to raise the dead.

My last lover said he'd never seen anything hotter
than a girl behind the wheel.
Well, I'm a woman now, and I've got
the Hubs of Hades to rattle at my will.
You wanna drag? I'll drag you *down*
with blazing flames for wings.
Hell hath no fury like a woman scorned
and my Fury's more than a match for hers.

The light winks green as a jealous lover's eye
and I leave him in the blackest wake I can muster
with the screech of tires chasing behind.
It's a blur of lights as I hurl us down
It's a blur of lights as I pull ahead
It's a blur of lights
It's a blur of lights
Christ, I've got fire shooting out my ass.
I may not be much of a looker,
but you should see me fucking *drive*.

SNAKE CHARMING

A woman who lives
in the back woods of Kentucky
says
you put three drops of menstrual blood
in your man's morning coffee

if you wanna keep him true.

These little spells never seem to work for me.
I'd smear myself all over town
if I thought it would draw your love
better than these cheap mojo candles.

I've been hauling on you
like a chain-smoked pack of cigarettes, so
every time you sleep in someone else's bed
I feel like I'm breathing.

To death.
& I know I'm to blame
'cause I picked your ass out of a crowded bar
I decided
                    three tequilas short of paradise
that you

                    your name escaping me
                    after that all-too-brief introduction
that you
would love me.

See
I picked you out.
You had no part in the matter.
I picked you out
power dripping off my newly painted nails
drawing you in like magnetic blood
smoke-hazed magic seemed
sympathetic
to my cause.

I brought you home with me
Wild crazed   out-of-control
        you came.

In about
thirty seconds.

As you rolled over
large lumbering bear snores
the sex-smell of your breathing
fermenting in the air
I wished I had checked my spell book

a little more carefully.

It seemed
strange

to me
that a body as beautiful as yours
round   &   hard
                    in *just the right* places
could fail so miserably
at a test
as simple
as this.

& yet this voice said in me
                    a voice that when it speaks up
                    I should decline to listen
                    or just paint the person in question
                    rather than fuck him
that squeaking small voice
compassionate
compelling
told me you were *so* beautiful
& you were probably just

drunk

                    or

tired

                    or

excited

silencing that pain in my groin that said perhaps
you were just
a lousy lay.

See
you pay the price when you start relying on spells

the magic always seems to work better on you
than the intended victim.
The contagion of blood desire spills over onto you
wanting it to work so much
that you will do *anything*
just to have that person
you imagined
you saw
in that crowded bar.

& when that person seems transformed &
serpentine
not quite what you expected
the temptation is just a little too much
& one spell leads to another
& I'm praying
& I'm putting my *blood* in your *coffee*
& I'm putting on clothes that I think you'll like
I'm trying so hard to be that person
you dreamed of
even though I was the dreamer
all along.

You see, I'm sick
of handling snakes.
I haven't the faith
of a Southern Pentecostal
I seem to get stung
more often than I see God.

& now it's time
to drop the trappings & the traps I laid
it's time
I'm tossing out
incense candles makeup & lingerie
it's time
it's time

it's time
to get that stinging
gone.

Mark Bibbins

YOUR SHIRT

maintains its shape
on the hanger
regardless of you.

It can't remember
the warm touch
of your living

flesh against it,
and does not know
or care where you are.
It does not need
to wrap its own
arms around itself

in the dark
and imagine they belong
to you.

BLIND
for Derek Jarman

There was no dawn today.
Rain on the windowpane
waits to be licked clean
by sun that forgot to shine.
Outside, your voice rises

through a subway grate
and metal wheels shake out
a list of names. I wait to see
if I remember yours.
All I feel now is blue—a cliché

under any light, even none,
but I let it engulf me.

I scoop out my eyes
and offer them to you
in a darkened theater

where a puzzled audience
whispers at an empty screen,
and I start to inch back blindly
toward the arms and mouths
from which I have fallen.

ORACLE

How swift we had been,
when you died, to change
your answering machine message:
The dead shouldn't
speak unless spoken to.

Your voice had become another
of so many photographs,
pairs of shoes, souvenirs
left for us to decide
whether or not to keep.

Now, three years later,
I am startled at finding
just a second of a message
you had left on my machine,

a tiny mass of ions adrift
on a narrow stream of tape—
floating like the paper boat
the child runs beside
before it sails out of sight.

THE PARTS OF THIS WE REMEMBER

For Salaam al-Saidi, who, on April 20,
1995, was stillborn at seven months
when citizens of Oklahoma City stoned
his parents' house.

Without television, they might have been
no more than stolen coins left
on a railroad track and flattened,

making it difficult to imagine faces
with mouths telling us
that love is not a feeling
but a decision some people don't make—
and heaven is even better than peace.
In a laundromat in Manhattan

a Korean man stands bewildered
as he stares at his wet clothes
falling in circles behind the glass

like seaweed in a wave,
as if they might have an answer.
The owner of the laundromat is convinced

the Korean man will understand English
if he yells his words and repeats them.
There are men even worse than this

on the radio tonight, telling us
we need tougher immigration laws.
It is hard to think

of a building as being alive
until we see its entrails trying to close
themselves around a wound

and failing. We can almost see
the sky pull back
during the next few days,

affording space in which to die.

Somewhere, an Iraqi woman is driven
through the rooms of her house

by pale, stone-throwing hands
until her premature contractions
push a stillborn son

into the righteous Midwestern air.
No one says, "Bring us a picture
of this baby to put on our news."

When this, too, becomes mythology,
theologians will argue whether or not
an angel came to whisper in the ears
of people who needed to know:
When you try to count the babies,
one will always be missing.

Ron Drummond

ATTENTION TO GRAY

early
again
still
dark

again
awake
dark
light

awake
it's
light
too

it's

still
too
early

THE CROSSING

The rear axle of a schoolbus
is suspended over railroad ties.

A force more demanding than
screams has its way.

Some children are killed at once.
Somersaults snap others.

A boy up front

heard the southbound train
and turned around in time

to see a friend's profile
just before the wreck.

He dreams about a nuclear flash,
about flesh pulling away from flesh.

Shafiq

TACKY TACK

Tacky tic tack toe as we roll across the floor of green underbellied
bits and pieces of new world billybats of decadence
you know as I slip slappity slide stride down Queen Street
the slight smiles and cocky airs ride by in rage

Tacky tic tack wacks as I dose in on the specimens of life
that garner lifeless the city smell of gas-imbued death threats
I smile as cats and racoons scattle and reaw rack reaw at each other
the puzzle pieces present me with a picture to just take in.

Tacky tic tack toe as they roll in on me like roller blades
Questions of sensuality, questions of sexuality rack my back with ungratifying
    anxious... But listen,

There's a Chinese poet in New York who found it only
one of his works of art to tie himself to a woman
without touching her for three hundred and sixty-five days ... no joke
there's a Chinese poet in New York whose gallery display
was to take a shit in that posh stosh-aired Dada exhibit for champagne
connoisseurs to see
No mistake Jake, this Jack knows that freedom ain't doin' whatever
But whatever we're doin' to do it in such fervor
with such undivided concentration and love
that few can refute the part-purity of that passion

Tacky tic tack wacky gets organic living in the midst of phallic concrete towers
    and giant dustbins for massive electrifying entertainment
The last breath of the only true poet living seems to remain a mystery
Tell me something, did you sit up last night singing Billy blues and wondering
    why shit, why shit, why shit, this life is all so sweet?!
Damn, if I knew the galaxies as thoroughly as I feel I wanted to
would there be pain beyond understanding?
Or would there be love in the air, love in the air, love in the air?
Homo
Hetero
Billy Goat
Bi
Try this
smile ties
giving guides to little children
it all satisfies my....
and this is an abstract word for soul thank you Billy Holiday...
"Southern trees bear a strange fruit
Blood on the leaves
And blood at the root
Black bodies swingin'
In the southern trees
Strange fruit hangin'
From the poplar trees."
Bees we natural boys and girls
Bees we rancid troll and perpetual rolls of weed
Tacky tic tack rackin' life of its paradoxes
Let's stick it to them, stick it to them real please.

Thoth Harris

THE IRWIN ALLEN EXPERIENCE

This is how it always begins, always begins in horror a sense of menace and unbeing. Always someone's vanity gets us into trouble.

And the fact is we will never get back to earth or the twentieth century. Stuck in this nightmare paradise with an uncontrollable family, whether it be my partner (and therefore brother, scientific brother) or with the wretched, vain and greedy Dr. Smith and the ever so conformist 50s parents and children with their synthetic sweaters and—goodness gracious how did they even have the scientific ingenuity, if you can call it that, with the crackpot spaceship that looks like a deranged toy manufacturer's bad acid trip—anyway, horror of horrors, we're here, we always end up here, in this warped land, as if communist Russia did take over. This is what Americans always wanted. The strange face of Dr. Smith, always plotting, or chiding, or pretending to be nice. The Irwin Allen Arketypes, of the Arks of Late Twentieth Century Time Warps will always take us into the menace of Man's inner reality. That, my friends is why Irwin Allen is so brilliant! The terror in our hearts will go unheeded and speed dangerously along unless we listen to the visions and prophecies of Irwin Allen.

The mist and fog in our spirits will hang thickly. We will see the inevitable fact of insidiousness in our lives and our society. Our accomplishments which to our ultimate horror amount to nothing. Nothing ends in nothing, they say.

Whenever Land of the Giants comes on, we encounter a kind of gloom upon which we have never, never ... ever been set. We set forth as ... Leetle Peeple! An extremely vain, pompous, but likeable Alexander Fitsu always gets us into trouble with the giants. Always, we are forced to hide in matchboxes, use giant paperclip climbing devices ... every minute we are sent to our doom. We always must escape the giant police chief who wants to use us for our technology and thus rule not only our planet, but his. The law prevents the giants from harboring us. We are always blamed by the police for any catastrophe of significance.

And this is the crux of the matter. We live in a land of corporations ... global economy ... not much we can do if we get crushed or squashed by a giant foot ... we have no power. We get crushed, defeated and trapped everywhere! Unlike the far more optimistic Time Tunnel, where the two time travelers (with polyester sweaters, no less) save the past and the future, and confirm twentieth century America's place as Great and Godly. But Lost in Space and Land of the Giants shows us something far more disturbing: the point we have come to, the point of no return! ... The point where everything we touch becomes at that moment, or very soon, alien and vile ... The point where we are split as a family, where the one child on our 'mission' is practically an orphan, who has as much maturity and caution as the scientists and the two women, and much more than fumbling Fitsu. The true predecessor to contemporary programs like Millennium and X-Files, we lie paralyzed by premonitions. Irwin is the true prophet. He foresaw what our lives would be like as they are now, and what we will be like for sometime. No escape. The destiny of ciphers, fumblers, opportunists, and outright suicides. The warp of reality ... the warp of time ... the warp of mind(s) ... the warp of dementia ... the warp of dimensions...and we relentlessly and willingly approach infinite horror ... for ever and ever...

We stand before a great future. The greatness of the Abyssal Night, the night of truth and power. Before the Abyss where our earth, that piece of trash must be thrown!

Tina Chang

FACE

"Mrs. Michiko Sako, whose face was totally destroyed by the blast of the Hiroshima A-bomb at the age of 13, is one of the 25 'Hiroshima Maidens' who were invited to the United States in 1955 for a series of plastic surgeries." —The New York Times

I smell hibiscus.
The white sun is round
and unstoppable. Blood rushes
through the universe
of my veins like fitful wine.
Wild birds flock to peck
at my intricately floral body.

In America, I give them my face
a headful of hair singed to thin wire
my mouth but a box of broken teeth
eyes ebb in cataract clouds of pastel blue.
Scabbed shadows gnaw on the surface
of a wall.

In half sleep, needles pierce
the tender linen of my cheeks.

They sew my dangling tongue, mold
the nose to breathe fresh air,
the eyes are carved out
and replaced with iridescent pearls.

I am glued and mended. Blackbirds
chant in the hollows of my bones.

We were girls holding pomegranates
in our hands. There was a path
that led to school, a place
where I would sit and calculate
the birds from my desk by the window.

And then the sky cracked onto my back,
the sun dropped deep into my belly.
A cloud took me in, swallowed
me, then spit me out, flailing flesh,
whittleboned. Fire spun orange
out of the roots of trees. Orange swells,
orange oceans rose to eat this city whole.
The faces of young girls fell
apart in my hands.
The fine powder of their bodies
sparkled and scattered Westbound
with a gust of wind.

Among the buildings of Hiroshima,
among the hens, church bells,
school girls, trees unmasked to black.
Houses are skeletal and contorted,
nailed to the landscape.

If I could raise a hand to touch
my face, I'd peel the skin like a fine fruit,
to reveal the soft pink muscle beneath. To find
my beauty sleeping on a mattress of bone,
to leave the fragile scarves of flesh on a field
before the surge, the drop-fire molecules
in my mouth that leave me
raw, perfect, breathing.

ODE TO SOY SAUCE
OR MARTHA STEWART COOKS CHINESE

Spill it on a half ruptured egg for lunch.
Watch the black seep into the yellow yolk.
Spoon it into the open mouth.
My snake in a rice bowl.

Splatter it onto deep red beef.
Let it rest inside the walls of rare tenderloin
until salt mixes with threads of blood.
Its own little milk.

Pour it into soup, and watch the artful
dark tongue mix its own remedy. It is the same
as looking at hard men cry as they watch
cream weave through coffee.

Drizzle it onto a pile of clams
and learn the way to reject
a lover. It just doesn't stick. Sauce
drains into the shell's cold hand.

Rub it into the legs of a duck.
This is a way to avoid loneliness
on Sundays. The aroma of it
in your nose, something close to honey.

Kiss dumplings on the mouth
during dinner. Dip your finger in
and taste ginger snapping
like mint on your taste buds.

Let it boil up into the hearts
of artichokes. Let it hover
over the quivering flesh of squid. Love
takes time. At least 45 minutes
according to many recipes.

And when you say it is over,
having placed your oven mitt by
the door. You can't tell me you weren't sad,
when you found the bottle empty.

Alphabetical Listing of Authors

Algarin, Miguel 65
Allen, Robert 151
Anderson, Fortner 46
Arima, Phlip 227

B., Cheryl 255
Baines, Mercedes 217
Bak, Louise 134
Baraka, Ras 75
Battson, Jill 55
Beatty, Paul 149
Bell, Chris 101
Benson, Tish 241
Bibbins, Mark 301
bissett, bill 36
Blackman, Nicole 68
Blades, Joe 206
Bonanza, Buffy 172
Boutros, Alex 248

Cabico, Regie 77
Camlot, Jason 119
Carbo, Nick 146
Castro, Guillermo 277
Chang, Tina 308
Chin, Justin 207
Cisneros, Sandra 81
Cochrane, Mark 140
Compton, Wayde 243
Conway, Jeffery 284
Crosbie, Lynn 137
Crysler, Julie 296

De la Rosa, Audrey 93
Death Waits 263
Dembowski, Nancy 222

Dougherty, Sean Thomas 235
Doughty, M. 213
Downing, Emily S. 273
Drummond, Ron 304
Duhamel, Denise 41, 141
Durand, Marcella 139
Dutton, Paul 73

Eden, Evert 193
Elliott, Anne 166

Ferrier, Ian 204
Filip, Raymond 150
Franklin, Noel 223
Fried, Golda 274

Georgiou, Elena 266
Gilbert, Sky 236
Ginsberg, Allen 29
Goff, Cindy 104
Goldstein, Jonathan 294
Gotham, Lee 57
Gotman, Kélina 209
Grace, Mary Elizabeth 216

Hahn, Kimiko 76
Hanni, Carl 173
Harris, Thoth 307
Harrison, Richard 153
Heighton, Steven 158
Holman, Bob 37
Holmes, Michael 144

Jager, David 261
Jones, C.D. 180
Jordan, Melody 61
Joseph, Clifton 40

Karasick, Adeena 91
Keon, Wayne 162
Kidd, Catherine 177

Langworthy, Christian 257
Lau, Evelyn 117
Lee, John B. 130
Lewis, Ben Porter 171
Lisick, Beth 95
Liu, Timothy 161

Mali, Taylor 238
Maybe, Ellyn 44
McDaniel, Jeffrey 129
McGimpsey, David 108
McGrath, Carmelita 96
McGrath, Donald 114
mclennan, rob 234
Medina, Tony 86
Minister Faust 219

O'Hara, Alexis 249
O'Leary, Daniel 106
O'Neill, Heather 279

Parrish, Rittah 228
Pearlberg, Gerry Gomez 118
Penelope 74
Power, Donal 264
Priest, Robert 231

Redmond, Bob 39
Renegade, DJ 188
Rogal, Stan 157
Roop, Daniel 186
Rosenfeld, Carol 253
Rux, Carl Hancock 175

Sampsell, Kevin 210
Savageau, Cheryl 98
Seaton, Maureen 141
Shafiq 305
Sia, Beau 169
Siegel, Micki 64
Sigler, Eric 116
Sirowitz, Hal 51
Smith, Marc 58
Smith, Patricia 71
Smith, Steven Ross 159
Stephens, Ian 54
stillpoint, horehound 200
Stone, Anne 250
Sutherland, W. Mark 59
Swift, Todd 88

Tabios, Eileen 115
Taylor, Cheryl Boyce 182
Tayson, Richard 155
Thompson, Andrea 31
Torres, Edwin 197
Tran, Barbara 94

Williams, Crystal 259
Wilson, Sheri-D 83

Yamanaka, Lois-Ann 132

Contributors' Notes – Canadian

Robert Allen. Essayist, novelist and poet, Rob Allen was born in Bristol, England. He teaches in the Creative Writing department at Concordia University, Montreal, and is the editor of *The Moosehead Anthology* and *Matrix*, Quebec's premier English-language literary journal.

Fortner Anderson. Educated in the streets of Berkeley, Paris, and Montreal, he immigrated to Canada from the U.S. in 1976. He founded Dromos Editions, ran Montreal's Dial-a-Poem service, and published the spoken word zine, *Brazen Oralities*. Fortner currently hosts *Dromostexte*—a weekly radio show on CKUT-FM (Montreal), and is co-producer (with Ian Ferrier) of the *Wired on Words* recording series.

Phlip Arima is the author of *Beneath the Beauty* (Insomniac Press, 1996) as well as seven chapbooks, including *Blood Guts and Automatic Beds* (1994). His work for video includes the self-titled *Performance Poet Phlip Arima*, showcasing a live show at Toronto's The Little Alex theater space.

Mercedes Baines is a writer, performer, director, drama teacher and performance poet born and raised in Vancouver. She has co-written, produced and performed in three plays, including *l'Erotique*. Her poetry has been collected in *Miscegenation Blues* (Sister Vision Press), *Colour: An Issue* (West Coast Line) and *North: New African-Canadian Writing* (West Coast Line).

Louise Bak is a Toronto-based writer, editor, radio broadcaster, performance artist and sexuality counselor. Her poetry book, *Gingko Kitchen*, was published by Coach House Books in 1997. Louise can be heard every Tuesday morning on CIUT-FM 89.5 as co-host of "Sex City." Her performance work has appeared in the independent films *Amidst Us* (Total Eclipse Productions, 1996) and *The Wall* (1997).

Jill Battson. Her groundbreaking *Word Up* anthology is still a touchstone. She produced the spoken word TV series *Word Up* for *MuchMusic*, as well as many live poetry events including the Poetry Express, Poetburo's Slam Sessions, Festival of the Spoken Word, Poets' Refuge and the hugely popular Fightin' Words—which featured slam poets competing in a boxing ring in an old gym. *Hard Candy* was published by Insomniac Press.

Chris Bell is a Montreal author, poet and multimedia artist. Some of his previous works include *Tales of The Lost Cheebah-Ha*, a novel and spoken word performance (ga press, 1995); and *Capturing Shadowtalk*, a novel published on the Web.

bill bissett. bill—in his own words—was "born halifax nova scotia nov 1939 came 2 vancouver 58 startid blewointment press 63-83 readings sound work seek 2 keep on exploring byond narrativ as well as lyrik politikul romanse n storee telling singr n lyricist with LUDDITES band alternativ rock basd in london ont moovd 2 ontario 85 now basd in toronto sins 1992 invitid 2 partisipate in sound poetree festivals glasgow london england new york amsterdam paris toronto n st johns nufoundland did european tour with adeena karasick 92"—and the beat goes on.

Joe Blades is a writer, artist and book publisher living in Fredericton, New Brunswick. He has created audio installation pieces and poetry videos for exhibits, and currently produces and hosts a weekly show on CSHR-FM. He also runs River Readings, a monthly reading series. He has published *Cover Makes A Set* (Spare Time Editions) and has *River Suite* forthcoming from Insomniac Press.

Buffy Bonanza. Pop-culture columnist and editor-at-large for Montreal's alternative weekly *Hour.* A veteran of the Montreal spoken word scene, Bonanza has performed at events/venues throughout central Canada and the East coast. She is the editor of the webzine *CultureSwab*, and is the author of the recently released book about Sarah McLachlan's feminist-based rock tour, *From Lilith to Lilith Fair* (Madrigal Press).

Alex Boutros. A Montreal-based performance artist whose sound has largely been influenced by the work of beat and dub poets. Her musical background—including an honors degree in classical music—has brought musical structures and forms, as well as instrumentation, to her texts. She has performed at a number of events/venues, including Unusual Suspects, Yawp!, and Funky Ass Folk Babes.

Jason Camlot has performed his songs across North America with his performance group, Letterbomb and has released three compilations of songs, including *Letterbomb* (DNA, 1996). He has a Ph.D. in English literature from Stanford University and is beginning research for a book about the influence of sound-recording technology upon poetry.

Mark Cochrane. Mark's poetry has been featured inside Vancouver and Victoria busses and skytrains as part of the BC Poetry in Transit project. He has performed his poems on CBC radio and at a fitness centre while people worked out. Mark is currently writing *Soft Men*, poems and prose relating athletics—particularly hockey and bodybuilding—to sexual identity.

Wayde Compton. Both poet and activist, he serves as the Chair of Communications for the Black Cultural Association of British Columbia, and works with Anti-Racist Action-Vancouver. His first poetry collection, *49th Parallel Psalm* is forthcoming from Arsenal Pulp Press.

Lynn Crosbie is the author of the controversial novel, *Paul's Case*, based on a true account of a serial killer. Her poetry collections are stylish, often sensuous, and daring. She has published three books of poems, *Miss Pamela's Mercy*, *VillainElle* and *Pearl*. She recently edited the anthology *Click: Becoming Feminists* (Macfarlane Walter & Ross).

Julie Crysler lives in Toronto where she programs a reading series at Buddies in Bad Times Theatre. As a member of the 1995 Montreal Vox Hunt slam team (having been a Montreal champion) she competed at the U.S. National Poetry Championships in Ann Arbor, Michigan. While living in Montreal she ran the influential Coolest Girl in the World cabaret series. She has published two chapbooks, *Vision Songs* (1995) and *All Consuming* (1997).

Nancy Dembowski has organized poetry readings at The Art Bar and Ted's Collision and has performed her poetry at events/venues all over Toronto. She co-hosted *The Scream in High Park* in the summer of 1996. From 1996 on she has been editor of *Plus Zero Magazine*. Her book *Ninety-Seven Posts with the Heads of Dead Men* was published by Tortoiseshell & Black.

Emily S. Downing. A perennial winner of the Montreal slam competitions held through Vox Hunt, her evocative voice and subtle gesturing at the mic gained many fans. Her work has been collected on the CD anthology *Millennium Cabaret*, produced by Ian Ferrier, and has also appeared on CBC radio. She recently moved to Europe.

Paul Dutton. A member of the hugely influential sound poetry quartet The Four Horsemen (with Rafael Barreto-Rivera, Steve McCaffery, and bpNichol), Paul is now a member of CCMC—a free improvisation band—currently a trio (with Michael Snow and John Oswald). He has performed solo and in ensembles at literary and musical events/venues throughout Europe and North America, and has published five books and has issued five sound recordings.

Minister Faust is an Edmonton teacher, broadcaster, artist, and activist. He has researched ancient spirituality in Egypt as well as early African-Canadian settlements in Alberta. He participated and reported on the Million Man March radio program, *The Terrordome: Black Radio in the Hour of Chaos* and *The Phantom Pyramid* (CJSR FM-88).

Ian Ferrier. In 1993 his pioneer series *Wired On Words* placed poems and spoken word pieces on self-rewinding cassettes and distributed them to radio stations so that DJs could play them like songs. The best of the series was later released as a tape, and the entire project won a Standard Broadcasting Award for excellence in radio programming. He has just finished a CD anthology *Millennium Cabaret*.

Raymond Filip. A teacher of music and literature at John Abbott College near Montreal, he also runs his DO-RE-MIDI studio. He has performed his work across North America and Europe. In 1989 his tape *Playing the Poet* was released, and also that year his poems and songs were featured off-Broadway in *Etched in Amber*. He wrote the music for playwright David Fennario's *Dr. Neil Crean: Mysteries of McGill* and *Banana Boots*. He is the 1994 winner of the QSPELL award for poetry.

Golda Fried. One of Canada's rising new voices. In 1993 she came third in the *Books in Canada* Student Writing Awards. In 1994 she won the Chester McNaughten Prize in Creative Writing from McGill University. Golda has published, among others, *Check the Floor*, a poetry chapbook from Alphabeat Press, and a collection of short stories, *Darkness Then a Blown Kiss* (Gutter Press).

Sky Gilbert. Writer, filmmaker, director, and drag queen extraordinaire, Sky is one of Canada's most controversial artistic forces. His hit plays *Drag Queens on Trial* and *Drag Queens in Outer Space* (published by Playwright's Canada Press, 1996) have been produced in New York and other major cities. His first novel, *Guilty*, was published by Insomniac Press in April 1998 and his complete poems will be published by ECW Press in late1998.

Jonathan Goldstein is a Montreal-based performance poet originally from Brooklyn. A nouveau hipster, he has slammed his poems successfully at the Nuyorican Poets Cafe and the infamous Green Mill Lounge in Chicago. Jonathan has been anthologized in *Agent*, *Revival*, *Concrete Forest*, *The Headlight Anthology*, and *Burning Ambitions*.

Lee Gotham. For four years Lee edited the little magazine, *Pawn*. He also produced and hosted the spoken word poetry event, Enough Said, which had a profound impact on the Montreal poetry revival. He recently opened for Ray Manzarek and Michael McClure at Yawp!. His work has been heard on CBC radio and can also be found on the Web in the E-zines *Euphony* and *Cyberhyme*.

Kélina Gotman was born and raised in Montreal. She has edited and/or contributed to various literary journals, including *Clerestory* and *Ophelia*. She recently worked on a performance art installation with James Bewley, a graduate of the Sculpture program at the Rhode Island School of Design. She will be attending Oxford in 1998.

Mary Elizabeth Grace is a Toronto-based performance poet and musician who has been featured at reading events and festivals in Canada, Ireland and the UK. Her first book, *Bootlegging Apples on the Road to Redemption* also featured a companion CD. One of her poems, *Rosa's Time*, was the inspiration for, and the title of, a short film screened at the 1998 Sundance Festival, directed by Daniel Hawks.

Thoth Harris. Second generation *poète maudite* Thoth Harris has been in Montreal since 1990. He recently became an active, if startling, presence on that city's spoken word scene with his monthly, eclectic, late-night cabaret show *The Devil's Voice*. His work has been featured in the Web magazine *switchmag* (www.switchmag.com) and he recently released a short story cycle/novel, *Blank*, which pushes the envelope.

Richard Harrison. His first three books of poems were critically-acclaimed for their resonant investigation of women's issues and male identity. They are *Fathers Never Leave You*, *Recovering The Naked Man,* and *Hero of the Play*. A TV adaptation of his work was aired on *Adrienne Clarkson Presents*. He teaches Creative Writing and English at Mount Royal College in Calgary.

Steven Heighton. A Governor General's Poetry Award finalist for *The Ecstasy of Skeptics*, Granta has published two books of his short stories. He has done many public readings and organized a reading series. Steven is perhaps one of a handful of the present generation of Canadian writers that can already be considered a major new voice both in prose and poetry.

Michael Holmes is a writer and cultural critic living in Toronto. He has a Ph.D. in English Literature from York University. He is the author of three books of poetry, including the acclaimed *james i wanted to ask you* (ECW Press, 1994). He is also the editor of the anthology *The Last Word* from Insomniac Press.

David Jager. An accomplished classical pianist and lounge crooner, David moved to Montreal in the mid-90s, becoming a fixture in the retro-cabaret movement spearheaded by Vox Hunt Slam. David is a two-time member of the Vox Hunt Montreal Slam Team and has competed at the U.S. National Poetry Championships in Ann Arbor, Michigan, and Middleton, Connecticut.

C. D. Jones. Charlene (C.D.) is a well-known Toronto performance poet. Her work has been published in a variety of journals, including *Prairie Schooner*, *cold-drill*, *Canadian Women's Studies*, *Boise Magazine*, and *Tiger Lilly*.

Clifton Joseph has performed widely across Canada, the United States, the UK, and the Caribbean. One of the engines behind the first International Festival of Dub Poetry held in Toronto in 1994, Clifton has published a book of poetry, *Metropolitan Blues* (1983); and released *Oral Trans/missions*, an album of poetry and music. He is one of Canada's most respected and popular performance poets.

Adeena Karasick. Dedicated to language-centered writing, feminist and Jewish concerns, Adeena is the author of three books of poetry and poetic theory, *Genrecide* (Talonbooks, 1996), *Mêmewars* (Talonbooks, 1994) and *The Empress Has No Closure* (Talonbooks, 1992). With her fusion of academic savvy (she has a Ph.D.) and opulent, erotic eloquence on stage, she is as good a justification for this anthology as any that could be found.

Wayne Keon is an Ojibway poet and financial analyst living in Ontario, whose poetry has been published in journals across North America. He has published several collections of poems, notably *Storm Dancer* (Mercury Press, 1993). His poems, placed in a musical context—*Storm Dances* (1994-96)—were performed recently in Toronto by William Beauvais, Julian Knight and Mhari Fyfe.

Catherine Kidd. Her performances combine dance-like choreography of movement with dramatic vocal range and are often complimented by elaborate sound-and-light shows. Her texts have appeared in numerous journals, including *Matrix*, and a number of *ga press* productions—notably her multi-media book/cassette *Everything I Know About Love I Learned From Taxidermy*.

Evelyn Lau. Perhaps the only person in this collection to have had a Movie of the Week made about her life—CBC's *Runaway*, based on her best-selling teen auto-biography detailing a life on the street. Since her spectacular debut she has become an accomplished novelist and poet, with six books translated into a dozen languages. She was the youngest-ever nominee for Canada's top literary prize, the Governor General's Award, for her book of poems *Oedipal Dreams*. Her poetry has appeared in *Best American Poetry*. She currently lives in the Vancouver area.

John B. Lee's work has been published on the Internet, and on radio and TV, including *Morningside*, and *MuchMusic*. As a writer/performer of children's songs and poems he has performed in children's festivals across North America. He is the only person to have won the annual Milton Acorn Memorial People's Poetry Award twice.

David McGimpsey. Author of two successful books of poetry which are groundbreaking in their accomplished fusion of high culture and low-brow pop iconography—*Lardcake* and *Dogboy*, both published by ECW. Known to strum on a ukulele while reciting, he has read his poetry on CBC radio's *Morningside* and *Sunday Morning*.

Carmelita McGrath. A Newfoundlander, she writes fiction, non-fiction and also works as an editor and reviewer. She co-edited *Their Lives and Times, Women in Newfoundland and Labrador* and edited *Signatures* (Killick Press, 1996)—an anthology of writing and visual art. She has won seven Newfoundland and Labrador Arts and Letters Awards for her writing and has published two books of poems, *Poems on Land and Water* and *To the New World*.

Donald McGrath. Brother of Carmelita McGrath, Don now lives in Montreal. Known for his eloquent and witty performances of lyric verse—often revealing glimpses of a skewed Catholic childhood, he has moved from the page to the stage in a uniquely gentle manner. His first book of poems, *At First Light* (Wolsak & Wynn, 1996) was published to much praise.

rob mclennan. Since founding above/ground press in 1993, he has published dozens of chapbooks by other writers, and continues to edit two different zines, *STANZAS* and *Missing Jacket*. He runs the poetry 101 reading series, the WHIPlash Poetry Festival, the Ottawa Small Press Book Fair (since 1994) and the TREE Reading Series (with b. stephen harding) now into its 18th year.

Alexis O'Hara. A member of the electronic jam collective, Stellaform, she performs in both of Canada's official languages. In 1997 she competed on the Vox Hunt Montreal Slam team at the U.S. National Poetry championships. She has performed at numerous spoken word events/venues, including Yawp! and SenseArt.

Daniel O'Leary. After eight years in Montreal—where he became a legendary performance presence and leader of a group of contemporary gnostic artists, O'Leary recently moved to Vancouver to complete his dissertation at the University of British Columbia and to be poetry editor of *Prism International*. Daniel's first book of verse was *The Sorcerer of Les Trois Frères*.

Heather O'Neill. This twenty-three-year-old performance poet rose to prominence in the spoken word community due to her searing and lyrical appearances at such events/venues as Vox Hunt and Yawp! and the 1997 U.S. National Poetry Championships. She recently published her first poetry collection with DC Books.

Penelope. Author of a best-selling book of poems and photographs, *Image 5 Seeds of the Spacefields* (Martlet Press), she acted in and wrote an award-winning feature film (*Zero the Fool*, Ann Arbor Festival). Active in the 60s, she only recently returned to the world of arts, poetry and politics as a performer in the 90s.

Donal Power. He has performed at Budapest's *Kacat Kabaré* and was an editor at *Frank* magazine both on the East coast and in Ottawa, before leaving the country to live in Europe for several years. He is working on his first collection of poems.

Robert Priest is a poet, successful pop songwriter (he co-wrote thehit by Alannah Myles, *Song Instead of a Kiss*), novelist, playwright, children's writer, and performer. He won the Milton Acorn People's Poetry Award in 1989. His latest CD *Tongue'n Groove* (EMI/Artisan) features a smorgasbord of poems, songs, sayings, chants and iterations. ECW Press recently published *Resurrection in the Cartoon*.

Stan Rogal is an artistic director of Bald Ego Theatre and has had his plays performed in several Canadian cities, most notably The Threepenny EPIC Cabaret, in 1996. He has also been the coordinator of the popular Toronto institution, the Idler Pub Reading Series since 1990. He has three collections of poems, the latest being *Personations* (Exile Editions, 1997).

Shafiq. Born in Dominica, and raised in Hamilton, Ontario, performance artist/ poet Shafiq has worked with free-form jazz-meisters Handslang, and performed at Lollapallooza '94 in Barrie. A member of Crossroads Cant Collective, his poetry is featured in the four-author book *Crossroads Cant* issued from Broken Jaw Press in 1997.

Eric Sigler could be mistaken for a creation of Henry James, as an American expatriate living in Westmount, Quebec in the early 90s. Blessed with a remarkable reciting voice and the guts to perform aloud, he cut a truly romantic figure.He currently resides in Mystic, Connecticut.

Steven Ross Smith. A poet, fiction writer, and sound/performance poet, he's published six books, and put out five audiocassettes. His work has also been broadcast on CBC radio. Since 1992 he has performed and recorded with the sound/music ensemble DUCT. His latest book is *fluttertongue Book 1*.

Ian Stephens. A pioneer of performance poetry in Canada, his contribution spanned three decades beginning in the late 1970s and ending with his untimely death in 1996. His book *Diary of a Trademark* was published by The Muses' Company in 1994. It includes *Weary State of Grace,* the acclaimed essay about his life with AIDS. Some of Ian's last releases were a poetry video and audio tracks for the *Word UP* CD.

Anne Stone. Her work has appeared in numerous publications, including *Index*, *Matrix*, the *Moosehead Anthology* (1997), and the chapbook *Sweet Dick All*. Her first novel, *jacks: a gothic novel*, was published in fall 1998. Her performances have been recorded and broadcast on radio. She has performed her work at a number of events/ venues, among them Kali Gallery, Mainlines, Volume, Yawp!, The Devil's Voice, Legba, and Vox Hunt Slam.

W. Mark Sutherland. Mark is a language-based artist, poet and musician. His written work has been collected in several anthologies, notably *The Last Word*

(Insomniac Press, 1995). His poetry tapes, music, and soundscapes have received air play throughout North America and Europe. His work is also included on the audio anthology *Modern Sounds* by The CAGE Group (Cincinnati) and *Baobab—The New Worlds* (Cento, Italy).

Todd Swift. He created and emceed the monthly Vox Hunt spoken word series, the first of its kind in Canada. As a poet and essayist, Swift's work has appeared in *Prism International*, *Quarry*, and *Matrix* and he has published six poetry chapbooks. In 1988 he co-edited *Map-Maker's Colours: New Poets of Northern Ireland*. He provided the lyrics for choreographer/dancer José Navas' dance piece *Sterile Fields*, which premiered in New York at the *St. Mark's Dance Space* in 1996 and has since been performed worldwide. His work with Tom Walsh appears on the spoken word CD *Millennium Cabaret*.

Andrea Thompson has read at events/venues across North America, including the Word On the Street Festival (Vancouver) and the U.S. National Poetry Championships (Portland and Middleton). Andrea has worked to give a greater voice to the Vancouver spoken word community as host of CITR radio's *Hearsay* and as host/coordinator of the *Word On The Street's Poets Corner*

Death Waits. Toronto native Death, as his friends call him, wears many hats, not all of them tall and black. He is a (performance) poet, playwright, choreographer, Artistic Director of Candid Stammer Theatre and a singer/songwriter with the band Glitter Wimp. He has published several books of poems.

Sheri-D Wilson is an artist known for her innovative and dramatic performance style. She has performed at Bumbershoot (Seattle), The Harbourfront Reading Series (Toronto), and The Brainwash Reading Series (San Francisco). She has published three collections of poetry, the most recent being *Girl's Guide to Giving Head* (Arsenal Pulp Press, 1996). She is one of Canada's leading spoken word divas.

Contributors' Notes — U.S.

Miguel Algarin. Founder of the Nuyorican Poets Cafe, the mecca of spoken word poetry. He is co-editor of *Aloud: Voices From The Nuyorican Poets Cafe* and *Action: The Nuyorican Poets Cafe Theater Festival.* His recent collection of poems *Love Is Hard Work* (Scribner, 1997) was nominated for a Pulitzer Prize.

Cheryl B. Cheryl received her BFA in Playwriting from NYU and is the recipient of an Australian Playwriting Fellowship. She is the author of *Pubic Enemy # 1* and performs in the band Hot Sauce Gizzard. Her work combines the audacity of a New Jersey Mall Chick with the angst of a Black Sabbath Roadie. Featured in *Revival: Spoken Word Poetry From Lollapalooza 1995.*

Ras Baraka. Son of the internationally acclaimed poet/playwright/activist Amiri Baraka and Amini Baraka. He co-edited the ground-breaking *In the Tradition*, featuring the newest generation of African-American writers.

Paul Beatty. One of the few Nuyorican poets to make a transition from the Poetry Slam to print. He is the author of *Big Bank, Take Little Bank* (Penguin, 1995) and the widely praised novel *White Boy Shuffle* (Holt, 1996). Seen on MTV's "Unplugged," Beaty remanipulates the lower case to make accessible hip hop race with a wry, rhythmic machine gun of gen-Xer lingo.

Tish Benson. A Grand Slam Champion of the Nuyorican Poets Cafe. Tish's poetry is featured on several compilations including *Flippin' The Script* (Mouth Almighty). Take a sweaty, Texan drawl, with the sensuality of Mae West, give her a daishiki and you'll get Tish—the only poet to total three perfect scores of thirty in her Grand Slam.

Mark Bibbins lives in New York City where he teaches a poetry workshop at The New School. His work has been been published in *The Paris Review*, *The Yale Review*, and *The Antioch Review*. His first collection, *Swerve*, appears in *Take Three: 3 (AGNI/ Graywolf Press*, 1998).

Nicole Blackman. If Charlie's Angels had adopted a niece, they would have picked this sassy spoken word diva, mesmerizing a café and rock crowd with her edgy lyrics and pristine, soft-voiced phrasing. She is the author of three books of poetry: *Pretty*, *Sweet*, and *Nice*, and can be heard performing her work with The Golden Palominos on their CD *Dead Inside*.

Cheryl Boyce Taylor. Author of *Raw Air*, Cheryl was a student of Audre Lorde and carries her teacher's politics and poetics even further with her erotic love poems and Trinidanian dialect. Currently she is collaborating with her son Malik, one of the members of A Tribe Called Quest.

Regie Cabico received his BFA in Drama from NYU's Tisch School of the Arts and has been featured in the film *Boys Life* (Strand Releasing) as the Act-Up Boy. He left acting to go into something more lucrative like poetry. He teaches a class, Rant Without Whining, at The Writers Voice and Muscial Theater Works in Manhattan. He has participated in the 1993, 1994 and 1997 U.S. National Poetry Slams and took a First Place prize with the winning team, Mouth Almighty, Manhattan.

Nick Carbo. Carbo's magical surrealistic poems, like a sorcerer, conjure Filipino creation myths and catapults them gleefully into a pot of American pop culture. Editor of *Returning A Borrowed Tongue: Contemporary Filipino Poetry* (Coffee House Press) and author of *EL Grupo McDonald's* (Tia Chucha). He is married to the poet Denise Duhamel.

Guillermo Castro. Author of *Toy Storm* (Big Fat Press). If Charles Simic spoke Spanish, he'd channel Guillermo Castro's dark verses. His poems cover the immigrant struggle and exile, juxtaposing the Manhattan landscape with his Argentina collapsing in the hands of fascism.

Tina Chang. Columbia Graduate in Creative Writing, Tina Chang's lush poems barrage the reader's ear with the musicality of the persona she inhabits. In "Hiroshima," she meticulously captures the inner life of a victim with the haunting sound of a wind instrument. She was a finalist for the Allen Ginsberg Awards for poetry.

Justin Chin. The sharp poetry and prose of Chin are beautifully fused in his work as a performance artist. His collections of poetry are *Bite Hard* (Manic D Press) and *Mongrel* (St. Martin's Press). He was a member of the 1994 and 1995 San Francisco Slam Team.

Sandra Cisneros. *House on Mango Street* is the widely-acclaimed novel that has influenced a generation of writers. *My Wicked, Wicked Ways* and *Loose Women* are her collections of poetry. Heartbreaking and sexy, Cisneros' delivery is tequila spitfire wrapped in the vulnerability of the woman poet in love.

Jeffery Conway. In Conway's world, sex and humor intertwine like a dark tango dipped in a confessional pool of 80s pop imagery—he is our post-modern Cavafy. He is the author of *Blood Poisoning* and featured in the anthology *Plush* (Coach House Press).

Denise Duhamel has been featured in *Best American Poetry* three times and is the author of seven books of poetry. Her work has been published in many journals and anthologies. Duhamel's feminist politics and her confessional poetry is like a slumber party from Barbie to virginity. She is married to the poet Nick Carbo.

Audrey de la Rosa. One of the newest Latina writers to address racial identity with new Feminism and the lyricism of a contemporary Sor Juana Ines de la Cruz. As mother and as Argentine-American, her poems are meditations—deeply spiritual and intense.

Sean Thomas Dougherty. Editor of *The Red Brick Review*, and author of numerous collections of poetry including *Love Song of the Young Couple, The Dumb Job* (Dance Floor, 1995). Sean Thomas' "Looking For Lorca In Your Letters" is a slam classic that never compromises the page for the stage and when delivered produces a big fat 10. He just completed his MFA in Creative Writing at Syracuse Unversity.

Ron Drummond captures the flavor of the New York School of Poetry with his witty remanipulation of the pantoum in "Attention To Gray." A former actor and theater manager, Drummond has swept the heart of the downtown literary community. In the tradition of James Schuyler meets Felix the Cat—"he's got a bag of metaphors up his sleeve."

M. Doughty has moved from Brooklyn to London to Pensacola in the space of three years. He is the guitar player and lyricist for the band Soul Coughing. He is author of *Slanky* and featured in *Verses that Hurt*, a collection of poemphone poets.

Marcella Durand. Currently, the director of the St. Mark's Poetry Project, Durand also was co-coordinator of the Sunday Reading series at Biblio's cafe, New York City and the Zinx Bar for three years. She is the author of *Lapsus Linguae* (Situations Press, 1995)." City of Ports" is a collaborative piece with visual artist, Carin Riley, under the direction of poet Mei-mei Berssenbrugge and artist Kiki Smith at The Poets Theater

Evert Eden. Two-time U.S. National Slam finalist Eden is a South African urban-voiced bard who spews his verse like a volcano of sexual innuendo. He is the author of *Suck My Poem*. His one-man-show, "How to Cook A Man" is currently playing off-off Broadway at The Gene Frankel Theater.

Anne Elliott. One of the most innovative Nuyorican slam poets. Influenced by Jerome Rothenberg and Karen Finley, Elliott masterfully evokes the paranoia and isolation in the big city. "She Thought Starvation Was Somehow Holy" is sung in Gregorian chant. Perhaps the only slam poet with an MFA in Performance Art, she is the editor and publisher of Big Fat Press, NYC.

Noel Franklin. President of Eleventh Hour productions and co-founder of the Seattle Poetry Festival. She was a member of the 1997 Seattle Poetry Slam and has performed at the Albuquerque Poetry festival and the Internet broadcast from Seattle's Moe's Mo' Rockin' café.

Elena Georgiou is a co-editor of *Gay & Lesbian Poets of the New Millenium* (St. Martin's Press, forthcoming year 2000). A Cyprian originally from London, Elena has written the truly Aquarian line in "a buoy drifting warily out to sea." She is the recipient of an Astrea Fellowship for Poetry.

Gerry Gomez Pearlberg is the editor of *Marianne Faithfull's Cigarette* (Cleis, 1998) and edited *The Key to Everything* and *The Zenith of Desire*. Gerry is Sappho and Superman rolled into one.

Allen Ginsberg. The grandfather of spoken word poetry (if Whitman is the great-grandfather of performance poetry) made "Howl" a household word and textbook American classic. His last album was *Ballad of the Skeletons* and he performed up until his death in April 1997.

Cindy Goff. Goff's quirky poems cover taboos with surrealistic precision and an Appalachian flavor. She received her MFA from George Mason University and was featured in *Last Call: Poems on Addiction, Alcoholism and Deliverance* (Sarabande Books). She now lives in Warrenton, Virginia.

Kimiko Hahn. Kimiko's collections of poetry include *Air Pocket* and *Ear Shot* by Hanging Loose Press and most recently, *The Unbearable Heart* (Kaya Press) which received a Before Columbus American Book Award. Kimiko captures the calamity and tragedy she experiences with breathtaking, generous observations and sense memories. Her next poetry book is forthcoming from Norton.

Carl Hanni. Hanni's first full collection of poetry, *Night Shift*, was published by Quiet Lion Press in 1996. He produced the CD *Talking Rain: Spoken Word and Music from the Pacific Northwest* for Tim/Kerr Records in 1994. His work also appears in *Roadside Distractions* (Orange Ocean Press) and *Playing With A Full Deck* (Unnumb Press). He lives in Portland Oregon, but dreams about deserts of the Southwest.

Bob Holman. The impressario of the contemporary poetry and spoken word explosion. His exuberant love for poetry is evident in *Aloud:Voices From the Nuyorican Poets Cafe*, which he co-edited with Miguel Algarin—a bible for poetry into the 21st century. He is the author of *Collect Call of the Wild* (Henry Holt) and the producer for the unprecedented PBS series "The United States Of Poetry." His pork-pie hat, glasses, and raspy MC slam voice are iconographic.

Melody Jordan. Published in the Lollapalooza *Revival Anthology* (Manic D Press) and *Poetry Is Dead* (Future Tense), among others. She can be heard on *Talking Rain*, a compilation CD featuring spoken word performers from the Pacific Northwest. Melody is active in Portland's cabaret community and enjoys gardening. She's a red-headed Rimbaud who has attempted to form 6-person pyramids at slams.

Christian Langworthy. Langworthy redefines the definitions of multi-culturalism with his Vietnam memory pieces. The work in his chapbook, *Geography of War* (a winner of the 1993 Poet Magazine's National Chapbook Contest) is accomplished, regal, and breathtaking.

Ben Porter Lewis. Born in Saigon, raised in New York City, and now living in Los Angeles, he is one of the most active spoken word performers on the West Coast. He has particiated in the U.S. National Poetry Championships and runs a reading/slam series in Los Angeles.

Beth Lisick. San Francisco Slam finalist. Beth's book *Monkey Girl* is a delicious collection of bad girl, West Coast narratives. One of the few slam poets to be featured in *Best American Poetry, 1997*, edited by James Tate.

Taylor Mali. The most ferocious slam poet in North America, Mali delivers his work with the zest of a Shakespearean thespian. Featured in Paul Devlin's acclaimed documentary "Slam Nation," Mali coached the 1996 Providence team to victory and repeated the win in 1997 with Mouth Almighty, Manhattan. He is featured in the documentary, *Slam Nation*. He teaches math and history at the Browning School, NYC.

Jeffery McDaniel. Author of *Alibi School* and *Forgiveness Parade*, McDaniel reads his poetry in a dark, strident belt that conjurs Bukowski, Anthony Perkins, and Pugsley from "The Addams Family." He captured the editing eye of A.R. Ammons who placed his work in *Best American Poetry, 1996*. He currently writes reviews and literary interviews for *CUPS* magazine in Los Angeles.

Ellyn Maybe is the author of *The Cowardice of Amnesia* (2.13.61). She was the Los Angeles representative on the MTV Spoken Word tour. Her work can be heard on KPFK, KCRW & KXLU.

Tony Medina. Co-editor of *In Defense of Mumia* (Writers and Readers, 1996), a classic of contemporary political poetry. A fierce reader, Medina's radical vision has influenced a new generation of writers. He is the author of *No Noose is Good Noose*.

Ritah Parrish is the author of *Ribbed for Your Pleasure*. She is an actress as well as a poet and has performed in solo shows. Her latest book, *Pink Menace*, is a collection of short stories published by Future Tense.

Bob Redmond. A poet and organizer from Seattle, his work has appeared in various zines around the Northwest and on stage at Bumpershoot, the Green Mill and other venues. Besides directing the Seattle Poetry Festival, Bob DJ's a weekly show at KBCS and works at *Real Change* street newspaper.

DJ Renegade aka Hoel Dias-Porter was born and raised in Pittsburgh, Pennsylvania. After high school he enlisted in the USAF. After leaving the service he became a professional disk jockey, in the Washington, DC area. In 1991 he quit his job and began living in homeless shelters, while undergoing an extensive Afrocentric studies program. He also began to write poetry and is a four-time U.S.National Slam Finalist. He has been the subject of numerous documentaries, appearing on NBC's "Today" show and in the feature film "Slam" which won the Grand Jury Prize at the Sundance Film Festival.

Daniel Roop. If River Phoenix wrote poetry, he would have sounded like Daniel Roop, the young bard of Tennessee who made a splash with his debut in the 1997 Slam representing the group AGOCAP.

Carol Rosenfeld. A late-blooming lesbian, "Dike-otomy" represents Rosenfeld at her best—comic yet vulnerable narratives which earned her a "Best Femme Poet in Hiking Boots" trophy at the First Poetry Ball Slam held at the Kit Kat Club, NYC. She is co-chair of "In Our Own Write" where she hosted the first Astrea Lesbian Writers Poetry Slam.

Carl Hancock Rux has a gospel intensity that jams the roofs off of auditoriums and coffee houses. His play, *Smoke, Lilies, Jade*, was presented at The Public Theater. He is the writer for several downtown dance companies. He was featured as one of *New York Magazine*'s Top Artists Under 30 and in *The Village Voice Literary Supplement*'s "Writers On The Verge." His prose and poetry collection, *Pagan Operetta*, was released by Fly By Night Press. He is currently releasing his spoken word album, *Rux*.

Kevin Sampsell runs the quirky but influential small press Future Tense Books in Portland, Oregon and works at the Powell's corporation as an events coordinator. He is also a freelance journalist and father. His latest collections are *Haiku You* and *Invisible Radios*. He once read with Jim Carrol on acid.

Cheryl Savageau. Her second book of poetry, *Dirt Home Road*, was a finalist for the 1996 Paterson Prize. She is the recipient of numerous poetry fellowships including a National Endowment for the Arts and the Massachusetts Artist Foundation. She received a Writer of the Year Award from Wordcraft Circle of Native Writers and Storytellers for her children's book, *Muskrat Will Be Swimming*, which was chosen a Notable Children's Book by *Smithsonian Magazine*. She is of Abenaki and French Canadian heritage.

Beau Sia. With his spoken word CD *Attack! Attack! GO!* released on Mouth Almighty / Mercury Records, he hopes to have sex with more girls. Beau's performance is a hurricane of death, love, financial success and Fiona Apple. His stage antics and breakdancing moves, and pistol delivery, are riotously hilarious and unique. He is a film major at NYU and author of *A Night Without Armour II: Revenge*.

Micki Siegel brought academic and performance poets together in the ground-breaking reading series Burnt Words, which ran for five years. Her poems are incantations influenced by Eavan Boland and Yeats. She was featured in the compilation *Relationships From Hell*.

Hal Sirowitz. This National Endowment for the Arts recipient is the King Of Droll and the ultimate son paying homage to Mother. He is the author of *Mother Said* (Crown, 1996) and *Therapist Said* (Crown, 1998). Hal has appeared on MTV's "Unplugged", NPRs "All Things Considered" and PBS' "The United States Of Poetry." He lives in Flushing, Queens.

Maureen Seaton. Seaton's books of poetry are *Fear of Subways, The Sea Among the Cupboards* and *Furious Cooking* which received a 1997 Lamba Literary Award. Her first collaborative book with Denise Duhamel, *Exquisite Politics*, was published by Tia Chucha Press, 1997.

Marc Smith The original Slam Master, Marc continues his weekly slam and jazz series at the Green Mill in Chicago. He has given the world a new art form.

Patricia Smith is the author of *Close to Death*, *Big Towns*, *Big Talk*, and *Life According to Motown*. A video of Smith performing her poem "Undertaker" won a 1998 Cable Ace Award, as well as Kudos from Sundance and the San Francisco film festivals.

Smith is the author of *Africans in America*, a companion book to a four-part PBS documentary series. She co-hosts the Boston Poetry Slam at The Cantab Lounge with her husband the poet, Michael Brown.

horehound stillpoint. Is he an herb or a slutty dog? He will tell you that he is both. His work can be found in *Queer View Mirror II, beyond definition, Sex Spoken Here* and *Best Gay Erotica 1998*. This two-time National Slam team member fromSan Francisco delivers with a discreet ferocity, at times channeling Patti Smith and David Bowie.

Eileen Tabios is the author of a poetry collection *Beyond Life Sentences* (Anvil, 1998) and *Black Lightning: Poetry-In-Progress*, a collection of essays about Asian American poets (Asian American Writers Workshop, 1998). She is currently editing *Doveglion: The Selected Works of Jose Garcia Villa* (Kaya Productions, 1999). She is the editor of *The Asian Pacific American Journal*.

Richard Tayson. Tayson's first book of poems, *The Apprentice Of Fever*, was awarded the 1997 Wick Poetry prize and published by The Kent State Univeristy Press. Tayson has been awarded a Pushcart Prize and *Prairie Schooner*'s Bernice Slote Award for emerging writers. His first book of non-fiction, *Look Up for Yes,* will be published in paperback by Viking Press, 1998.

Edwin Torres is an artist/poet/performer living in NYC attempting deflection through refraction. He has received a variety of acknowledgements for his various existences and is happy to have stalked some territory in this nation of poets, as he *edwin torreses* down the street. (i.e. **e-dwin TOR-res** (*nomadus palabras*): to travel the outskirts of language through the inskirts of poetry; to perform and misguide generations of listening; to have a debut CD on Kill Rock Stars called *Holy Kid*.)

Crystal Williams. Her "Aunt Jemima" was performed at the Apollo Theater stage on Amateur Night where she rocked the house with head-snapping charm. She was editor of *Icarus* magazine and is presently pursuing her MFA at Cornell University.

Lois-Ann Yamanaka. Yamanaka has made Hawaiian Pidgin part of the American canon. Her collection of poems *Saturday Night At The Pahala Theater* celebrates the landscape, people and musicality of the islands she grew up in. Her novels are *Bully Burgers* and *Blues* from Farrar, Strauss & Giroux.

Credits — Canadian

Fortner Anderson: "The Bovine Spongiform Encephalopathy Blues" and "My Friend" appear by permission of the author.

Mercedes Baines: "Clit Sing Along" and "The Last Time I Saw You" appear by permission of the author.

Louise Bak: "Double take," "M.," and "Heteroflexidome" appeared in *Gingko Kitchen* (Coach House Books). Reprinted by permission of the author.

Jill Battson: "Hitching" appears by permission of the author.

Chris Bell: "The Quest for Immortality" appeared in *Tales of the Lost Cheebah-Ha* (ga Press, 1995). Reprinted by permission of the author.

bill bissett: "loving without being vulnrabul" appeared in *loving without being vulnrabul* (Talonbooks). Reprinted by permission of the author and publisher.

Joe Blades: "Continuation (of Services Rendered by the Falmouth Lifeboats of the Royal National Lifeboat Institution)" appeared in *The Cormorant* magazine and in the chapbook, *eurotrip* (Poka Press, 1996). Reprinted by permission of the author.

Alex Boutros: The excerpt from "baby boy blues" appears by permission of the author.

Jason Camlot: "Kit Discovers Sound," "Phono Kit," and "Crypto Kit" appear courtesy of the author.

Mark Cochrane: "Mapplethorpe" appeared in *Boy Am I* (Wolsak & Wynn, 1995). Reprinted by permission of the author and publisher.

Wayde Compton: "Come To" and "Band" appear courtesy of the author. "Band" originally appeared (in a slightly different form) in *West Coast Line* (Spring/Summer 1997).

Julie Crysler: "Snake Charming" and "The Fury" appear by permission of the author.

Nancy Dembowski: "Life on Venus Avenue" appears courtesy of the author.

Emily S. Downing: "War Movies: Men in Armor in Arms" appears courtesy of the author.

Paul Dutton: "T'her" appeared in *Aurealities* (Coach House Books, 1991, 1998). Reprinted by permission of the author.

Ian Ferrier: "Exploding Head Man" and "You Want Me" appear courtesy of the author.

Ray Filip: "Motormouth" appeared originally in *Flowers in Magnetic Fields* (Guernica Editions, 1994). Reprinted by permission of the author.

Golda Fried: "The Diner," "Sticky Aisles," and "The Poetess in Late Afternoon Underwear" appears by permission of the author.

Sky Gilbert: "Romantic Possibilities of the Telephone" appears by permission of the author.

Lee Gotham: "I'd Love to But" appears by permission of the author.

Kélina Gotman: "Globular Mud" appears by permission of the author.

Thoth Harris: "The Irwin Allen Experience" appears by permission of the author.

Richard Harrison: "Love and the Hockey Pool" originally appeared in *Hero of the Play* (Wolsak & Wynn). Reprinted by permission of the author and publisher.

Steven Heighton: "Elegy as a Message Left on an Answering Machine" was originally published in *The Ecstasy of Skeptics* (Anansi, 1994). Reprinted by permission of the author and publisher.

Michael Holmes: "bramalea limited" and "in high school everyone you half know dies on Friday" originally appeared in *james I wanted to ask you* (ECW Press, 1994). Reprinted by permission of the author and publisher.

David Jager: "Words" appears by permission of the author.

Charlene D. Jones: "Coming of Age" appears by permission of the author.

Adeena Karasick: "Albeit Erstwhile" appeared in *Genrecide* (Talonbooks, 1996). Reprinted by permission of the author and publisher.

Wayne Keon: "high travellin" and "to teotihaucan" originally appeared in *Storm Dancers* (Mercury Press, 1993). Reprinted by permission of the author and publisher.

Evelyn Lau: "Vancouver Public Library Opening Gala, May 24, 1995" was originally published in *The Vancouver Sun*. Reprinted by permission of the author.

John B. Lee: "The Sergeant Pepper Sonnets" was originally published in *The Beatles Landed Laughing in New York* (Black Moss Press, 1995). Reprinted by permission of the publisher and author.

Alexis O'Hara: "Nipples' Hindsight Revenge" appears by permission of the author.

Daniel O'Leary: The excerpt from "Tarsus" appears by permission of the author.

Donal Power: "Pornography" and "Excavations" appear by permission of the author.

David McGimpsey: "In Memoriam: A.H. Jr." appeared in *Lardcake* (ECW Press). Reprinted by permission of the author and publisher, ECW Press.

Carmelita McGrath: "The Half-life of Taffeta" appeared in *To the New World* (Killick Press, 1996). Reprinted by permission of the author.

Donald McGrath: "The Stable" appeared in *First Light* (Wolsak & Wynn). Reprinted by permission of the author.

rob mclennan: "Dukes of Hazard Monologue" originally appeared in *Descant* and then *Open 24 Hours* (Broken Jaw Press). Reprinted by permission of the author.

Penelope Schafer: "Stein Tribute" appears by permission of the author.

Stan Rogal: "Vowels" appears by permission of the author.

Steven Ross Smith: "Bren Gun Girl 1941" appeared in *Transient Light* (Mercury Press, 1990). Reprinted by permission of the author and publisher. "fluttering,4," "fluttering 8," and "fluttering 9" appear by permission of the author.

Ian Stephens: "Home" appears by permission of Alex Espinosa.

W. Mark Sutherland: "Fuck" and "Art Blakey" appear by permission of the author.

Sheri-D Wilson: "Bukowski on the Block Ah-ha" appears by permission of the author.

Credits — U.S.

Miguel Algarin: "Nuyorican Angel of Wordsmithing (Note for a Poet)," "Nuyorican Angel Papo (the Bi-sexual Super Macho)," and "Nuyorican Angel Of Despair (December 31, at the End of the Millenium)"–all Copyright © 1998 by Miguel Algarin–appear in *Love Is Hard Work;* reprinted by permission of Susan Bergholtz Literary Services, New York. All rights reserved.

Cheryl B.: "You are Not the Hetero Diva" first appeared in *Motor Oil Queen!* 1998. Reprinted by permission of the author

Ras Baraka: "For the Brothers Who Ain't Here" appears in *In the Tradition.* Reprinted by permission of the publisher.

Paul Beatty: For "Stall Me Out," Copyright © 1994 by Paul Beatty, reprinted with the permission of The Wylie Agency, Inc.

Tish Benson: "no parts spared" printed by permission of the author 1998.

Mark Bibbins: "The Parts of This We Remember" originally appeared in *The Paris Review,* 1998; "Blind" was first published in *A & U* magazine; "Your Shirt" reprinted by permission of the author, 1998.

Nicole Blackman: "Girls" appeared in *Pretty,* 1994, reprinted by permission of the author. "Liberation Barbie" appeared in Singapore *Elle,* 1997, reprinted by permission of the author. "Oracle" appeared in *Chiron Review,* Reprinted by permission.

Cheryl Boyce Taylor: "Wind" and "Plenty Time Pass fast, Fas Dey So" appears in "Raw Air", 1997. Reprinted by permission of the author.

Regie Cabico: "Antonio Banderas in His Underwear," "In a Legendary Light," and "Check One" appear by permission of the author.

Nick Carbo: "For My Friend Who Says He Can't Dance and Has a Severe Case of Writers Block" appears in *El Grupo McDonalds.* "Mal de Ojo" and "Ang Tunay Na Lalaki (The Real Man) is Baffled by Cryptic Messages is reprinted by permission of the author.

Guillermo Castro: "Balloons From Hell," "Ship of Fools" and "The Fascist Manifesto" appear in *Toy Storm,* 1997 . Reprinted by permission of the author.

Tina Chang: "Face" first appeared in *International Quarterly,* 1998, reprinted by permission of the author.

Justin Chin: "Ex-Boyfriends Named Michael" appears in "Bite Hard", 1997. reprinted by permission of the author.

Sandra Cisneros: "You Bring Out The Mexican In Me," from *Loose Woman*, Copyright © 1994 by Sandra Cisneros. Published by Vintage Books, a division of Random House, Inc., and originally in hardcover by Alfred A. Knopf, Inc. Reprinted by permission of Susan Bergholtz Literary Services, New York. All rights reserved.

Denise Duhamel: "The Difference Between Pepsi & Pope" & "Happy Ending" first appeared in *The Salt Hill Journal*, 1996. Reprinted by permission of the author.

Audrey De larosa: "I Am Not White Señores" appears courtesy of the author.

Sean Thomas Dougherty: "Looking For Lorca In Your Letters," appeared in *Love Song of the Young Couple, The Dumb Job* (Red Dancefloor, 1995); reprinted by permission of the author.

Ron Drummond: "The Crossing" first appeared in *Fresh Ground*, 1998; reprinted by permission of the author. "Attention to Gray" appears courtesy of the author, 1998.

M. Doughty: "In The Mind Of the Mind" "I'll Be your Babydoll, I'll be your Seven Day Fool," "For charlotte, Unlisted," and "Rootless," first appeared in *Slanky*, 1996; reprinted by permission of the author.

Marcella Durand: "City Of Ports 2" appears courtesy of the author, 1998.

Evert Eden: "Big Breasts"was recorded on the CD *Nuyorican Symphony*, reprinted by permission of the author. "Mandela" appears courtesy of the author, 1998.

Anne Elliott: "When I Returned From My Mother's Funeral, He Said I Was Too Rebellious", first appeared in *Excursus Literary Journal, 1995;* reprinted by permission of the author. "She Thought Starvation was Somehow Holy" first appeared in *Interview,* 1993. "Recipes" reprinted by permission of the author.

Noel Franklin: "blood quantum" and "long-distance ex" first appeared in *theo*, 1997; reprinted by permission of the author.

Elena Georgiou: "A Week In The Life Of The Ethnically Indeterminate" and "Lessons In Honesty," reprinted by permission of the author.

Gerry Gomez Pearlberg: "The Death Of Superman" appears in *Marianne Faithful's Cigarette* (Cleis, 1998); reprinted by permission of the author.

Allen Ginsberg: For "Death & Fame," Copyright © 1997 by Allen Ginsberg, reprinted with the permission of The Wylie Agency, Inc.

Cindy Goff: "The Pole in His Back Was as Strong as My Family Tree," "Appalachian Flood," "The First Sober Morning," and "Addiction" appear by permission of the author. Kimiko Hahn: "The Unbearable Heart" appears in *The Unbearable Heart* (Kaya

Production, 1996); reprinted by permission of the author.

Carl Hanni: "Not Making It in Mexico" first appeared in *Night Shift* (Quiet Lion Press, 1996).

Bob Holman: "The Death Of Poetry" appears in *The Collect Call Of The Wild*; reprinted by permission of the author.

Christian Langworthy: "How Could I Interpret The Events Of My Youth, Events I Do Not Remember Except In Dreams" first appeared in *Premonitions (Kaya Production, 1995);* reprinted by permission of the author.

Beth Lisick: "Monkey Girl" appears in *Monkey Girl (Manic D Press, 1997)*; reprinted by permission of the author.

Taylor Mali: "Labeling Keys" and "Switching Sides" are printed by permission of the author.

Jeffery McDaniel: "Poetry Nation" is reprinted by permission of the author 1998.

Ellyn Maybe: "I Have Never Fallen In Love With Anyone Who Felt Comfortable In America" first appeared in *The Cowardice Of Amnesia (2.13.61), 1998;* reprinted by permission of the author.

Tony Medina: "Bloodsong" was published by *African Voices magazine, Winter 1996/97;* reprinted by permission of the author. "How To Be A United States Citizen" appears courtesy of the author, 1998.

Ritah Parrish: "The Rules" appears by permission of the author.

Bob Redmond: "The Poet" appears courtesy of the author, 1998.

D.J. Renegade: "Subterranean Night-Colored Magi" and "Mama After Midnite" appears in *4,000 Shades Of Blue* (Karibu Books, 1996) reprinted by permission of the author. "Father, Son, and the Wholly Ghost" appears courtesy of the author, 1998.

Daniel Roop: "Handing Out Condoms" is printed by permission of the author, 1998.

Carol Rosenfeld: "Dyke-otomy" appeared in *Excursus*, 1996; reprinted by permission of the author.

Carl Hancock Rux: "Red Velvet Dress Lullabye" appears in *Pagan Operetta* (Fly By Night Press, 1998); reprinted by permission of the author.

Kevin Sampsell: "Ulysses," "Answering Machine Love," "Jack Nance," "Rikki Lake," and "David Duke" appear by permission of the author.

Cheryl Savageau: "Too'kay" and "After Listening to a Reading of Romantic poems About Columbus: One More Thought" first appeared in *Dirt Road Home*, Curbstone Press, 1995; reprinted by permission of the author. "Looking For Indians" first appeared in *Home Country* (Alice James Books, 1992); reprinted by permission of the author.

Beau Sia: "A Little Known Truth About Financial Success" first appeared in *Fuck Me #1*, 1995; reprinted by permission of the author.

Micki Siegel: "Penamanship" & "Skin Tones" appear courtesy of the author.

Hal Sirowitz: "No More Birthdays," "Does God Exist," "Damaged Body," "Different Versions", "Two Burials For The Same Person," "How To Wash Clothes" appear in *Mother Said* (Crown, 1996); reprinted by permission of the author.

Maureen Seaton: "Exquistie Majority," "Let Me Explain," "Xena, the Warrior Princess" first appeared in *Exquisite Politics* (Tia Chucha Press, 1997); reprinted by permission of the authors.

Marc Smith: "My Father's Coat" originally appeared in *Crowdplese* (Collage Press) and appears by permission of the author.

Patricia Smith: "Biting Back" appears by permission of the author.

horehound stillpoint: "All Right I'm Okay, You're Okay, Everybody Is Okay And Nothing Human Is Alien And All That, Fine, But There Is Still A Few People I Would Like to See take A Long Hike Off A Short Pier" first appeared in *Excursus vol. 1*; reprinted by permission of the author. "Reincaranation Woes" appears courtesy of the author.

Eileen Tabios: "Rapunzel Enrapt" first appeared in *beyond Life Sentences* (Anvil, 1998); reprinted by permission of the author.

Richard Tayson: "Remembering The Man Who Molested Me" and "Sacred Anus" appeared in *The James White Review*; reprinted by permission of the author.

Edwin Torres: "15 minutes," "Catching The Rain in the Palm of My Hand," and "With Heart Sky Drowning," appear courtesy of the author.

Barbara Tran: "Love and Rice" first appeared in the *Antioch Review*. Reprinted by permission of the author.

Crystal Williams: "In Search Of Aunt Jemmima" appeared in *Icarus*; reprinted by permission of the author.

Lois-Ann Yamanaka: "Yarn Wig" appears in *Saturday Night at the Pahala Theater*, Copyright © 1993 by Lois-Ann Yamanaka. Published by Bamboo Ridge Press. First published in Bamboo Ridge: *The Hawai'i Writers Quarterly*. Reprinted by permission of Susan Bergholtz Literary Services, New York. All rights reserved.

Regie Cabico and Todd Swift